Corporate Governance
in Developing Economies

Robert W. McGee
Editor

Corporate Governance in Developing Economies

Country Studies of Africa, Asia and Latin America

Springer

Editor
Dr. Robert W. McGee
Florida International University
3000 NE., 151st Street
North Miami FL 33181
USA
bob414@hotmail.com

ISBN: 978-0-387-84832-7   e-ISBN: 978-0-387-84833-4
DOI 10.1007/978-0-387-84833-4

Library of Congress Control Number: 2008931854

Printed on acid-free paper

springer.com

Preface

Much has been written about the economic and political problems of countries that are in the process of changing from centrally planned systems to market systems. Most studies have focused on the economic, legal, political, and sociological problems these economies have had to face during the transition period. However, not much has been written about the dramatic changes that have to be made to the accounting and financial system of a transition economy. This book was written to help fill that gap.

This book is the sixth in a series to examine accounting and financial system reform in transition and developing economies. The first book (*Accounting and Financial System Reform in a Transition Economy: A Case Study of Russia*) used Russia as a case study. The second volume in the series (*Accounting and Financial System Reform in Eastern Europe and Asia*) examined some additional aspects of the reform in Russia and also looked at the accounting and financial system reform efforts that are being made in Ukraine, Bosnia and Herzegovina, Armenia, Eastern Europe, and Central Asia. The third volume (*Taxation and Public Finance in Transition and Developing Economies*) examined taxation and public finance in transition and developing economies. The fourth volume (*Accounting Reform in Transition and Developing Economies*) examines accounting reform in transition and developing economies.

The fifth volume focused attention on the current state of corporate governance in transition economies and the recent changes that have taken place in this area. The present volume uses the same approach to examining corporate governance in developing economies.

It is divided into three parts. Part I examines selected issues in corporate governance. Part II consists of case studies and comparative studies. Part III consists of studies of more than 20 developing countries.

Contents

Part III   Country Studies

Asia

Latin America

Africa & the Middle East

Contributors

Ruth V. Aguilera University of Illinois at Champaign-Urbana, Champaign, IL, USA, ruth-agu@uiuc.edu

Arsen M. Djatej Eastern Washington University, Cheney, WA, USA, adjatej@ewu.edu

Vu Dinh Hien National Economics University, Hanoi, Vietnam, vdhien@fpt.vn

Danielle N. Igoe University of Florida, Gainesville, FL, USA, dnigoe@gmail.com

Robert W. McGee Florida International University, Miami, FL, USA, bob414@hotmail.com

Judith Muhoro St. Paul's University, Limuru, Kenya, nduturas@yahoo.com

Robert H. S. Sarikas Ohio University, Athens, OH, USA, sarikas@ohio.edu

Thomas Tarangelo Florida International University, Miami, FL, USA, tarangel@fiu.edu

Michael Tyler Barry University, Miami Shores, FL, USA, mtyler@mail.barry.edu

Xiaoli Yuan California State University, East Bay, Hayward, California, USA, acg2021@gmail.com

Part I
Selected Issues in Corporate Governance

Chapter 1
Corporate Governance in Developing Economies

Robert W. McGee

Introduction

Corporate governance issues are especially important in developing economies, since these countries do not have a strong, long-established financial institution infrastructure to deal with corporate governance issues.

Corporate governance has become an important topic in developing economies in recent years. Directors, owners, and corporate managers have started to realize that there are benefits that can accrue from having a good corporate governance structure. Good corporate governance helps to increase share price and makes it easier to obtain capital. International investors are hesitant to lend money or buy shares in a corporation that does not subscribe to good corporate governance principles. Transparency, independent directors, and a separate audit committee are especially important. Some international investors will not seriously consider investing in a company that does not have these things.

Several organizations have popped up in recent years to help adopt and implement good corporate governance principles. The Organisation for Economic Co-operation and Development (OECD), the World Bank, the International Finance Corporation, the U.S. Commerce and State Departments, and numerous other organizations have been encouraging governments and firms in Eastern Europe to adopt and implement corporate codes of conduct and good corporate governance principles.

The Center for International Private Enterprise (2002) lists some of the main attributes of good corporate governance. These include

- Reduction of risk;
- Stimulation of performance;
- Improved access to capital markets;
- Enhancement of marketability of goods and services;
- Improved leadership; and
- Demonstration of transparency and social accountability.

R.W. McGee (✉)
Florida International University, Miami, FL, USA
e-mail: bob414@hotmail.com

R.W. McGee (ed.), *Corporate Governance in Developing Economies*,
DOI 10.1007/978-0-387-84833-4_1, © Springer Science+Business Media, LLC 2009

This list is by no means exhaustive. However, it does summarize some of the most important benefits of good corporate governance. All countries, whether developed or developing, face similar issues when it comes to corporate governance. However, transition economies face additional hurdles because their corporate boards lack the institutional memory and experience that boards in developed market economies have. They also have particular challenges that the more developed economies do not face to the same extent. Some of these extra challenges include

- Establishing a rule-based (as opposed to a relationship-based) system of governance;
- Combating vested interests;
- Dismantling pyramid ownership structures that allow insiders to control and, at times, siphon off assets from publicly owned firms based on very little direct equity ownership and thus few consequences;
- Severing links such as cross shareholdings between banks and corporations;
- Establishing property rights systems that clearly and easily identify true owners even if the state is the owner (when the state is an owner, it is important to indicate which state branch or department enjoys ownership and the accompanying rights and responsibilities);
- Depoliticizing decision-making and establishing firewalls between the government and management in corporatized companies where the state is a dominant or majority shareholder;
- Protecting and enforcing minority shareholders' rights;
- Preventing asset stripping after mass privatization;
- Finding active owners and skilled managers amid diffuse ownership structures; and
- Cultivating technical and professional know-how (CIPE, 2002).

Review of the Literature

Actually, the literature on the topic of corporate governance is too large to review in any detail. A full review of just the Russian literature in the English language would require a book. Then there is the Russian language literature and the English and national language literature for each of the other former Soviet republics, plus each country in Central and Eastern Europe, the Balkans, and China. Then there is the literature on developing countries, either individually or as a group or region.

Generic Literature

One subfield of the corporate governance literature may be labeled generic literature. This literature does not focus on any particular country but rather on general principles of corporate governance.

Hundreds of articles and dozens of books have been written about corporate governance in the last few years alone. One book that should be mentioned is *Corporate Governance* by Monks and Minow (2004). This book was required reading for the ACCA Diploma in Corporate Governance program before that program was discontinued. Davis Global Advisors publishes an annual *Leading Corporate Governance Indicators*, which measures corporate governance compliance using a variety of indicators.

The Cadbury Report (1992) published the findings of the Committee on Financial Aspects of Corporate Governance. The Greenbury Report (1995) discusses directors' remuneration. The Hampel Committee Report (1998) addresses some of the same issues as the Cadbury and Greenbury reports. It has separate sections on the principles of corporate governance, the role of directors, directors' remuneration, the role of shareholders, accountability and audit, and issued conclusions and recommendations.

The *Encyclopedia of Corporate Governance* is a good reference tool for obtaining information on corporate governance. It is available online. The OECD's *Principles of Corporate Governance* (1999, 2004) has been used as a benchmark for a number of corporate governance codes in transition and developing economies. OECD has also published a *Survey of Corporate Governance Developments in OECD Countries* (2003c). The European Corporate Governance Institute maintains many links to codes of corporate conduct for many countries on its website.

Several academic journals are devoted either exclusively or partially to corporate governance issues. The following four journals are devoted exclusively to corporate governance issues:

Corporate Governance: An International Review
Corporate Governance: International Journal of Business in Society
Journal of Management and Governance
Corporate Ownership and Control

Governance is an international monthly newsletter devoted exclusively to corporate governance issues. *Economics of Governance* also publishes articles on corporate governance, in addition to articles on governance in the nonprofit and governmental sectors.

Several websites are also devoted to corporate governance issues and contain many articles, research papers, and reports on a wide variety of corporate governance issues. These include

British Accounting Association Corporate Governance Special Interest Group;
Corporate Monitoring;
European Corporate Governance Institute;
Global Corporate Governance Forum;
International Corporate Governance Network;
OECD; and
World Bank.

Corporate Governance in Developing Economies

There is a growing body of literature that focuses on corporate governance in developing countries, either as a category, a region, or individually. Some comparative studies have also been done on this subtopic. The following discussion merely skims the surface and limits the discussion to the literature that is available in the English language.

The OECD (2007) has published a study that provides an overview of the state of corporate governance in Asia as of 2007 for 13 Asian economies and updates its 2003 White Paper on Corporate Governance in Asia (OECD, 2003a). It also completed a study of corporate governance of Asian banks (OECD, 2006a).

Cheung and Chan (2004) examined the state of corporate governance in some Asian-Pacific countries. Clarke (2000) discussed the relationship between corporate governance and the Asian financial crisis. Cheung and Jang (2006) constructed a corporate governance scorecard for East Asia based on a survey using the OECD Principles of Corporate Governance categories.

The OECD has done a white paper on corporate governance in Latin America (OECD, 2003d) that discusses the various corporate governance categories as outlined in its principles document and also summarizes Latin American corporate governance initiatives and has some case studies. It also published a series of case studies of good corporate governance practices in Latin America (OECD, 2006b).

Cruces and Kawamura (2006) examined insider trading in Latin America. Da Silva and de Lira Alves (2004) examined the voluntary disclosure of financial information on the Internet and the firm value effect it had on companies across Latin America. Reyes (2008) published a law review article on corporate governance in Latin America that took a legal perspective.

Apreda (2001) conducted a survey to determine how the corporate governance model in Argentina is shifting. Black, de Carvalho, and Gorga (2008) provide an overview of corporate governance in Brazil. The Instituto Brasileiro de Governanca Corporativa (2004) published a *Code of Best Practice of Corporate Governance*. Standard & Poor's did a country governance study of Brazil (2004).

Gatamah (2004) has written about governance, citizenship, and social responsibility in Africa. Rwegasira (2000) argues that African countries should adopt an institutionally based corporate governance model.

Hussain and Mallin (2002) examine the existing state of corporate governance in Bahrain. They later looked at the structure, responsibilities, and operation of corporate board in Bahrain (Hussain & Mallin, 2003).

Corporate Governance in Transition Economies

Within the field of corporate governance literature is a subfield of corporate governance in transition economies. The OECD has published a *White Paper on Corporate Governance in South Eastern Europe* (OECD, 2003b) that is used for guidance by enterprises in that part of the world. This *white paper* contains sections on shareholder rights and equitable treatment, the role of stakeholders, transparency and disclosure, the responsibilities of the board, and implementation and enforcement. Much of what is contained in this *White Paper* is applicable to corporate governance in Russia as well, although the *White Paper* is not specifically addressed to Russian enterprises. The OECD and World Bank websites have numerous publications on corporate governance in other east European countries as well.

The OECD website section on corporate governance is subdivided by country. There is a link for Russia that contains studies, papers, and announcements pertaining to Russia. One important paper is the OECD's *White Paper on Corporate Governance in Russia* (2002), which contains recommendations for improving corporate governance in Russia. The Russian Corporate Governance Roundtable website also contains documents and announcements pertaining to corporate governance in Russia. The International Finance Corporation, which is affiliated with the World Bank, has a Russia Corporate Governance Project. Its website provides up-to-date information about several aspects of corporate governance in Russia. The Global Corporate Governance Forum website provides links to more than 60 organizations that are involved in corporate governance issues.

Several Russian organizations also have websites and publication on corporate governance. The Russian Institute of Directors website contains news items as well as publications. Some of its publications and links include *Code of Corporate Governance* (2002), several Foreign Best Practices Codes, and several corporate codes of conduct. They also publish surveys and provide training for corporate directors in Russia. The Independent Directors Association also has a website that provides current information and various documents on corporate governance, mostly pertaining to directors. It also publishes a newsletter, which is available on its website. The Institute of Corporate Law and Corporate Governance also has a website that contains publications about corporate governance in Russia. One of its studies is *Managing Corporate Governance Risks in Russia* (2002). It also provides corporate governance ratings of Russian firms.

Detailed or even brief descriptions of all the papers that have been written on corporate governance, in general, corporate governance in transition economies or corporate governance in Russia, would take us far afield of the limited focus of the present chapter. Citing the sources above is intended to give other researchers some good leads that will aid them in their own research. However, a few papers are worthy of special mention.

A rich body of literature about corporate governance in Russia has evolved and grows larger with each passing year. Judge, Naoumova, and Kutzevol (2003) conducted survey research of Russian managers in December 2002 that found a negative correlation between leadership and firm performance where the same person served as CEO and board chair. This finding is especially curious given the fact that Russian federal legislation has made it illegal since 1996 for the same person to serve as both CEO and board chair at the same time. They also found that the correlation between the proportion of inside directors serving on the board and firm performance becomes increasingly negative the more vigorously a firm pursues a retrenchment strategy. But there was no significant correlation between the proportion of inside directors and firm performance when the firm was not in retrenchment mode, which seems to support the view that inside directors generally fulfill their fiduciary duties to the owners except when their jobs are threatened. Their study complements an earlier study by Wagner, Stimpert, and Fubara (1998), which found that very high and very low levels of insider representation on the board had an effect on board performance, whereas moderate levels of representation did not.

Puffer and McCarthy (2003) discuss the substantial progress made in corporate governance in Russia in recent years and track the emergence of corporate governance in Russia through four stages – commercialization, privatization, nomenklatura, and statization – beginning in the mid-1980s. They place special emphasis on problems on nondisclosure and nontransparency that have made Russia one of the riskiest countries for investment. In an earlier work (2002), they examine the question of whether the Russian corporate governance model will evolve into something that looks like the U.S. model or whether it will look more like the European model. They conclude that it will evolve into something that is uniquely Russian, taking into account Russian values, culture, and tradition.

Buck (2003) discusses corporate governance in Russia from a historical perspective and the hostile attitude that is taken toward Western and outside investors. He also discusses the persistently strong state influence in Russian corporate governance. Roth and Kostova (2003) tested data from 1,723 firms in 22 countries in Central and Eastern Europe and the Newly Independent States and conclude that cultural factors must be considered when explaining corporate governance in transition economies.

Filatotchev, Wright, Uhlenbruck, Tihanyi, and Hoskisson (2003) discuss the effect that privatization has had on corporate governance in Eastern and Central European countries. They suggest that excessive management control and ignorance of the governance process are causing problems that could be reduced by increasing the influence of outside directors. Their arguments are supported by case studies.

Peng, Buck, and Filatotchev (2003) conducted a survey of 314 privatized Russian firms and tested two hypotheses of agency theory that outside directors and new managers correlate positively to firm performance. They found little support for the hypotheses, a finding that goes against much of the prior research and thinking on this relationship. Their findings question whether this issue must be viewed from other perspectives.

Robertson, Gilley, and Street (2003) collected data from 112 U.S. and 74 Russian respondents and looked for patterns of ethical conduct. McCarthy and Puffer (2003) focus on large Russian companies and provide a framework for analyzing corporate governance in transition economies where the corporate governance process is still evolving. They draw on agency theory, stakeholder theory, and the cultural embeddedness model in their analysis.

Muravyev (2001) challenges the view that good corporate governance does not exist in Russia and shows through an empirical study that Russian executives can be fired for poor performance. He also challenges the view that the state is a passive shareholder in Russian enterprises and presents evidence of how the ownership of a corporation influences managerial succession.

Filatotchev, Buck, and Zhukov (2000) examined enterprises in Russia, Ukraine, and Belarus and looked at the relationship between downsizing and outside, noninstitutional shareholding. They found that downsizing is positively correlated with outside, noninstitutional shareholding, but that the firm's ability to downsize is negatively correlated with the degree of management shareholding. In other words, when management is entrenched and has a sufficiently large block of voting shares, it can block downsizing in an effort to protect jobs.

Timeliness of Financial Reporting

Several studies have been done on various aspects or components of corporate governance. In the area of timeliness of financial reporting, for example, the Accounting Principles Board (1970) recognized the general principle several decades ago. The Financial Accounting Standards Board (1980) recognized the importance of timeliness in one of its Concepts Statements. Ashton, Graul, and Newton (1989) examined the relationship of timeliness and the delay of audits. Atiase, Bamber, and Tse (1989) examined the relationship of timeliness, the firm size effect, and stock price reactions to annual earnings announcements. Basu (1997) applied the principle of conservatism to the asymmetric timeliness of earnings. Chai and Tung (2002) studied the effect of earnings-announcement timing on earnings management. Chambers and Penman (1984) looked at the timeliness of reporting and the stock price reaction to earnings announcements.

Davies and Whittred (1980) looked at the association between selected corporate attributes and the timeliness of corporate reporting. Dwyer and Wilson (1989) investigated the factors affecting the timeliness of reporting by municipalities. Gigler and Hemmen (2001) explored the relationship among conservatism, optimal disclosure policy, and the timeliness of financial reports. Givoli and Palmon (1982) looked at some empirical evidence regarding the timeliness of earnings announcements. Han and Wild (1997) examined the relationship between timeliness of reporting and earnings information transfers. Haw, Qi, and Wu (2000) looked at the relationship between the timeliness of annual report releases and market reactions to earnings announcements in China. Jindrichovska and Mcleay (2005) looked at the relationship between the timeliness of financial reporting and the announcement of good news or bad news in the Czech Republic. Rees and Giner (2001) examined the same issue for France, Germany, and the UK. Soltani (2002) did an empirical study of timeliness in France. Whittred and Zimmer (1984) examined the relationship between timeliness and financial distress.

Keller (1986) looked at the relationship between the timeliness of financial reporting and the presence of a qualified audit opinion. Whittred (1980) also looked at the relationship between audit qualification and the timing of financial data publication. Krishnan examined the relationship between audit firm expertise and the timeliness of financial reporting. Kross and Schroeder (1984) conducted an empirical investigation on the effect of quarterly earnings-announcement timing on stock returns. Trueman (1990) looked at the timing of earnings announcements. Leventis and Weetman (2004) examined the applicability of disclosure theories in emerging capital markets. Pope and Walker (1999) looked at the international differences in the timeliness of financial reporting.

Studies on the timeliness of financial reporting have been done of the Russian energy sector (McGee, 2006, 2007b&c), the Russian telecom industry (McGee, 2007a, 2007c), and the Russian banking industry (McGee & Tarangelo, 2008b). Another study compared the timeliness of financial reporting by companies in the new and old European Union (EU) countries (McGee & Igoe, 2008). Yet another study examined the timeliness of financial reporting in China (McGee & Yuan, 2008).

Other studies focusing on the timeliness of financial reporting included an overview of the subject (McGee, 2008c), a comparative study of timeliness in the USA and China (McGee & Yuan, 2008), a comparative study of Russian and non-Russian banks (McGee & Tarangelo, 2008a), the Russian transportation industry (McGee & Gunn, 2008), Russian and non-Russian companies in general (McGee & Tyler, 2008), a comparative study of Russian and the U.S. companies (McGee, Tarangelo & Tyler, 2008), a comparative study of companies in Russia and the EU (McGee, Tyler, Tarangelo & Igoe, 2008), a comparative study of Russia and China (McGee, Yuan, Tarangelo & Tyler, 2008), and a trend analysis of timeliness in Russia (McGee, 2008d). Several chapters of the present study expand the literature on this subtopic by including a study on timeliness of financial reporting in Kenya as well as several comparative studies of Kenya and various other countries or regions.

Other studies examined other principles of corporate governance outlined in the OECD (2004) White Paper. Studies were done on insider trading (McGee, 2008a) and the market for corporate control (McGee, 2008b), for example.

Guidelines for Emerging Economies

Numerous articles, documents, and reports have been published in recent years that provide some policy guidelines for good corporate governance. Such documents are especially valuable for developing economies, since the subject of corporate governance is relatively new for them and even their top government and private-sector leaders have little or no experience governing market-oriented private firms that have a public constituency along the lines of the more developed economies. The World Bank has published more than 40 studies on corporate governance in various countries that use the OECD principles (OECD, 2004) as a template. More than 20 of those studies are of developing economies and are listed in the reference section.

The OECD (2004) principles are subdivided into the following categories:

I. Ensuring the Basis for an Effective Corporate Governance Framework

> The corporate governance framework should promote transparent and efficient markets, be consistent with the rule of law and clearly articulate the division of responsibilities among different supervisory, regulatory, and enforcement authorities.

II. The Rights of Shareholders and Key Ownership Functions

The corporate governance framework should protect and facilitate the exercise of shareholders' rights.

III. The Equitable Treatment of Shareholders

The corporate governance framework should ensure the equitable treatment of all shareholders, including minority and foreign shareholders. All shareholders should have the opportunity to obtain effective redress for violation of their rights.

IV. The Role of Stakeholders in Corporate Governance

The corporate governance framework should recognize the rights of stakeholders established by law or through mutual agreements and encourage active co-operation between corporations and stakeholders in creating wealth, jobs, and the sustainability of financially sound enterprises.

V. Disclosure and Transparency

The corporate governance framework should ensure that timely and accurate disclosure is made of all material matters regarding the corporation, including the financial situation, performance, ownership, and governance of the company.

VI. The Responsibilities of the Board

The corporate governance framework should ensure the strategic guidance of the company, the effective monitoring of management by the board, and the board's accountability to the company and the shareholders.

One of the better documents in this area was published by the Institute of International Finance (IIF). Its *Policies for Corporate Governance and Transparency in Emerging Markets* (2002) provides a set of guidelines that corporate officers and directors can use when establishing or revising their own company's corporate governance rules. Here are some of the main suggestions.

Minority Shareholder Protection

The company should have a formal policy that defines voter rights and which corporate actions require shareholder approval. There should also be a mechanism that allows minority shareholders to voice their objections to majority decisions. Minority shareholders should have the legal right to vote on all important matters, including mergers and the sale of substantial assets.

Firms should be encouraged to allow proxy voting, and proxy systems should be available to all shareholders, foreign and domestic.

Multiple voting classes should be eliminated where they exist. The number of nonvoting and supervoting shares should be reduced or eliminated and all new issues should have a "one share, one vote" policy.

Cumulative voting should be permitted. Shareholder approval of takeovers, mergers, and buyouts should be required. Any anti-takeover measures such as poison pills, golden parachutes, and issuances of bonds with special rights in the event of a takeover should have to be approved by shareholders. Spin-offs should also require a majority vote of all shareholders.

Dilution of ownership or voting rights should require a majority vote of all shareholders, at the very least. The IIF recommends a supermajority vote as a "Best Practice."

In the event of a takeover or delisting, all shareholders should be offered the same terms.

Shareholder approval should be required before a company can sell additional shares to existing majority shareholders after some threshold. Any capital increases should first be offered to any existing shareholders. Significant share buybacks should require shareholder approval.

Shareholders should be notified a sufficient time in advance of shareholder meetings. The "Best Practice" is to send a notice of the meeting and agenda at least 1 month prior to the meeting. Reasonable efforts should be taken to prevent vote fraud and to allow for a recount in the event an election is contested. Minority shareholders should be able to call special meetings and petition the board with some minimum share threshold.

Foreign and domestic shareholders should be treated equally. A policy should be established to clearly define who retains the right to vote when shares are traded close to the meeting date. Quorum rules should not be set too low or too high. The IIF recommends around 30%, which should include some independent minority shareholders.

Structure and Responsibilities of the Board

The company should define independence, disclose the biographies of board members, and make a statement on independence. The IIF recommends that as a Best Practice a board member cannot (a) have been an employee of the firm in the past 3 years; (b) have a current business relationship with the firm; (c) be employed as an executive of another firm in which any of the company executives serve on that firm's compensation committee; and (d) be an immediate family member of an executive officer of the firm or any of its affiliates.

At least one-third of the board should be nonexecutive, a majority of whom should be independent. The Best Practice calls for a majority of independent directors.

The board should meet every quarter for large companies. The audit committee should meet every 6 months. Minutes of meetings should become part of the public record. The Best Practice would be to apply this rule to all companies.

The quorum requirement should be specified by the firm and should consist of executive, nonexecutive, and independent nonexecutive members. Best Practice calls for representation by both executive and independent directors.

Nominations to the board should be made by a committee that is chaired by an independent nonexecutive. There should be a mechanism in place that would allow minority shareholders to put forth the names of potential directors at annual general meetings and extraordinary general meetings.

For large firms, directors should need to be re-elected every 3 years. The Best Practice rule would apply the 3-year requirement to firms of any size.

For large companies, the compensation and nomination committees should be chaired by an independent nonexecutive director. The Best Practice would be to extend this requirement to firms of any size.

The board should formally evaluate directors before their election, in the case of large firms. The Best Practice is to extend this requirement to firms of any size.

The board should disclose immediately any information that affects the share price, including major asset sales or pledges. Procedures should be established for releasing information. Best Practice calls for releasing information on the company website through the stock exchange.

Remuneration for all directors and senior executives should be disclosed in the annual report. All major stock option plans should be disclosed and subjected to shareholder approval.

The company's articles of association or bylaws should clearly state the responsibilities of directors and managers. This document should be accessible to all shareholders.

The chairman or CEO should publish a statement of corporate strategy in the annual report.

Any actual or potential conflict of interest involving a board member or senior executive should be disclosed. Board members should abstain from voting in cases where they have a conflict of interest. The audit or ethics committee is required to review conflict-of-interest situations.

The integrity of the internal control and risk management system should be a function of the audit committee, according to the Best Practice guideline.

The company should have an investor relations program. Best Practice requires the CFO or CEO to assume this responsibility as part of the job.

The company should make a policy statement concerning environmental and social responsibility issues.

Accounting and Auditing

The company should disclose which accounting principles it is using. It should comply with local practice and file consolidated annual statements where appropriate. Companies should file annual audited reports and semi-annual unaudited reports. Best Practice calls for filing quarterly unaudited reports.

Audits should be conducted by an independent public accountant. Best Practice calls for adherence to the standards developed by the International Forum on Accountancy Development.

Off-balance-sheet transactions (e.g., operating leases and contingent liabilities) should be disclosed.

The audit committee should issue a statement on risk factors (See Anonymous, December 2000/January 2007b). For large companies, the audit committee should be chaired by an independent director. Best Practice calls for the audit committee chair to be an independent director regardless of company size. The chair must have a financial background. A minimum of 1 week should be allocated for any committee review of an audit. Communication between the internal and external auditor should be in the absence of executives.

Any departures from accounting standards must be explained in the annual report.

Transparency of Ownership and Control

Best Practice calls for significant ownership (20–50%, including cross-holdings) to be deemed as control.

For buyout offers to minority shareholders, Best Practice calls for ownership exceeding 35% to be considered as triggering a buyout offer in which all shareholders are treated equally.

Companies should disclose directors' and senior executives' shareholdings and all insider dealings made by directors and senior executives within 3 days of their execution.

Best Practice calls for shareholders with minimally significant ownership (3–10%) of outstanding shares to disclose their holdings.

There should be independence between industry and government. There should be rules outlining acceptable employee and management conduct.

This IIF document is not the only comprehensive set of guidelines on corporate governance practices. The OECD (www.oecd.org) has several comprehensive documents as well. Private groups have also issued comprehensive guidance documents. Gregory (2000) has published a major study that compares various sets of guidelines.

Merely having rules and guidelines is not enough to ensure success, however. Culture, institutions, and organizational structure also play an important role. Roth and Kostova (2003) conducted a major study of 1,723 firms in 22 countries in Central and Eastern Europe and the Newly Independent States and that a firm's adopting a new governance structure will be helped or hindered based on these factors.

Concluding Comments

The evidence clearly shows that much work still needs to be done in the area of corporate governance in both developing and transition economies. However, corporate governance standards are improving and it is expected that the trend will continue, especially in the countries that are becoming integrated into the EU. The EU integration process will serve as a source of constant and steady pressure to improve corporate governance. Even those countries that are not yet being integrated into the EU will continue to experience pressure to reform their corporate governance practices, not from EU pressure directly, but rather from competition with the EU and elsewhere for foreign direct investment.

However, most developing countries do not have the option of joining the EU. That does not necessarily mean they are on their own, of course. Various organizations are willing, ready, and able to assist them to improve their corporate governance structure, including the World Bank, USAID, TACIS, the Asian Development Bank, and the African Development Bank, to name a few.

Russia presents a special case, but not a case that is all that much different from those of other transition economies. Russian financial statements still suffer from a lack of transparency. It is difficult to overcome generations of Russian culture and the Russian mentality, which prefers secrecy to disclosure. But the trend is toward more transparency, more independent directors, and financial statements that have a degree of international credibility.

Poor corporate governance policies cause the shares of firms to sell for billions of dollars less than they would if their companies had good corporate governance policies, according to James Fenkner of Troika Dialog, Russia's largest brokerage firm (Anon., 2001a). Bernard Black, using data from Troika, conducted a study to determine whether corporate governance matters, in terms of share price. He found that it made a huge difference (Black, 2000). Likewise, Russian companies that improved their corporate governance practices by adopting and implementing the Corporate Governance Code saw their share prices increase (Miller, 2002). So can other countries.

However, much still needs to be done. It is difficult to superimpose a corporate code of conduct on any country's culture, especially if the code is drawn up by foreigners. Codes of conduct and the corporate governance policies they espouse will only take a firm hold in these countries when a significant number of local directors and managers actually believe that having and utilizing such codes is the right thing to do.

References

Accounting Principles Board. (1970). *Basic concepts and accounting principles underlying financial statements of business enterprises – statement no. 4.* New York: American Institute of Certified Public Accountants.

Anonymous. (2001a, February 24). Minority what? *Economist., 358*(8210), 72.

Anonymous, (December 2000/January 2001b). S&P devises scoring system for corporate governance risk. Central European., 10(10), 20–21.

Apreda, R. (2001). Corporate Governance in Argentina: the outcome of economic freedom (1991–2000). *Corporate Governance, 9*(4), 298–310.

Ashton, R. H., Graul, P. R., & Newton J. D. (1989). Audit delay and the timeliness of corporate reporting. *Contemporary Accounting Research, 5*(2), 657–673.

Atiase, R. K., Bamber, L. S., & Tse S. (1989). Timeliness of financial reporting, the firm size effect, and stock price reactions to annual earnings announcements. *Contemporary Accounting Research, 5*(2), 526–552.

Basu, S. (1997). The conservatism principle and the asymmetric timeliness of earnings. *Journal of Accounting & Economics 24*, 3–37.

Black, B. (2000, June). Does corporate governance matter? A crude test using Russian data. *University of Pennsylvania Law Review, 149*(6), 2131–2150.

Black, B. S., de Carvalho, A. G., & Gorga, E. (2008). An overview of Brazilian corporate governance. Cornell Law School Research Paper No. 08–014. Available at www.ssrn.com.

British Accounting Association Corporate Governance Special Interest Group website retrieved from http://www.baacgsig.qub.ac.uk/

Buck, T. (2003). Modern Russian corporate governance: Convergent forces or product of Russia's history? *Journal of World Business, 38*(4), 299–313.

Cadbury Report. (1992). *Report of the Committee on Financial Aspects of Corporate Governance, December 1*, London: Gee Publishing Ltd. Available at http://www.worldbank.org/html/fpd/privatesector/cg/docs/cadbury.pdf.

Center for International Private Enterprise. (2002). *Instituting corporate governance in developing, emerging and transitional economies: A handbook*. Washington, DC: Author. retrieved from www.cipe.org.

Chai, M. L., & Tung, S. (2002). The effect of earnings-announcement timing on earnings management. *Journal of Business Finance & Accounting, 29* (9&10), 1337–1354.

Chambers, A. E., & Penman, S. H. (1984). Timeliness of reporting and the stock price reaction to earnings announcements. *Journal of Accounting Research, 22*(1), 21–47.

Cheung, S. Y. L., & Chan, B. Y. (2004). Corporate governance in Asia. *Asia-Pacific Development Journal, 11*(2), 1–31.

Cheung, S. Y. L., & Jang, H. (2006). *Scorecard on corporate governance in East Asia*. Working Paper No. 13. Waterloo, Ontario, Canada: The Centre for International Governance Innovation.

Clarke, T. (2000). Haemorrhaging tigers: the power of international financial markets and the weakness of Asian modes of corporate governance. *Corporate Governance, 8*(2), 101–116.

Corporate Monitoring retrieved from http://www.corpmon.com/

Cruces, J. J., & Kawamura, E. (2006). *Insider trading and corporate governance in Latin America: A sequential grade model approach*. Available at www.ssrn.com.

Da Silva, W. M., & de Lira Alves, L. A. (2004). *The voluntary disclosure of financial information on the internet and the firm value effect in companies across Latin America*. Available at www.ssrn.com.

Davies, B., & Whittred, G. P. (1980). The association between selected corporate attributes and timeliness in corporate reporting: Further analysis. *Abacus, 16*(1), 48–60.

Davis Global Advisors. (2007). *Leading corporate governance indicators*, Newton, MA: Author. Annual publication. retrieved from http://www.davisglobal.com/publications/lcgi/index.html

Dwyer, P. D., & Wilson, E. R. (1989). An empirical investigation of factors affecting the timeliness of reporting by municipalities. *Journal of Accounting and Public Policy, 8*(1), 29–55.

Encyclopedia of Corporate Governance retrieved from http://www.encycogov.com/

European Corporate Governance Institute website retrieved from http://www.ecgi.org/

European Corporate Governance Institute link to Codes retrieved from http://www.ecgi.org/codes/all_codes.htm

Feinberg, P. (2000, November 13). Historically indifferent Russia starts to heed corporate governance rules, *Pensions & Investments, 28*(23), 18–19.

Filatotchev, I., Buck, T., & Zhukov, V. (2000). Downsizing in privatized firms in Russia, Ukraine, and Belarus. *Academy of Management Journal, 43*(3), 286–304.

Filatotchev, I., Wright, M., Uhlenbruck, K., Tihanyi, L., & Hoskisson, R. (2003). Governance, organizational capabilities, and restructuring in transition economies. *Journal of World Business, 38*(4), 331–347.

Financial Accounting Standards Board. (1980). *Statement of financial accounting concepts no. 2, qualitative characteristics of accounting information*. Stamford, CT: Author.

Gatamah, K. (2004). The corporate enterprise in Africa: Governance, citizenship and social responsibility. *Corporate Ownership & Control, 1*(3), 139–144.

Gigler, F. B., & Hemmer, T. (2001). Conservatism, optimal disclosure policy, and the timeliness of financial reports. *The Accounting Review, 76*(4), 471–493.

Givoli, D., & Palmon D. (1982). Timeliness of annual earnings announcements: Some empirical evidence. *The Accounting Review, 57*(3), 486–508.

Global Corporate Governance Forum retrieved from http://www.gcgf.org/

Greenbury Report. (1995). *Directors' remuneration: report of a study group chaired by Sir Richard Greenbury.* London: Gee Publishing Ltd. Retrieved July 17, from http://www.baacgsig.qub.ac.uk/

Gregory, H. L. (2000). *International comparison of corporate governance guidelines and codes of best practice: Investor viewpoints.* New York: Weil, Gotshal & Manges and Egon Zehnder International.

Haigh, A. (2001). We view Russia's future with optimism. *Kommersant-Daily*, January 26 retrieved from www.pwcglobal.ru/.

Hampel Committee. (1998). *Hampel Committee report*, London: Gee Publishing Ltd., January. Available at http://www.ecgi.org/codes/country_documents/uk/hampel_index.htm

Han, J. C. Y., & Wild, J. J. (1997). Timeliness of reporting and earnings information transfers. *Journal of Business Finance & Accounting, 24*(3&4), 527–540.

Haw, I.-M., Qi, D., & Wu, W. (2000). Timeliness of annual report releases and market reaction to earnings announcements in an emerging capital market: The case of China. *Journal of International Financial Management and Accounting, 11*(2), 108–131.

Hussain, S. H., & Mallin, C. (2002). Corporate Governance in Bahrain. *Corporate Governance, 10*(3), 197–210.

Hussain, S. H., & Mallin, C. (2003). The dynamics of corporate governance in Bahrain: Structure, responsibilities and operation of corporate boards. *Corporate Governance, 11*(3), 249–261.

Independent Directors Association website retrieved from www.independentdirector.ru

Independent Directors Association. (2003). *Independent director code* (April 15 Draft), Moscow: Independent Directors Association. Available at www.independentdirector.ru.

Institute of Corporate Law and Corporate Governance website retrieved from www.iclg.ru

Institute of Corporate Law and Corporate Governance. (2002). *Managing corporate governance risks in Russia.* Moscow: Institute of Corporate Law and Corporate Governance, May.

Institute of International Finance. (2002). Policies for corporate governance and transparency in emerging markets. Retrieved February from www.iif.com/data/public/NEWEAG_Report.pdf.

Instituto Brasileiro de Governanca Corporativa. (2004). Code of Best Practice of Corporate Governance.

International Corporate Governance Network website retrieved from http://www.icgn.org/

International Finance Corporation, Russia Corporate Governance Project website retrieved from http://www2.ifc.org/rcgp/english.htm

Iskyan, K. (2002). Clean-up time in Russia. *Global Finance*, February, 32–35.

Jindrichovska, I., & Mcleay, S. (2005). Accounting for good news and accounting for bad news: Some empirical evidence from the Czech Republic. *European Accounting Review, 14*(3), 635–655.

Judge, W. Q., Naoumova, I., & Kutzevol, N. (2003). Corporate governance in Russia: An empirical study of Russian managers' perception. Paper presented at the Gorbachev Foundation Conference on Corporate Governance in Transition Economies held at Northeastern University, Boston, April 2003. Published in *Journal of World Business*, November, 2003, 38(4), 385–396 under the title Corporate Governance and Firm Performance in Russia: An Empirical Study.

Keller, S. B. (1986). Reporting timeliness in the presence of subject to audit qualifications. *Journal of Business Finance & Accounting, 13*(1), 117–124.

Krishnan, G. V. (2005). The association between big 6 auditor industry expertise and the asymmetric timeliness of earnings. *Journal of Accounting, Auditing & Finance, 20*(3), 209–228.

Kross, W., & Schroeder, D. A. (1984). An empirical investigation of the effect of quarterly earnings announcement timing on stock returns. *Journal of Accounting Research, 22*(1), 153–176.

Leventis, S., & Weetman, P. (2004). Timeliness of financial reporting: Applicability of disclosure theories in an emerging capital market. *Accounting and Business Research, 34*(1), 43–56.

McCarthy, D. J., & Puffer, S. M. (2002). Corporate governance in Russia: Towards a European, US, or Russian model? *European Management Journal, 20*(6), 630–641.

McCarthy, D. J., & Puffer, S. M. (2003). Corporate governance in Russia: A framework for analysis. *Journal of World Business, 38*(4), 397–415.

McGee, R. W. (2006). Timeliness of financial reporting in the energy sector. *Russian/CIS Energy & Mining Law Journal, 4*(2), 6–10.

McGee, R. W. (2007a). Corporate governance in Russia: A case study of timeliness of financial reporting in the telecom industry. *International Finance Review, 7*, 365–390.

McGee, R. W. (2007b). *Corporate governance and the timeliness of financial reporting: A case study of the Russian energy sector.* Fifth International Conference on Accounting and Finance in Transition. London, July 12–14.

McGee, R. W. (2007c). Transparency and disclosure in Russia, in T. M. Mickiewicz (ed.), *Corporate governance and finance in Poland and Russia* (pp. 278–295). London: Palgrave Macmillan.

McGee, R. W. (2008a). Insider trading in transition economies. In R. W. McGee (ed.), *Corporate governance in transition economies.* New York: Springer.

McGee, R. W. (2008b). Some thoughts on the market for corporate control. In R. W. McGee (ed.), *Corporate governance in transition economies.* New York: Springer.

McGee, R. W. (2008c). Corporate governance and the timeliness of financial reporting: An overview. In R. W. McGee (ed.), *Corporate governance in transition economies.* New York: Springer.

McGee, R. W. (2008d). The timeliness of corporate governance in Russia: A trend analysis. In R. W. McGee (ed.), *Corporate governance in transition economies.* New York: Springer.

McGee, R. W., & Gunn, R. (2008). The timeliness of financial reporting: A comparative study of Russian and Non-Russian companies in the transportation industry. In R. W. McGee (ed.), *Corporate governance in transition economies.* New York: Springer.

McGee, R, W., & Igoe, D. N. (2008). Corporate governance and the timeliness of financial reporting: A comparative study of selected EU and transition countries. *Proceedings of the 43rd Annual Western Regional Meeting of the American Accounting Association, San Francisco, May 1–3*, 2008, 74–87. Revised and reprinted in R. W. McGee (ed.), *Corporate governance in transition economies.* New York: Springer.

McGee, R. W., & Preobragenskaya, G. G. (2005). *Accounting and financial system reform in a transition economy: A case study of Russia.* New York: Springer.

McGee, R. W., Preobragenskaya, G. G. (2006). *Accounting and financial system reform in Eastern Europe and Asia.* New York: Springer.

McGee, R. W., & Tarangelo, T. (2008a). The timeliness of financial reporting: A comparative study of Russian and Non-Russian banks. In R. W. McGee (ed.), *Corporate governance in transition economies.* New York: Springer.

McGee, R. W., & Tarangelo, T. (2008b). The timeliness of financial reporting and the Russian banking system: An empirical study. In R. W. McGee (ed), *Accounting reform in transition and developing economies*, New York: Springer.

McGee, R. W., Tarangelo, T., & Tyler, M. (2008). The timeliness of financial reporting: A comparative study of companies in Russia and the USA. In R. W. McGee (ed.), *Corporate governance in transition economies.* New York: Springer.

McGee, R. W., & Tyler, M. (2008). The timeliness of financial reporting: A comparative study of Russian and Non-Russian companies. In R. W. McGee (ed.), *Corporate governance in transition economies.* New York: Springer.

McGee, R. W., Tyler, M., Tarangelo, T., & Igoe, D. N. (2008). The timeliness of financial reporting: A comparative study of companies in Russia and the European Union. In R. W. McGee (ed.), *Corporate governance in transition economies.* New York: Springer.

McGee, R. W., & Yuan, X. (2008). Corporate governance and the timeliness of financial reporting: An empirical study of the People's Republic of China. *International Journal of Business, Accounting and Finance*, forthcoming.

McGee, R. W., Yuan, X., Tarangelo, T., & Tyler, M. (2008). The timeliness of financial reporting: A comparative study of the People's Republic of China and Russia. In R. W. McGee (ed.), *Corporate governance in transition economies*. New York: Springer.

Metzger, B., Dean, R. N., & Bloom, D. (2002, March/April). Russia's code of corporate conduct: An innovative approach to solving shareholder rights abuses. *The Corporate Governance Advisor, 10*(2), 12–17.

Miller, S. (2002, March). Law and order makes its mark. *Banker, 152*(913), 44–45.

Monks, R.A.G., & Minow, N. (Eds.) (2004). Corporate governance (3rd ed.), London: Blackwell Publishers.

Muravyev, A. (2001). Turnover of top executives in Russian companies. *Russian Economic Trends, 10*(1), 20–24.

National Association of Corporate Directors website retrieved from http://www.nacdonline.org/

Organisation for Economic Co-operation and Development. (1999). *Principles of Corporate Governance*. Paris: Author. Available at www.oecd.org/dataoecd/47/50/4347646.pdf.

Organisation for Economic Co-operation and Development. (2002). *White Paper on Corporate Governance in Russia*. Paris: Author, Retrieved April 15, from http://www.oecd.org/dataoecd/10/3/2789982.pdf.

Organization for Economic Co-operation and Development. (2003a). *White Paper on Corporate Governance in Asia*. Paris: Author.

Organisation for Economic Co-operation and Development. (2003b). *White Paper on Corporate Governance in South Eastern Europe*. Paris: Author. Retrieved from www.oecd.org.

Organisation for Economic Co-operation and Development. (2003c). *Survey of Corporate Governance Developments in OECD Countries*. Paris: Author.

Organisation for Economic Co-operation and Development. (2003d). *White Paper on Corporate Governance in Latin America*. Paris: Author.

Organisation for Economic Co-operation and Development. (2004). *Principles of Corporate Governance*. Paris: Author. Available at www.oecd.org.

Organisation for Economic Co-operation and Development. (2006a). *Policy Brief on Corporate Governance of Banks in Asia*. Paris: Author.

Organisation for Economic Co-operation and Development. (2006b). *Case Studies of Good Corporate Governance Practices*. Paris: Author. Also available in Spanish and Portuguese.

Organisation for Economic Co-operation and Development. (2007). *Asia: Overview of Corporate Governance Frameworks in 2007*. Paris: Author.

Organisation for Economic Co-operation and Development website retrieved from http://www.oecd.org/document/62/0,2340,en_2649_37439_1912830_1_1_1_37439,00.html

Peng, M., Buck, T., & Filatotchev, I. (2003). Do outside directors and new managers help improve firm performance? An exploratory study in Russian privatization. *Journal of World Business, 38*(4), 348–360.

Pistor, K., Raiser, M., & Gelfer, S. (2000). Law and finance in transition economies. *Economics of Transition, 8*(2), 325–368.

Pope, P. F., & Walker, M. (1999). International differences in the timeliness, conservatism, and classification of earnings. *Journal of Accounting Research, 37*(Supp.), 53–87.

Puffer, S. M., & McCarthy, D. J. (2003). The emergence of corporate governance in Russia. *Journal of World Business, 38*(4), 284–298.

Rees, W. P., & Giner, B. (2001). On the asymmetric recognition of good and bad news in France, Germany and the UK. *Journal of Business Finance & Accounting, 28*(9&10): 1285–1332.

Reyes, F. (2008). Corporate governance in Latin America. *Inter-American Law Review*, forthcoming.

Robertson, C. J., Gilley, K. M., & Street, M. D. (2003). The relationship between ethics and firm practices in Russia and the United States. *Journal of World Business, 38*(4), 375–384.

Roth, K., & Kostova, T. (2003). Organizational coping with institutional upheaval in transition economies. *Journal of World Business, 38*(4), 314–330.

Russian Corporate Governance Roundtable website retrieved from http://www.corp-gov.org/

Russian Institute of Directors website retrieved from www.rid.ru

Russian Institute of Directors. (2002). *Corporate governance code*, Moscow: Author, Retrieved April 5, from www.rid.ru.

Russian Institute of Directors. (2003). *Structure and activities of boards of directors of Russian joint-stock companies.* Moscow: Author. Retrieved from www.rid.ru

Rwegasira, K. (2000). Corporate governance in emerging capital markets: Whither Africa? *Corporate Governance 8*(3), 258–267.

Soltani, B. (2002). Timeliness of corporate and audit reports: Some empirical evidence in the French context. *The International Journal of Accounting, 37,* 215–246.

Standard & Poor's. (2004). Country Governance Study: Brazil.

Trueman, B. (1990). Theories of earnings-announcement timing. *Journal of Accounting & Economics, 13*: 285–301.

Wagner, J., Stimpert, J., & Fubara, E. (1998). Board composition and organizational performance: Two studies of insider/outsider effects. *Journal of Management Studies, 35*(5), 655–677.

Whittred, G., & Zimmer, I. (1984). Timeliness of financial reporting and financial distress. *The Accounting Review, 59*(2), 287–295.

Whittred, G.P. (1980). Audit qualification and the timeliness of corporate annual reports. *The Accounting Review, 55*(4): 563–577.

World Bank Corporate Governance website retrieved from http://www.worldbank.org/html/fpd/privatesector/cg/

World Bank. (2001), *Report on the Observance of Standards and Codes (ROSC), Corporate Governance Country Assessment, Republic of Croatia, September.* Author. Retrieved from www.worldbank.org.

World Bank. (2002a), *Report on the Observance of Standards and Codes (ROSC), Corporate Governance Country Assessment, Bulgaria, September.* Washington, DC: Author. Retrieved from www.worldbank.org.

World Bank. (2002b), *Report on the Observance of Standards and Codes (ROSC), Corporate Governance Country Assessment, Czech Republic, July.* Washington, DC: Author. Retrieved from www.worldbank.org.

World Bank. (2002c), *Report on the Observance of Standards and Codes (ROSC), Corporate Governance Country Assessment, Georgia, March.* Washington, DC: Author. Retrieved from www.worldbank.org.

World Bank. (2002d), *Report on the Observance of Standards and Codes (ROSC), Corporate Governance Country Assessment, Latvia, December.* Washington, DC: Author. Retrieved from www.worldbank.org.

World Bank. (2002e), *Report on the Observance of Standards and Codes (ROSC), Corporate Governance Country Assessment, Republic of Lithuania, July.* Washington, DC: Author. Retrieved from www.worldbank.org.

World Bank. (2002f), *Report on the Observance of Standards and Codes (ROSC), Corporate Governance Country Assessment, Mauritius, October.* World Bank: Author, Retrieved from www.worldbank.org.

World Bank. (2003a), *Report on the Observance of Standards and Codes (ROSC), Corporate Governance Country Assessment, Chile, May.* World Bank: Author, Retrieved from www.worldbank.org.

World Bank. (2003b), *Report on the Observance of Standards and Codes (ROSC), Corporate Governance Country Assessment, Colombia, August.* World Bank. Retrieved from www.worldbank.org.

World Bank. (2003c), *Report on the Observance of Standards and Codes (ROSC), Corporate Governance Country Assessment, Republic of Korea, September.* World Bank:. Retrieved from www.worldbank.org.

World Bank. (2003d), *Report on the Observance of Standards and Codes (ROSC), Corporate Governance Country Assessment,* Mexico, September. World Bank: Retrieved from www.worldbank.org.

World Bank. (2003e), *Report on the Observance of Standards and Codes (ROSC), Corporate Governance Country Assessment, Republic of South Africa, July.* World Bank. Retrieved from www.worldbank.org.

World Bank. (2003f), *Report on the Observance of Standards and Codes (ROSC), Corporate Governance Country Assessment, Hungary, February.* Washington, DC: Author. Retrieved from www.worldbank.org.

World Bank. (2003g), *Report on the Observance of Standards and Codes (ROSC), Corporate Governance Country Assessment, Slovak Republic, October.* Washington, DC: Author. Retrieved from www.worldbank.org.

World Bank. (2004a), *Report on the Observance of Standards and Codes (ROSC), Corporate Governance Country Assessment, Moldova, May.* Washington, DC: World Bank. Retrieved from www.worldbank.org.

World Bank. (2004b), *Report on the Observance of Standards and Codes (ROSC), Corporate Governance Country Assessment, Romania, April.* Washington, DC: Author. Retrieved from www.worldbank.org.

World Bank. (2004c), *Report on the Observance of Standards and Codes (ROSC), Corporate Governance Country Assessment, Slovenia, May.* Washington, DC: Author. Retrieved from www.worldbank.org.

World Bank. (2004d), *Report on the Observance of Standards and Codes (ROSC), Corporate Governance Country Assessment, Egypt, March.* World Bank. Retrieved from www.worldbank.org.

World Bank. (2004e), *Report on the Observance of Standards and Codes (ROSC), Corporate Governance Country Assessment, India, April.* World Bank. Retrieved from www.worldbank.org.

World Bank. (2004f), *Report on the Observance of Standards and Codes (ROSC), Corporate Governance Country Assessment, Republic of Indonesia, April.* World Bank. Retrieved from Retrieved from www.worldbank.org.

World Bank. (2004g), *Report on the Observance of Standards and Codes (ROSC), Corporate Governance Country Assessment, Jordan, June.* World Bank. Retrieved from www.worldbank.org.

World Bank. (2004h), *Report on the Observance of Standards and Codes (ROSC), Corporate Governance Country Assessment, Panama, June.* World Bank. Retrieved from www.worldbank.org.

World Bank. (2004i), *Report on the Observance of Standards and Codes (ROSC), Corporate Governance Country Assessment, Republic of Peru, June.* World Bank. Retrieved from www.worldbank.org.

World Bank. (2005a), *Report on the Observance of Standards and Codes (ROSC), Corporate Governance Country Assessment, Brazil, May.* World Bank. Retrieved from www.worldbank.org.

World Bank. (2005b), *Report on the Observance of Standards and Codes (ROSC), Corporate Governance Country Assessment, Ghana, May.* World Bank. Retrieved from www.worldbank.org.

World Bank. (2005c), *Report on the Observance of Standards and Codes (ROSC), Corporate Governance Country Assessment, Malaysia, June.* World Bank. Retrieved from www.worldbank.org.

World Bank. (2005d), *Report on the Observance of Standards and Codes (ROSC), Corporate Governance Country Assessment, Nepal, April.* World Bank. Retrieved from www.worldbank.org.

World Bank. (2005e), *Report on the Observance of Standards and Codes (ROSC), Corporate Governance Country Assessment, Pakistan, June.* World Bank. Retrieved from www.worldbank.org.

World Bank. (2005f), *Report on the Observance of Standards and Codes (ROSC), Corporate Governance Country Assessment, Thailand, June.* World Bank. Retrieved from www.worldbank.org.

World Bank. (2005g), *Report on the Observance of Standards and Codes (ROSC), Corporate Governance Country Assessment, Uruguay. September.* World Bank. Retrieved from www.worldbank.org.

World Bank. (2005h), *Report on the Observance of Standards and Codes (ROSC), Corporate Governance Country Assessment, Armenia, April.* Washington, DC: Author. Retrieved from www. worldbank.org.

World Bank. (2005i), *Report on the Observance of Standards and Codes (ROSC), Corporate Governance Country Assessment, Azerbaijan, July.* Washington, DC: Author. Retrieved from www.worldbank.org.

World Bank. (2005j), *Report on the Observance of Standards and Codes (ROSC), Corporate Governance Country Assessment, Macedonia, June.* Washington, DC: Author. Retrieved from www. worldbank.org.

World Bank. (2005k), *Report on the Observance of Standards and Codes (ROSC), Corporate Governance Country Assessment, Poland, June.* Washington, DC: Author. Retrieved from www.worldbank.org.

World Bank. (2006a), *Report on the Observance of Standards and Codes (ROSC), Corporate Governance Country Assessment, Bosnia and Herzegovina, June.* Washington, DC: Author. Retrieved from www.worldbank.org.

World Bank. (2006b), *Report on the Observance of Standards and Codes (ROSC), Corporate Governance Country Assessment, Ukraine, October.* Washington, DC: Author. Retrieved from www.worldbank.org.

World Bank. (2006c), *Report on the Observance of Standards and Codes (ROSC), Corporate Governance Country Assessment, Bhutan, December.* World Bank. Retrieved from www.worldbank.org.

World Bank. (2006d), *Report on the Observance of Standards and Codes (ROSC), Corporate Governance Country Assessment, Philippines, May.* World Bank. Retrieved from www.worldbank.org.

World Bank. (2006e), *Report on the Observance of Standards and Codes (ROSC), Corporate Governance Country Assessment, Senegal, June.* World Bank. Retrieved from www.worldbank.org.

World Bank. (2006f), *Report on the Observance of Standards and Codes (ROSC), Corporate Governance Country Assessment, Vietnam, June.* World Bank. Retrieved from www.worldbank.org.

World Bank. (n.d.), *Report on the Observance of Standards and Codes (ROSC), Corporate Governance Country Assessment, Turkey.* World Bank. Retrieved from www.worldbank.org.

World Bank. (n.d.), *Report on the Observance of Standards and Codes (ROSC), Corporate Governance Country Assessment, Zimbabwe.* World Bank. Retrieved from www.worldbank.org.

Chapter 2
Shareholder Rights Issues

Robert W. McGee

Introduction

One of the Organisation for Economic Co-operation and Development (OECD, 2004) principles of corporate governance is that

> The corporate governance framework should protect and facilitate the exercise of shareholders' rights.

This chapter examines this principle in some depth.

Methodology

The OECD has published a number of studies on corporate governance. In one study (OECD, 2004) it outlined a series of benchmarks intended for use by investors, policy makers, corporations, and other stakeholders. Corporations that follow the guidelines provided in this document will have a strong corporate governance system.

The World Bank has conducted a number of studies on corporate governance practices in more than 40 countries, using these OECD guidelines as a template. More than 20 of those studies were of developing economies. The World Bank studies examined the corporate governance practices identified by the OECD and classified them into the following five categories:

O = Observed
LO = Largely Observed
PO = Partially Observed
MNO = Materially Not Observed
NO = Not Observed

R.W. McGee (✉)
Florida International University, Miami, FL, USA
e-mail: bob414@hotmail.com

R.W. McGee (ed.), *Corporate Governance in Developing Economies*,
DOI 10.1007/978-0-387-84833-4_2, © Springer Science+Business Media, LLC 2009

The present study assigned point values to those categories, where O = 5, LO = 4, PO = 3, MNO = 2, and NO = 1, then compared how closely the developing countries came to meeting the various OECD benchmarks. This study reports on those findings in the category of shareholder rights.

Findings

The following pages summarize the findings.

Protection of Shareholder Rights

Table 2.1 shows the World Bank rankings for protection of shareholder rights by country. Only Egypt, India, and South Africa received the highest ranking. The Largely Observed category was the category most frequently listed. Nepal and Ghana were the only two countries in the MNO category. No countries ranked in the lowest category.

Table 2.1 Protection of shareholder rights

Country	O	LO	PO	MNO	NO
Bhutan			X		
Brazil		X			
Chile		X			
Colombia		X			
Egypt	X				
Ghana				X	
India	X				
Indonesia			X		
Jordan		X			
Korea		X			
Malaysia		X			
Mauritius			X		
Mexico		X			
Nepal				X	
Pakistan		X			
Panama		X			
Peru		X			
Philippines		X			
Senegal		X			
South Africa	X				
Thailand		X			
Uruguay			X		
Vietnam			X		

Shareholder Participation in Decision Making

Table 2.2 shows the World Bank rankings for the category of shareholder participation in decision making. Only Chile, India, and Korea earned the top ranking. The next two categories had a nearly equal number of countries. No countries were listed in the last two categories.

Shareholder Participation and Voting

Table 2.3 shows the World Bank rankings in the category of shareholder participation and voting. Only India earned the top ranking for this category. Most countries fell into the LO or PO categories. Only Bhutan was in the MNO category and no country fell into the lowest category.

Capital Structures and Arrangements

Table 2.4 shows the results for the category of capital structures and arrangements. Only South Africa earned the top ranking in this category. The most frequent category

Table 2.2 Shareholder participation in decision making

Country	O	LO	PO	MNO	NO
Bhutan			X		
Brazil		X			
Chile	X				
Colombia			X		
Egypt		X			
Ghana		X			
India	X				
Indonesia		X			
Jordan		X			
Korea	X				
Malaysia			X		
Mauritius			X		
Mexico			X		
Nepal		X			
Pakistan		X			
Panama			X		
Peru		X			
Philippines		X			
Senegal		X			
South Africa		X			
Thailand			X		
Uruguay			X		
Vietnam			X		

Table 2.3 Shareholder participation and voting

Country	O	LO	PO	MNO	NO
Bhutan				X	
Brazil			X		
Chile		X			
Colombia			X		
Egypt		X			
Ghana		X			
India	X				
Indonesia		X			
Jordan		X			
Korea		X			
Malaysia		X			
Mauritius			X		
Mexico			X		
Nepal			X		
Pakistan		X			
Panama			X		
Peru			X		
Philippines			X		
Senegal		X			
South Africa			X		
Thailand		X			
Uruguay			X		
Vietnam			X		

Table 2.4 Capital structures and arrangements – disproportionate control

Country	O	LO	PO	MNO	NO
Bhutan			X		
Brazil			X		
Chile			X		
Colombia				X	
Egypt		X			
Ghana			X		
India		X			
Indonesia				X	
Jordan			X		
Korea		X			
Malaysia		X			
Mauritius			X		
Mexico			X		
Nepal				X	
Pakistan			X		
Panama				X	
Peru			X		
Philippines			X		
Senegal			X		
South Africa	X				
Thailand		X			
Uruguay				X	
Vietnam			X		

was the Partially Observed category. Five countries were listed in the MNO category. No country was listed in the bottom category.

The Market for Corporate Control

Table 2.5 shows the World Bank rankings for the category of the market for corporate control. Only India earned the top ranking in this category. The next three categories each had a number of countries listed. Bhutan and Senegal were listed in the lowest category.

Costs and Benefits of Voting Rights

Table 2.6 shows the World Bank rankings for the category of costs and benefits of voting rights. None of the countries earned the top ranking in this category and the only three countries that earned the second highest ranking were Brazil, Chile, and Thailand. Most countries were in the third or fourth category. Five countries were ranked in the lowest category.

Table 2.5 Market for corporate control

Country	O	LO	PO	MNO	NO
Bhutan					X
Brazil		X			
Chile		X			
Colombia				X	
Egypt		X			
Ghana				X	
India	X				
Indonesia				X	
Jordan			X		
Korea		X			
Malaysia		X			
Mauritius			X		
Mexico		X			
Nepal				X	
Pakistan			X		
Panama		X			
Peru			X		
Philippines			X		
Senegal					X
South Africa		X			
Thailand			X		
Uruguay				X	
Vietnam				X	

Table 2.6 Costs and benefits of voting rights

Country	O	LO	PO	MNO	NO
Bhutan			X		
Brazil		X			
Chile		X			
Colombia					X
Egypt		X			
Ghana				X	
India				X	
Indonesia				X	
Jordan			X		
Korea			X		
Malaysia			X		
Mauritius					X
Mexico					X
Nepal				X	
Pakistan				X	
Panama				X	
Peru			X		
Philippines			X		
Senegal					X
South Africa					X
Thailand		X			
Uruguay				X	
Vietnam				X	

Concluding Comments

There is much room for improvement in all categories. In some categories not a single country earned the top ranking. In several categories one or more countries earned the lowest ranking.

References

OECD. (2004). *Principles of Corporate Governance.* Paris: Author.

World Bank. (2002). *Report on the Observance of Standards and Codes (ROSC), Corporate Governance Country Assessment, Mauritius, October.* World Bank. Retrieved from www.worldbank.org.

World Bank. (2003a). *Report on the Observance of Standards and Codes (ROSC), Corporate Governance Country Assessment, Chile, May.* World Bank. Retrieved from Retrieved from www.worldbank.org.

World Bank. (2003b). *Report on the Observance of Standards and Codes (ROSC), Corporate Governance Country Assessment, Colombia, August.* World Bank. Retrieved from www.worldbank.org.

World Bank. (2003c). *Report on the Observance of Standards and Codes (ROSC), Corporate Governance Country Assessment, Republic of Korea, September.* World Bank. Retrieved from www.worldbank.org.

World Bank. (2003d). *Report on the Observance of Standards and Codes (ROSC), Corporate Governance Country Assessment, Mexico, September.* World Bank. Retrieved from www.worldbank.org.

World Bank. (2003e). *Report on the Observance of Standards and Codes (ROSC), Corporate Governance Country Assessment, Republic of South Africa, July.* World Bank. Retrieved from www.worldbank.org.

World Bank. (2004a). *Report on the Observance of Standards and Codes (ROSC), Corporate Governance Country Assessment, Egypt, March.* World Bank. Retrieved from www.worldbank.org.

World Bank. (2004b). *Report on the Observance of Standards and Codes (ROSC), Corporate Governance Country Assessment, India, April.* World Bank. Retrieved from www.worldbank.org.

World Bank. (2004c). *Report on the Observance of Standards and Codes (ROSC), Corporate Governance Country Assessment, Republic of Indonesia, April.* World Bank. Retrieved from www.worldbank.org.

World Bank. (2004d). *Report on the Observance of Standards and Codes (ROSC), Corporate Governance Country Assessment, Jordan, June.* World Bank. Retrieved from www.worldbank.org.

World Bank. (2004e). *Report on the Observance of Standards and Codes (ROSC), Corporate Governance Country Assessment, Panama, June.* World Bank. Retrieved from www.worldbank.org.

World Bank. (2004f). *Report on the Observance of Standards and Codes (ROSC), Corporate Governance Country Assessment, Republic of Peru, June.* World Bank. Retrieved from www.worldbank.org.

World Bank. (2005a). *Report on the Observance of Standards and Codes (ROSC), Corporate Governance Country Assessment, Brazil, May.* World Bank. Retrieved from www.worldbank.org.

World Bank. (2005b). *Report on the Observance of Standards and Codes (ROSC), Corporate Governance Country Assessment, Ghana, May.* World Bank. Retrieved from www.worldbank.org.

World Bank. (2005c). *Report on the Observance of Standards and Codes (ROSC), Corporate Governance Country Assessment, Malaysia, June.* World Bank. Retrieved from www.worldbank.org.

World Bank. (2005d). *Report on the Observance of Standards and Codes (ROSC), Corporate Governance Country Assessment, Nepal, April.* World Bank. Retrieved from www.worldbank.org.

World Bank. (2005e). *Report on the Observance of Standards and Codes (ROSC), Corporate Governance Country Assessment, Pakistan, June.* World Bank. Retrieved from www.worldbank.org.

World Bank. (2005f). *Report on the Observance of Standards and Codes (ROSC), Corporate Governance Country Assessment, Thailand, June.* World Bank. Retrieved from www.worldbank.org.

World Bank. (2005g). *Report on the Observance of Standards and Codes (ROSC), Corporate Governance Country Assessment, Uruguay. September.* World Bank. Retrieved from www.worldbank.org.

World Bank. (2006a). *Report on the Observance of Standards and Codes (ROSC), Corporate Governance Country Assessment, Bhutan, December.* World Bank. Retrieved from www.worldbank.org.

World Bank. (2006b). *Report on the Observance of Standards and Codes (ROSC), Corporate Governance Country Assessment, Philippines, May.* World Bank. Retrieved from www.worldbank.org.

World Bank. (2006c). *Report on the Observance of Standards and Codes (ROSC), Corporate Governance Country Assessment, Senegal, June.* World Bank. Retrieved from www.worldbank.org.

World Bank. (2006d). *Report on the Observance of Standards and Codes (ROSC), Corporate Governance Country Assessment, Vietnam, June.* World Bank. Retrieved from www. worldbank.org.

World Bank. (n.d.). *Report on the Observance of Standards and Codes (ROSC), Corporate Governance Country Assessment, Turkey.* World Bank. Retrieved from www.worldbank.org.

World Bank. (n.d.). *Report on the Observance of Standards and Codes (ROSC), Corporate Governance Country Assessment, Zimbabwe*, World Bank. Retrieved from www.worldbank.org.

Chapter 3
Equitable Treatment of Shareholders

Robert W. McGee

Introduction

One of the Organisation for Economic Co-operation and Development (OECD, 2004) principles of corporate governance is that

> The corporate governance framework should ensure the equitable treatment of all shareholders, including minority and foreign shareholders. All shareholders should have the opportunity to obtain effective redress for violation of their rights.

This chapter examines this principle in some depth.

Methodology

The OECD has published a number of studies on corporate governance. In one study (OECD, 2004) it outlined a series of benchmarks intended for use by investors, policy makers, corporations, and other stakeholders. Corporations that follow the guidelines provided in this document will have a strong corporate governance system.

The World Bank has conducted a number of studies on corporate governance practices in more than 40 countries, using these OECD guidelines as a template. More than 20 of those studies were of developing economies. The World Bank studies examined the corporate governance practices identified by the OECD and classified them into the following five categories:

O = Observed
LO = Largely Observed
PO = Partially Observed
MNO = Materially Not Observed
NO = Not Observed

R.W. McGee (✉)
Florida International University, Miami, FL, USA
e-mail: bob414@hotmail.com

R.W. McGee (ed.), *Corporate Governance in Developing Economies*,
DOI 10.1007/978-0-387-84833-4_3, © Springer Science+Business Media, LLC 2009

The present study assigned point values to these categories, where O=5, LO=4, PO=3, MNO=2, and NO=1, then compared how closely the developing countries came to meeting the various OECD benchmarks. This study reports on those findings in the category of equitable treatment of shareholders.

Findings

The following pages summarize the findings.

Equitable Treatment of Shareholders

Table 3.1 shows the rankings of each country in the category of equitable treatment of shareholders. None of the countries scored in the top category. The category with the most entrants was Partially Observed. Four countries were in the Materially Not Observed category and no countries were in the bottom category.

Table 3.1 Equitable treatment of shareholders

Country	O	LO	PO	MNO	NO
Bhutan			X		
Brazil			X		
Chile		X			
Colombia			X		
Egypt		X			
Ghana			X		
India			X		
Indonesia			X		
Jordan			X		
Korea		X			
Malaysia			X		
Mauritius			X		
Mexico			X		
Nepal				X	
Pakistan		X			
Panama				X	
Peru			X		
Philippines			X		
Senegal				X	
South Africa			X		
Thailand			X		
Uruguay			X		
Vietnam				X	

Insider Trading and Abusive Self-Dealing

Table 3.2 shows the results in this category. Only South Africa had the top ranking. The most frequently listed category was Partially Observed. Four countries were in the Materially Not Observed category. Only Senegal was in the Not Observed category.

Disclosure of Material Interests

Table 3.3 shows the results in the disclosure of material interests category. None of the countries ranked at the top. The category containing the most countries was Partially Observed. Four countries were in the Materially Not Observed category. Only Colombia was in the Not Observed category.

Concluding Comments

There is much room for improvement in this category. For two out of three categories no country earned the top ranking. In the other case, only one country was listed in the top category. In two out of three cases there was a country listed in the lowest category. Most countries tended to rank in one of the three middle categories.

Table 3.2 Insider trading and abusive self-dealing

Country	O	LO	PO	MNO	NO
Bhutan			X		
Brazil		X			
Chile			X		
Colombia				X	
Egypt			X		
Ghana			X		
India			X		
Indonesia			X		
Jordan		X			
Korea			X		
Malaysia		X			
Mauritius			X		
Mexico		X			
Nepal			X		
Pakistan			X		
Panama		X			
Peru				X	
Philippines			X		
Senegal					X
South Africa	X				
Thailand		X			
Uruguay				X	
Vietnam				X	

Table 3.3 Disclosure of material interests

Country	O	LO	PO	MNO	NO
Bhutan			X		
Brazil			X		
Chile		X			
Colombia					X
Egypt		X			
Ghana				X	
India			X		
Indonesia			X		
Jordan		X			
Korea			X		
Malaysia		X			
Mauritius			X		
Mexico			X		
Nepal				X	
Pakistan		X			
Panama		X			
Peru				X	
Philippines			X		
Senegal			X		
South Africa					
Thailand		X			
Uruguay			X		
Vietnam				X	

References

OECD. (2004). *Principles of Corporate Governance*. Paris: Author.

World Bank. (2002). *Report on the Observance of Standards and Codes (ROSC), Corporate Governance Country Assessment, Mauritius, October*. World Bank. Retrieved from www.worldbank.org.

World Bank. (2003a). *Report on the Observance of Standards and Codes (ROSC), Corporate Governance Country Assessment, Chile, May*. World Bank. Retrieved from www.worldbank.org.

World Bank. (2003b). *Report on the Observance of Standards and Codes (ROSC), Corporate Governance Country Assessment, Colombia, August*. World Bank. Retrieved from www.worldbank.org.

World Bank. (2003c). *Report on the Observance of Standards and Codes (ROSC), Corporate Governance Country Assessment, Republic of Korea, September*. World Bank. Retrieved from www.worldbank.org.

World Bank. (2003d). *Report on the Observance of Standards and Codes (ROSC), Corporate Governance Country Assessment, Mexico, September*. World Bank. Retrieved from www.worldbank.org.

World Bank. (2003e). *Report on the Observance of Standards and Codes (ROSC), Corporate Governance Country Assessment, Republic of South Africa, July*. World Bank. Retrieved from www.worldbank.org.

World Bank. (2004a). *Report on the Observance of Standards and Codes (ROSC), Corporate Governance Country Assessment, Egypt, March*. World Bank. Retrieved from www.worldbank.org.

World Bank. (2004b). *Report on the Observance of Standards and Codes (ROSC), Corporate Governance Country Assessment, India, April.* World Bank. Retrieved from www.worldbank.org.

World Bank. (2004c). *Report on the Observance of Standards and Codes (ROSC), Corporate Governance Country Assessment, Republic of Indonesia, April.* World Bank. Retrieved from www.worldbank.org.

World Bank. (2004d). *Report on the Observance of Standards and Codes (ROSC), Corporate Governance Country Assessment, Jordan, June.* World Bank. Retrieved from www.worldbank.org.

World Bank. (2004e). *Report on the Observance of Standards and Codes (ROSC), Corporate Governance Country Assessment, Panama, June.* World Bank. Retrieved from www.worldbank.org.

World Bank. (2004f). *Report on the Observance of Standards and Codes (ROSC), Corporate Governance Country Assessment, Republic of Peru, June.* World Bank. Retrieved from www.worldbank.org.

World Bank. (2005a). *Report on the Observance of Standards and Co des (ROSC), Corporate Governance Country Assessment, Brazil, May.* World Bank. Retrieved from www.worldbank.org.

World Bank. (2005b). *Report on the Observance of Standards and Codes (ROSC), Corporate Governance Country Assessment, Ghana, May.* World Bank. Retrieved from www.worldbank.org.

World Bank. (2005c). *Report on the Observance of Standards and Codes (ROSC), Corporate Governance Country Assessment, Malaysia, June.* World Bank. Retrieved from www.worldbank.org.

World Bank. (2005d). *Report on the Observance of Standards and Codes (ROSC), Corporate Governance Country Assessment, Nepal, April.* World Bank. Retrieved from www.worldbank.org.

World Bank. (2005e). *Report on the Observance of Standards and Codes (ROSC), Corporate Governance Country Assessment, Pakistan, June.* World Bank. Retrieved from www.worldbank.org.

World Bank. (2005f). *Report on the Observance of Standards and Codes (ROSC), Corporate Governance Country Assessment, Thailand, June.* World Bank. Retrieved from www.worldbank.org.

World Bank. (2005g). *Report on the Observance of Standards and Codes (ROSC), Corporate Governance Country Assessment, Uruguay. September.* World Bank. Retrieved from www.worldbank.org.

World Bank. (2006a). *Report on the Observance of Standards and Codes (ROSC), Corporate Governance Country Assessment, Bhutan, December.* World Bank. Retrieved from www.worldbank.org.

World Bank. (2006b). *Report on the Observance of Standards and Codes (ROSC), Corporate Governance Country Assessment, Philippines, May.* World Bank. Retrieved from www.worldbank.org.

World Bank. (2006c). *Report on the Observance of Standards and Codes (ROSC), Corporate Governance Country Assessment, Senegal, June.* World Bank. Retrieved from www.worldbank.org.

World Bank. (2006d). *Report on the Observance of Standards and Codes (ROSC), Corporate Governance Country Assessment, Vietnam, June.* World Bank. Retrieved from www.worldbank.org.

World Bank. (n.d.). *Report on the Observance of Standards and Codes (ROSC), Corporate Governance Country Assessment, Turkey.* World Bank. Retrieved from www.worldbank.org.

World Bank. (n.d.). *Report on the Observance of Standards and Codes (ROSC), Corporate Governance Country Assessment, Zimbabwe.* World Bank. Retrieved from www.worldbank.org.

Chapter 4
The Role of Stakeholders in Corporate Governance

Robert W. McGee

Introduction

One of the Organisation for Economic Co-operation and Development (OECD, 2004) principles of corporate governance is that

> The corporate governance framework should recognize the rights of stakeholders established by law or through mutual agreements and encourage active co-operation between corporations and stakeholders in creating wealth, jobs, and the sustainability of financially sound enterprises.

This chapter examines this principle in some depth.

Methodology

The OECD has published a number of studies on corporate governance. In one study (OECD, 2004) it outlined a series of benchmarks intended for use by investors, policy makers, corporations, and other stakeholders. Corporations that follow the guidelines provided in this document will have a strong corporate governance system.

The World Bank has conducted a number of studies on corporate governance practices in more than 40 countries, using these OECD guidelines as a template. More than 20 of those studies were of developing economies. The World Bank studies examined the corporate governance practices identified by the OECD and classified them into the following five categories:

O = Observed
LO = Largely Observed
PO = Partially Observed
MNO = Materially Not Observed
NO = Not Observed

R.W. McGee (✉)
Florida International University, Miami, FL, USA
e-mail: bob414@hotmail.com

R.W. McGee (ed.), *Corporate Governance in Developing Economies*,
DOI 10.1007/978-0-387-84833-4_4, © Springer Science+Business Media, LLC 2009

The present study assigned point values to these categories, where O=5, LO=4, PO=3, MNO=2, and NO=1, then compared how closely the developing countries came to meeting the various OECD benchmarks. This study reports on those findings in the category of the role of stakeholders in corporate governance.

Findings

The tables below present the findings for the category of the role of stakeholders.

Recognition of Rights of Stakeholders

Table 4.1 shows the results for the category of the recognition of rights of stakeholders. Eight of the 23 countries earned the top ranking. The other countries ranked in categories two or three. No country ranked in either of the lowest two categories.

Table 4.1 Recognition of rights of stakeholders

Country	O	LO	PO	MNO	NO
Bhutan			X		
Brazil	X				
Chile		X			
Colombia	X				
Egypt	X				
Ghana		X			
India	X				
Indonesia			X		
Jordan	X				
Korea			X		
Malaysia		X			
Mauritius			X		
Mexico		X			
Nepal		X			
Pakistan	X				
Panama	X				
Peru		X			
Philippines		X			
Senegal			X		
South Africa	X				
Thailand		X			
Uruguay			X		
Vietnam			X		

Opportunity for Effective Redress of Grievances

Table 4.2 shows the results for the category of opportunity for effective redress of grievances. Six countries earned the top ranking. The other countries fell into either category two or three. None of the countries fell into either of the bottom two categories.

Performance-Enhancement Mechanisms

Table 4.3 shows the relative rankings for the category of performance-enhancement mechanisms for stakeholder participation. Five countries earned the top rank. Mauritius and Nepal ranked in the Materially Not Observed category. None of the countries earned the lowest ranking.

Access to Relevant Information

Table 4.4 shows the rankings for the category of access to relevant information. Seven countries earned the top ranking. Most countries fell into the second or third category. Four countries earned the Materially Not Observed ranking. No country fell into the lowest category.

Table 4.2 Opportunity for effective redress of grievances

Country	O	LO	PO	MNO	NO
Bhutan			X		
Brazil	X				
Chile			X		
Colombia			X		
Egypt	X				
Ghana			X		
India			X		
Indonesia			X		
Jordan	X				
Korea	X				
Malaysia		X			
Mauritius			X		
Mexico		X			
Nepal		X			
Pakistan			X		
Panama	X				
Peru		X			
Philippines			X		
Senegal			X		
South Africa	X				
Thailand		X			
Uruguay		X			
Vietnam			X		

Table 4.3 Performance-enhancement mechanisms for stakeholder participation

Country	O	LO	PO	MNO	NO
Bhutan			X		
Brazil		X			
Chile		X			
Colombia		X			
Egypt	X				
Ghana	X				
India	X				
Indonesia			X		
Jordan	X				
Korea		X			
Malaysia		X			
Mauritius				X	
Mexico		X			
Nepal				X	
Pakistan	X				
Panama		X			
Peru			X		
Philippines			X		
Senegal			X		
South Africa		X			
Thailand		X			
Uruguay			X		
Vietnam			X		

Table 4.4 Access to relevant information

Country	O	LO	PO	MNO	NO
Bhutan				X	
Brazil		X			
Chile	X				
Colombia	X				
Egypt		X			
Ghana			X		
India	X				
Indonesia			X		
Jordan	X				
Korea	X				
Malaysia		X			
Mauritius		X			
Mexico	X				
Nepal			X		
Pakistan		X			
Panama		X			
Peru		X			
Philippines			X		
Senegal				X	
South Africa	X				
Thailand		X			
Uruguay				X	
Vietnam			X		

Concluding Comments

Countries did better in this category than in the categories of shareholder rights or equitable treatment of shareholders, in the sense that more countries earned the top ranking. But most countries earned the second or third highest ranking, which indicates that more work needs to be done in the category of the role of stakeholders in corporate governance.

References

OECD. (2004). *Principles of Corporate Governance.* Paris: Author.

World Bank. (2002). *Report on the Observance of Standards and Codes (ROSC), Corporate Governance Country Assessment, Mauritius, October.* World Bank. Retrieved from www.worldbank.org.

World Bank. (2003a). *Report on the Observance of Standards and Codes (ROSC), Corporate Governance Country Assessment, Chile, May.* World Bank. Retrieved from www.worldbank.org.

World Bank. (2003b), *Report on the Observance of Standards and Codes (ROSC), Corporate Governance Country Assessment, Colombia, August.* World Bank. Retrieved from www.worldbank.org.

World Bank. (2003c), *Report on the Observance of Standards and Codes (ROSC), Corporate Governance Country Assessment, Republic of Korea, September.* World Bank. Retrieved from www.worldbank.org.

World Bank. (2003d). *Report on the Observance of Standards and Codes (ROSC), Corporate Governance Country Assessment, Mexico, September.* World Bank. Retrieved from www.worldbank.org.

World Bank. (2003e). *Report on the Observance of Standards and Codes (ROSC), Corporate Governance Country Assessment, Republic of South Africa, July.* World Bank. Retrieved from www.worldbank.org.

World Bank. (2004a). *Report on the Observance of Standards and Codes (ROSC), Corporate Governance Country Assessment, Egypt, March.* World Bank. Retrieved from www.worldbank.org.

World Bank. (2004b). *Report on the Observance of Standards and Codes (ROSC), Corporate Governance Country Assessment, India, April.* World Bank. Retrieved from www.worldbank.org.

World Bank. (2004c). *Report on the Observance of Standards and Codes (ROSC), Corporate Governance Country Assessment, Republic of Indonesia, April.* World Bank. Retrieved from www.worldbank.org.

World Bank. (2004d). *Report on the Observance of Standards and Codes (ROSC), Corporate Governance Country Assessment, Jordan, June.* World Bank. Retrieved from www.worldbank.org.

World Bank. (2004e). *Report on the Observance of Standards and Codes (ROSC), Corporate Governance Country Assessment, Panama, June.* World Bank. Retrieved from www.worldbank.org.

World Bank. (2004f). *Report on the Observance of Standards and Codes (ROSC), Corporate Governance Country Assessment, Republic of Peru, June.* World Bank. Retrieved from www.worldbank.org.

World Bank. (2005a). *Report on the Observance of Standards and Codes (ROSC), Corporate Governance Country Assessment, Brazil, May.* World Bank. Retrieved from www.worldbank.org.

World Bank. (2005b). *Report on the Observance of Standards and Codes (ROSC), Corporate Governance Country Assessment, Ghana, May.* World Bank. www.worldbank.org.

World Bank. (2005c). *Report on the Observance of Standards and Codes (ROSC), Corporate Governance Country Assessment, Malaysia, June.* World Bank. Retrieved from www.worldbank.org.

World Bank. (2005d). *Report on the Observance of Standards and Codes (ROSC), Corporate Governance Country Assessment, Nepal, April.* World Bank. Retrieved from www.worldbank.org.

World Bank. (2005e). *Report on the Observance of Standards and Codes (ROSC), Corporate Governance Country Assessment, Pakistan, June.* World Bank. Retrieved from www.worldbank.org.

World Bank. (2005f). *Report on the Observance of Standards and Codes (ROSC), Corporate Governance Country Assessment, Thailand, June.* World Bank. Retrieved from www.worldbank.org.

World Bank. (2005g). *Report on the Observance of Standards and Codes (ROSC), Corporate Governance Country Assessment, Uruguay. September.* World Bank. www.worldbank.org.

World Bank. (2006a). *Report on the Observance of Standards and Codes (ROSC), Corporate Governance Country Assessment, Bhutan, December.* World Bank. Retrieved from www.worldbank.org.

World Bank. (2006b). *Report on the Observance of Standards and Codes (ROSC), Corporate Governance Country Assessment, Philippines, May.* World Bank. Retrieved from www.worldbank.org.

World Bank. (2006c). *Report on the Observance of Standards and Codes (ROSC), Corporate Governance Country Assessment, Senegal, June.* World Bank. Retrieved from www.worldbank.org.

World Bank. (2006d). *Report on the Observance of Standards and Codes (ROSC), Corporate Governance Country Assessment, Vietnam, June.* World Bank. Retrieved from www.worldbank.org.

World Bank. (n.d.). *Report on the Observance of Standards and Codes (ROSC), Corporate Governance Country Assessment, Turkey.* Retrieved from World Bank. www.worldbank.org.

World Bank. (n.d.). *Report on the Observance of Standards and Codes (ROSC), Corporate Governance Country Assessment, Zimbabwe.* World Bank. Retrieved from www.worldbank.org.

Chapter 5
Disclosure & Transparency

Robert W. McGee

Introduction

One of the Organisation for Economic Co-operation and Development (OECD, 2004) principles of corporate governance is that

> The corporate governance framework should ensure that timely and accurate disclosure is made of all material matters regarding the corporation, including the financial situation, performance, ownership, and governance of the company.

This chapter examines this principle in some depth.

Methodology

The OECD has published a number of studies on corporate governance. In one study (OECD, 2004) it outlined a series of benchmarks intended for use by investors, policy makers, corporations, and other stakeholders. Corporations that follow the guidelines provided in this document will have a strong corporate governance system.

The World Bank has conducted a number of studies on corporate governance practices in more than 40 countries, using these OECD guidelines as a template. More than 20 of those studies were of developing economies. The World Bank studies examined the corporate governance practices identified by the OECD and classified them into the following five categories:

O = Observed
LO = Largely Observed
PO = Partially Observed
MNO = Materially Not Observed
NO = Not Observed

R.W. McGee (✉)
Florida International University, Miami, FL, USA
e-mail: bob414@hotmail.com

R.W. McGee (ed.), *Corporate Governance in Developing Economies*,
DOI 10.1007/978-0-387-84833-4_5, © Springer Science+Business Media, LLC 2009

The present study assigned point values to these categories, where O=5, LO=4, PO=3, MNO=2, and NO=1, then compared how closely the developing countries came to meeting the various OECD benchmarks. This study reports on those findings in the category of disclosure and transparency.

Findings

The findings for this category are presented below.

Timely and Accurate Disclosure of All Material Matters

Table 5.1 shows the results for the category of timely and accurate disclosure of all material matters. None of the countries achieved the top rating and only 7 of the 23 countries earned the second highest ranking. The most frequently listed category was Partially Observed. Four countries made the MNO rank. No countries were listed in the lowest category.

Table 5.1 Timely and accurate disclosure of all material matters

Country	O	LO	PO	MNO	NO
Bhutan			X		
Brazil			X		
Chile			X		
Colombia			X		
Egypt			X		
Ghana			X		
India		X			
Indonesia			X		
Jordan		X			
Korea		X			
Malaysia		X			
Mauritius			X		
Mexico		X			
Nepal				X	
Pakistan		X			
Panama			X		
Peru			X		
Philippines			X		
Senegal				X	
South Africa			X		
Thailand		X			
Uruguay				X	
Vietnam				X	

Standards of Preparation, Audit, and Disclosure of Information

Table 5.2 shows the results for the category of standards of preparation, audit, and disclosure of information. Only Jordan and Malaysia earned the top score in this category. Only five countries had the second highest ranking. The most frequent ranking was Partially Observed. Colombia and Nepal earned the fourth-level ranking. No countries were in the bottom ranking.

Independent Audit

Table 5.3 shows the results for the category of independent audit. None of the countries made the top ranking and only four countries earned the second highest rank. The most frequent ranking was Partially Observed. Five countries were in the MNO category. No countries were in the bottom category.

Fair, Timely, and Cost-Effective Access to Information

Table 5.4 shows the rankings in the category of fair, timely, and cost-effective access to information. Six countries earned the top ranking, making it the best category

Table 5.2 Standards of preparation, audit, and disclosure of information

Country	O	LO	PO	MNO	NO
Bhutan			X		
Brazil			X		
Chile			X		
Colombia				X	
Egypt		X			
Ghana			X		
India		X			
Indonesia			X		
Jordan	X				
Korea			X		
Malaysia	X				
Mauritius		X			
Mexico			X		
Nepal				X	
Pakistan		X			
Panama			X		
Peru			X		
Philippines		X			
Senegal			X		
South Africa			X		
Thailand			X		
Uruguay			X		
Vietnam			X		

Table 5.3 Independent audit

Country	O	LO	PO	MNO	NO
Bhutan			X		
Brazil			X		
Chile			X		
Colombia				X	
Egypt			X		
Ghana				X	
India				X	
Indonesia			X		
Jordan			X		
Korea		X			
Malaysia		X			
Mauritius			X		
Mexico			X		
Nepal				X	
Pakistan		X			
Panama			X		
Peru				X	
Philippines			X		
Senegal			X		
South Africa			X		
Thailand		X			
Uruguay			X		
Vietnam			X		

Table 5.4 Fair, timely, and cost-effective access to information

Country	O	LO	PO	MNO	NO
Bhutan			X		
Brazil	X				
Chile		X			
Colombia	X				
Egypt		X			
Ghana		X			
India	X				
Indonesia			X		
Jordan		X			
Korea	X				
Malaysia		X			
Mauritius		X			
Mexico	X				
Nepal			X		
Pakistan		X			
Panama	X				
Peru			X		
Philippines			X		
Senegal					X
South Africa		X			
Thailand		X			
Uruguay		X			
Vietnam			X		

in terms of top rankings. Ten countries earned the second highest ranking, which is also above average in the category of transparency and disclosure. Bhutan was the only country in the MNO category. Senegal was the only country in the Not Observed category.

Concluding Comments

Although there is a lot of room for improvement overall, countries seem to be doing relatively well in the fair, timely, and cost-effective access to information category.

References

OECD. (2004). *Principles of Corporate Governance.* Paris: Author.

World Bank. (2002). *Report on the Observance of Standards and Codes (ROSC), Corporate Governance Country Assessment, Mauritius, October.* World Bank. Retrieved from www.worldbank.org.

World Bank. (2003a). *Report on the Observance of Standards and Codes (ROSC), Corporate Governance Country Assessment, Chile, May.* Retrieved from World Bank. www.worldbank.org.

World Bank. (2003b). *Report on the Observance of Standards and Codes (ROSC), Corporate Governance Country Assessment, Colombia, August.* World Bank. www.worldbank.org.

World Bank. (2003c). *Report on the Observance of Standards and Codes (ROSC), Corporate Governance Country Assessment, Republic of Korea, September.* World Bank. Retrieved from www.worldbank.org.

World Bank. (2003d). *Report on the Observance of Standards and Codes (ROSC), Corporate Governance Country Assessment, Mexico, September.* World Bank. Retrieved from www.worldbank.org.

World Bank. (2003e). *Report on the Observance of Standards and Codes (ROSC), Corporate Governance Country Assessment, Republic of South Africa, July.* World Bank. Retrieved from www.worldbank.org.

World Bank. (2004a). *Report on the Observance of Standards and Codes (ROSC), Corporate Governance Country Assessment, Egypt, March.* World Bank. Retrieved from www.worldbank.org.

World Bank. (2004b). *Report on the Observance of Standards and Codes (ROSC), Corporate Governance Country Assessment, India, April.* World Bank. Retrieved from www.worldbank.org.

World Bank. (2004c). *Report on the Observance of Standards and Codes (ROSC), Corporate Governance Country Assessment, Republic of Indonesia, April.* World Bank. Retrieved from www.worldbank.org.

World Bank. (2004d). *Report on the Observance of Standards and Codes (ROSC), Corporate Governance Country Assessment, Jordan, June.* World Bank. Retrieved from www.worldbank.org.

World Bank. (2004e). *Report on the Observance of Standards and Codes (ROSC), Corporate Governance Country Assessment, Panama, June.* World Bank. Retrieved from www.worldbank.org.

World Bank. (2004f). *Report on the Observance of Standards and Codes (ROSC), Corporate Governance Country Assessment, Republic of Peru, June.* World Bank. Retrieved from www.worldbank.org.

World Bank. (2005a). *Report on the Observance of Standards and Codes (ROSC), Corporate Governance Country Assessment, Brazil, May.* World Bank. Retrieved from www.worldbank.org.

World Bank. (2005b). *Report on the Observance of Standards and Codes (ROSC), Corporate Governance Country Assessment, Ghana, May.* World Bank. Retrieved from www.worldbank.org.

World Bank. (2005c). *Report on the Observance of Standards and Codes (ROSC), Corporate Governance Country Assessment, Malaysia, June.* World Bank. Retrieved from www.worldbank.org.

World Bank. (2005d). *Report on the Observance of Standards and Codes (ROSC), Corporate Governance Country Assessment, Nepal, April.* World Bank. Retrieved from www.worldbank.org.

World Bank. (2005e). *Report on the Observance of Standards and Codes (ROSC), Corporate Governance Country Assessment, Pakistan, June.* World Bank. Retrieved from www.worldbank.org.

World Bank. (2005f). *Report on the Observance of Standards and Codes (ROSC), Corporate Governance Country Assessment, Thailand, June.* World Bank. Retrieved from www.worldbank.org.

World Bank. (2005g). *Report on the Observance of Standards and Codes (ROSC), Corporate Governance Country Assessment, Uruguay. September.* World Bank. Retrieved from www.worldbank.org.

World Bank. (2006a). *Report on the Observance of Standards and Codes (ROSC), Corporate Governance Country Assessment, Bhutan, December.* World Bank. Retrieved from www.worldbank.org.

World Bank. (2006b). *Report on the Observance of Standards and Codes (ROSC), Corporate Governance Country Assessment, Philippines, May.* World Bank. Retrieved from www.worldbank.org.

World Bank. (2006c). *Report on the Observance of Standards and Codes (ROSC), Corporate Governance Country Assessment, Senegal, June.* World Bank. Retrieved from www.worldbank.org.

World Bank. (2006d). *Report on the Observance of Standards and Codes (ROSC), Corporate Governance Country Assessment, Vietnam, June.* World Bank. Retrieved from www.worldbank.org.

World Bank. (n.d.). *Report on the Observance of Standards and Codes (ROSC), Corporate Governance Country Assessment, Turkey.* World Bank. Retrieved from www.worldbank.org.

World Bank. (n.d.). *Report on the Observance of Standards and Codes (ROSC), Corporate Governance Country Assessment, Zimbabwe.* World Bank. Retrieved from www.worldbank.org.

Chapter 6
The Responsibility of the Board

Robert W. McGee

Introduction

One of the Organisation for Economic Co-operation and Development (OECD, 2004) principles of corporate governance is that

> The corporate governance framework should ensure the strategic guidance of the company, the effective monitoring of management by the board, and the board's accountability to the company and the shareholders.

This chapter examines this principle in some depth.

Methodology

The OECD has published a number of studies on corporate governance. In one study (OECD, 2004) it outlined a series of benchmarks intended for use by investors, policy makers, corporations, and other stakeholders. Corporations that follow the guidelines provided in this document will have a strong corporate governance system.

The World Bank has conducted a number of studies on corporate governance practices in more than 40 countries, using these OECD guidelines as a template. More than 20 of those studies were of developing economies. The World Bank studies examined the corporate governance practices identified by the OECD and classified them into the following five categories:

O = Observed
LO = Largely Observed
PO = Partially Observed
MNO = Materially Not Observed
NO = Not Observed

R.W. McGee (✉)
Florida International University, Miami, FL, USA
e-mail: bob414@hotmail.com

R.W. McGee (ed.), *Corporate Governance in Developing Economies*,
DOI 10.1007/978-0-387-84833-4_6, © Springer Science+Business Media, LLC 2009

The present study assigned point values to these categories, where O=5, LO=4, PO=3, MNO=2, and NO=1, then compared how closely the developing countries came to meeting the various OECD benchmarks. This study reports on those findings in the category of board responsibility.

Findings

The following pages summarize the results for this category.

Due Diligence and Care

Table 6.1 shows the results for the category due diligence and care. None of the countries ranked in the top category but six countries made the second highest ranking. The most frequent ranking was Partially Observed. Nepal and Senegal ranked in the Materially Not Observed category. No countries were listed in the lowest category.

Table 6.1 Due diligence and care

Country	O	LO	PO	MNO	NO
Bhutan		X			
Brazil			X		
Chile			X		
Colombia			X		
Egypt		X			
Ghana			X		
India		X			
Indonesia			X		
Jordan		X			
Korea		X			
Malaysia			X		
Mauritius			X		
Mexico			X		
Nepal				X	
Pakistan			X		
Panama		X			
Peru			X		
Philippines			X		
Senegal				X	
South Africa			X		
Thailand			X		
Uruguay			X		
Vietnam			X		

Fair Treatment of Shareholders

Table 6.2 shows the results for the category fair treatment of shareholders. None of the countries earned the top ranking but five countries earned the second highest ranking. The most frequent category was Partially Observed. Five countries were in the Materially Not Observed category. Ghana was the only country in the lowest category.

Ensure Compliance with Law

Table 6.3 shows the results for the category ensure compliance with law. Only India and South Africa earned the highest ranking. Eleven countries earned the second highest ranking, making it the most frequently earned ranking. Eight countries were in the Partially Observed category. Only Uruguay and Vietnam were in the MNO category. No countries were in the lowest category. Six countries made it into the second best category. The next two categories were evenly mixed. No country was ranked in the lowest category.

Table 6.2 Fair treatment of shareholders

Country	O	LO	PO	MNO	NO
Bhutan			X		
Brazil			X		
Chile			X		
Colombia				X	
Egypt			X		
Ghana					X
India		X			
Indonesia			X		
Jordan			X		
Korea			X		
Malaysia		X			
Mauritius			X		
Mexico			X		
Nepal		X			
Pakistan			X		
Panama			X		
Peru				X	
Philippines			X		
Senegal				X	
South Africa		X			
Thailand		X			
Uruguay				X	
Vietnam				X	

Table 6.3 Ensure compliance with law

Country	O	LO	PO	MNO	NO
Bhutan			X		
Brazil		X			
Chile		X			
Colombia		X			
Egypt		X			
Ghana		X			
India	X				
Indonesia			X		
Jordan		X			
Korea			X		
Malaysia			X		
Mauritius			X		
Mexico		X			
Nepal		X			
Pakistan		X			
Panama		X			
Peru		X			
Philippines			X		
Senegal			X		
South Africa	X				
Thailand			X		
Uruguay				X	
Vietnam				X	

Fulfillment of Board Functions

Table 6.4 presents the results for the category of fulfillment of board functions. No country earned the top ranking but five countries earned the second best score. The Partially Observed category was the most frequent, with 15 countries. Three countries were in the fourth category and no countries were in the lowest category.

Table 6.4 Fulfillment of board functions

Country	O	LO	PO	MNO	NO
Bhutan			X		
Brazil			X		
Chile			X		
Colombia			X		
Egypt			X		
Ghana		X			
India		X			
Indonesia			X		
Jordan		X			
Korea		X			
Malaysia		X			
Mauritius			X		
Mexico			X		

Table 6.4 (continued)

Country	O	LO	PO	MNO	NO
Nepal			X		
Pakistan			X		
Panama			X		
Peru			X		
Philippines			X		
Senegal				X	
South Africa			X		
Thailand			X		
Uruguay				X	
Vietnam				X	

Independence form Management

Table 6.5 shows the rankings in the category of independence from management. None of the countries earned the top ranking and only Malaysia and Nepal earned the second highest ranking. Nine countries were in the Partially Observed category; 12 countries were in the Materially Not Observed category. No countries were in the lowest category.

Table 6.5 Independence from management

Country	O	LO	PO	MNO	NO
Bhutan				X	
Brazil				X	
Chile			X		
Colombia				X	
Egypt				X	
Ghana				X	
India			X		
Indonesia			X		
Jordan				X	
Korea			X		
Malaysia		X			
Mauritius				X	
Mexico			X		
Nepal		X			
Pakistan			X		
Panama				X	
Peru				X	
Philippines			X		
Senegal				X	
South Africa			X		
Thailand			X		
Uruguay				X	
Vietnam				X	

Table 6.6 Access to accurate, relevant, and timely information

Country	O	LO	PO	MNO	NO
Bhutan			X		
Brazil		X			
Chile		X			
Colombia	X				
Egypt	X				
Ghana		X			
India	X				
Indonesia			X		
Jordan	X				
Korea			X		
Malaysia		X			
Mauritius			X		
Mexico	X				
Nepal		X			
Pakistan	X				
Panama		X			
Peru			X		
Philippines		X			
Senegal			X		
South Africa		X			
Thailand		X			
Uruguay			X		
Vietnam			X		

Access to Accurate, Relevant, and Timely Information

Table 6.6 shows the rankings for the category of access to accurate, relevant, and timely information. Six countries earned the top rank. Nine countries earned the second best rank. Eight countries earned the Partially Observed ranking. No countries earned either of the lower two rankings.

Concluding Comments

There were no countries in the top category for four of the six categories and the second category was relatively sparsely populated as well, which means there is much room for improvement in this category.

References

OECD. (2004). *Principles of Corporate Governance*. Paris: Author.

World Bank. (2002). *Report on the Observance of Standards and Codes (ROSC), Corporate Governance Country Assessment, Mauritius, October.* World Bank. Retrieved from www.worldbank.org.

World Bank. (2003a). *Report on the Observance of Standards and Codes (ROSC), Corporate Governance Country Assessment, Chile, May.* World Bank. Retrieved from www.worldbank.org.

World Bank. (2003b). *Report on the Observance of Standards and Codes (ROSC), Corporate Governance Country Assessment, Colombia, August.* World Bank. Retrieved from www.worldbank.org.

World Bank. (2003c). *Report on the Observance of Standards and Codes (ROSC), Corporate Governance Country Assessment, Republic of Korea, September.* World Bank. Retrieved from www.worldbank.org.

World Bank. (2003d). *Report on the Observance of Standards and Codes (ROSC), Corporate Governance Country Assessment, Mexico, September.* World Bank. Retrieved from www.worldbank.org.

World Bank. (2003e). *Report on the Observance of Standards and Codes (ROSC), Corporate Governance Country Assessment, Republic of South Africa, July.* World Bank. Retrieved from www.worldbank.org.

World Bank. (2004a). *Report on the Observance of Standards and Codes (ROSC), Corporate Governance Country Assessment, Egypt, March.* World Bank. Retrieved from www.worldbank.org.

World Bank. (2004b). *Report on the Observance of Standards and Codes (ROSC), Corporate Governance Country Assessment, India, April.* World Bank. Retrieved from www.worldbank.org.

World Bank. (2004c). *Report on the Observance of Standards and Codes (ROSC), Corporate Governance Country Assessment, Republic of Indonesia, April.* World Bank. Retrieved from www.worldbank.org.

World Bank. (2004d). *Report on the Observance of Standards and Codes (ROSC), Corporate Governance Country Assessment, Jordan, June.* World Bank. Retrieved from www.worldbank.org.

World Bank. (2004e). *Report on the Observance of Standards and Codes (ROSC), Corporate Governance Country Assessment, Panama, June.* World Bank. Retrieved from www.worldbank.org.

World Bank. (2004f). *Report on the Observance of Standards and Codes (ROSC), Corporate Governance Country Assessment, Republic of Peru, June.* World Bank. Retrieved from www.worldbank.org.

World Bank. (2005a). *Report on the Observance of Standards and Codes (ROSC), Corporate Governance Country Assessment, Brazil, May.* World Bank. Retrieved from www.worldbank.org.

World Bank. (2005b). *Report on the Observance of Standards and Codes (ROSC), Corporate Governance Country Assessment, Ghana, May.* World Bank. Retrieved from www.worldbank.org.

World Bank. (2005c). *Report on the Observance of Standards and Codes (ROSC), Corporate Governance Country Assessment, Malaysia, June.* World Bank. Retrieved from www.worldbank.org.

World Bank. (2005d). *Report on the Observance of Standards and Codes (ROSC), Corporate Governance Country Assessment, Nepal, April.* World Bank. Retrieved from www.wowrldbank.org.

World Bank. (2005e). *Report on the Observance of Standards and Codes (ROSC), Corporate Governance Country Assessment, Pakistan, June.* World Bank. Retrieved from www.worldbank.org.

World Bank. (2005f). *Report on the Observance of Standards and Codes (ROSC), Corporate Governance Country Assessment, Thailand, June.* World Bank. Retrieved from www.worldbank.org.

World Bank. (2005g). *Report on the Observance of Standards and Codes (ROSC), Corporate Governance Country Assessment, Uruguay. September.* World Bank. Retrieved from www.worldbank.org.

World Bank. (2006a). *Report on the Observance of Standards and Codes (ROSC), Corporate Governance Country Assessment, Bhutan, December.* World Bank. Retrieved from www.worldbank.org.

World Bank. (2006b). *Report on the Observance of Standards and Codes (ROSC), Corporate Governance Country Assessment, Philippines, May.* World Bank. Retrieved from www.worldbank.org.

World Bank. (2006c). *Report on the Observance of Standards and Codes (ROSC), Corporate Governance Country Assessment, Senegal, June.* World Bank. Retrieved from www.worldbank.org.

World Bank. (2006d). *Report on the Observance of Standards and Codes (ROSC), Corporate Governance Country Assessment, Vietnam, June.* World Bank. Retrieved from www.worldbank.org.

World Bank. (n.d.). *Report on the Observance of Standards and Codes (ROSC), Corporate Governance Country Assessment, Turkey.* World Bank. Retrieved from www.worldbank.org.

World Bank. (n.d.). *Report on the Observance of Standards and Codes (ROSC), Corporate Governance Country Assessment, Zimbabwe.* World Bank. Retrieved from www.worldbank.org.

Chapter 7
Insider Trading in Developing Economies

Robert W. McGee

Introduction

Practically all the articles that have been written on insider trading in recent years have treated it as something evil. The notable exception is the work of Henry G. Manne (1966a, 1966b, 1966c, 1970, 1985). For two particularly hostile and vociferous attacks on Manne's position, see Hetherington (1967) and Schotland (1967). Inside traders are viewed as common criminals (McMenamin, 1988).

Whenever the term "insider trading" is used, the average listener/reader immediately classifies it as a bad practice, or something that is immoral or unethical. The Organisation for Economic Co-operation and Development (OECD) *Principles of Corporate Governance* (2004) seem to indicate that it is a practice that should be frowned upon, if not banned outright. Yet the application of utilitarian ethics leads one to conclude that insider trading has an overall beneficial effect on the economy, at least sometimes. Thus, the carpet ban on insider trading is inappropriate. Since transition and developing economies tend to follow the lead of the developed economies such as OECD member states, and since the OECD frowns on insider trading, pressure is being placed on these countries to treat insider trading as an undesirable activity, as something that constitutes bad corporate governance.

Whether insider trading is fraudulent is questionable. St. Thomas Aquinas said that fraud can be perpetrated in three ways, either by selling one thing for another or by giving the wrong quality or quantity (Dalcourt, 1965). A more modern definition is "intentional deception to cause a person to give up property or some lawful right." (Webster, 1964).

A typical case of insider trading occurs when a buyer with inside information calls his stock broker and tells him to buy, knowing that the stock price is likely to rise as soon as the inside information becomes public. In this case, the buyer does not deceive the seller into giving up property. Indeed, the buyer does not even know who the seller is, and the seller would have sold anyway, anonymously, through the

R.W. McGee (✉)
Florida International University, Miami, FL, USA
e-mail: bob414@hotmail.com

R.W. McGee (ed.), *Corporate Governance in Developing Economies*,
DOI 10.1007/978-0-387-84833-4_7, © Springer Science+Business Media, LLC 2009

same broker. The seller's action would have been the same whether an inside trader was the other party to the transaction or not. If the inside trader had not purchased the stock, someone else would have. Yet this "someone else" would not be accused of reaping unjust profits, even if the identical stock was purchased for the same price the insider would have paid.

Insider trading does not seem to fit the definition of fraud, so there does not seem to be anything fraudulent about it. Furthermore, according to Aquinas, there is no moral duty to inform a potential buyer that the price of the good you are trying to sell is likely to change in the near future (Aquinas; Barath, 1960; Bartell, 1962).

In the case Aquinas discusses, a wheat merchant

> ... carries wheat to a place where wheat fetches a high price, knowing that many will come after him carrying wheat ... if the buyers knew this they would give a lower price. But ... the seller need not give the buyer this information ... the seller, since he sells his goods at the price actually offered him, does not seem to act contrary to justice through not stating what is going to happen. If however he were to do so, or if he lowered his price, it would be exceedingly virtuous on his part: although he does not seem to be bound to do this as a debt of justice. (Aquinas)

Based on this view, an insider who knows the stock price is likely to rise in the near future has no moral duty to inform potential buyers of this fact. Where there is no moral duty, certainly there should be no legal duty either. In fact, the Supreme Court has ruled at least twice that those in possession of nonpublic information do not have a general duty to disclose the information to the marketplace (Chiarella, 1980; Dirks, 1983). Jonathan R. Macey (1988) has also spoken on this point.

Who Is Harmed by Insider Trading?

While the transaction of buying and selling stock by an insider does not meet either the dictionary's or Aquinas' definition of fraud, the question of justice still remains. If no one is harmed, the act is not unjust; if someone who does not deserve to be harmed is harmed, the act is unjust. The obvious question to raise is "Who is harmed by insider trading?"

The most obvious potential "victims" of insider trading are the potential sellers who sell their stock anonymously to an inside trader. But as was mentioned above, they would have sold anyway, so whether the inside trader buys from them or not does not affect the proceeds they receive from the sale. If the sellers are hurt by having an inside trader in the market, it is difficult to measure the damage, and it appears that there is no damage. In fact, the academic literature recognizes that insider trading does not result in any harm to any identifiable group (Manne, 1985) and those who sell to inside traders may actually be helped rather than harmed because they received a better price, so it appears illogical to allow them to sue for damages if, in fact, there are no damages (Carlton & Fischel, 1983; Easterbrook, 1981; Morgan, 1987).

From the perspective of utilitarian ethics (Crisp, 1997; Goodin, 1995; Shaw, 1999), buyers are no worse off as a result of having purchased from an insider than they would have been if they had purchased from a noninsiders. Thus, there is nothing wrong with the practice from the perspective of utilitarian ethics. Of course, utilitarian ethics has been criticized for having certain structural flaws (Frey, 1984; McGee, 1994; Rothbard, 1970), but time and space do not permit an adequate analysis of those arguments.

It has been argued that employers are harmed by insider trading because employees misappropriate corporate information for personal gain (Martin, 1986; Morgan, 1987; Scott, 1980). Yet employers whose employees misappropriate information for personal gain have a remedy at law already. If anyone sues, it should be the employer that sues the employee. Government should not be a party to such a lawsuit, since it is a private harm rather than a public harm that has been committed, if in fact any harm has been committed at all. Padilla (2002) sees insider trading as basically an agency problem.

Yet there has been little private restriction on trading on insider information, until recently, at least, and some authors have gone so far as to state that the gains derived from insider trading are equivalent to compensation that a corporation would otherwise pay to corporate officers for their entrepreneurial expertise (Carlton & Fischel, 1983; Easterbrook, 1981; Manne, 1966b, 1966c; Scott, 1980) and that employers are not harmed at all by insider trading.

What Are the Beneficial Effects of Insider Trading

Insider trading serves as a means of communicating market information, which makes markets more efficient (Carlton & Fischel, 1983; Kelly, Nardinelli & Wallace, 1987; Manne, 1985; Morgan, 1987; Wu, 1968). When insiders are seen trading, it acts as a signal to others that a stock's price will likely move in a certain direction. If a director of General Motors purchases a large quantity of General Motors stock, that act reveals evidence that the stock's price is likely to rise in the near future. Likewise, if the director sells, it is likely that the price will soon fall. A chain reaction will take place as the brokerage firm handling the transaction alerts other brokers and clients, and the stock price will start moving in the correct direction, closer to its true value.

There is no need to make a public announcement, because the market reacts almost immediately. Even if the insider is anonymous, an increase (or decrease) in demand for a particular stock will be noticed by the market, and the price will move accordingly. Placing prohibitions on insider trading has the effect of blocking this flow of information. Insiders will attempt to hide their trades, or perhaps not make them at all, thus preventing the market from learning this valuable information.

The potential acquirer in a takeover attempt may also benefit by insider trading. The investment banker hired by the acquirer may leak information to arbitragers, who then accumulate shares in the target company with the intent of tendering them shortly thereafter. The result is that the takeover's chances of success are increased, and the acquirer may actually benefit as a result of the investment banker's misconduct (Herzel & Katz, 1987).

The shareholders who sell at the time the arbitragers are buying may also benefit. The increased demand generated by the arbitragers increases the price the sellers receive when they sell. Without the leakage of the insider information to the arbitragers, the demand for the stock in question would have been lower, so the sellers (who would probably have sold anyway) would have received a somewhat lower price for their stock. Shareholders who do not sell also benefit, since the price of their shares rises as a result of insider trading.

A goal of most corporate managements is to increase shareholder wealth – in other words, increase the stock's price. Since insider trading has a tendency to increase the stock's price, inside traders assist management achieve its goal. Inside traders may benefit the corporation in another way as well.

> A decision by the board or its delegates to 'tip' inside corporate information to certain outsiders, to facilitate trading by them, could also be in the best interests of the corporation. For example, where the corporation has received valuable services from an outsider, one way of providing indirect compensation for those services is by providing the outsider with the authorized use of inside information owned by the corporation. Thus, if one accepts the notion that inside information is property of the corporation, even the tipping of that information to others ought not to be regarded as improper, if the board of directors or other authorized corporate decision maker has determined that such tipping is in the best interests of the corporation. (Morgan, 1987: 98)

Who Is Harmed by Prohibitions on Insider Trading?

Who is harmed by prohibitions on insider trading? The obvious answer is inside traders. If there is nothing morally wrong with insider trading (and Aquinas and others seem to think there is not), then preventing insiders from gaining from their knowledge becomes an unjust act.

There is a case to be made that the company's shareholders may be harmed by placing prohibitions on insider trading (Carlton & Fischel, 1983). For example, the Williams Act, the part of the Securities and Exchange Act of 1934 that requires anyone contemplating a tender offer to announce the intention well in advance (Sections 13d and e, and Sections 14d, e, and f), makes it easier for target managements to thwart a takeover. Several authors have argued that shareholders tend to benefit by takeovers, so making it easier to thwart a takeover may be against the stockholders' interest.

A number of authors have addressed this point. This line of reasoning is not new. It goes back to the 1980s, if not before. Some of the criticisms during that time were made by Jeffrey A. Johnson (1986), Henry Manne (1986), Doug Bandow (1988), David L. Prychitko (1987), John C. Coffee, Jr., Joseph A. Grundfest, Roberta Romano and Murray L. Weidenbaum (1988), Frank W. Bubb (1986), Roberta Romano (1987), Michael C. Jensen (1984), Gregg A. Jarell, James A. Brickley and Jeffrey M. Netter (1988), John E. Buttarazzi (1987), and Susan E. Woodward (1988).

A less obvious "victim" resulting from placing restrictions on insider trading is the brokerage industry. Since England and the United States were, until recently at least, practically the only countries that place restrictions on insider trading (McMenamin, 1988; Rider & Ffrench, 1979) it is likely that the U.S. brokerage industry will lose business to countries that do not regulate insider trading. Although other countries have, in recent years, passed legislation against at least some forms of insider trading, enforcement in these countries is comparatively weak.

Outlawing or restricting insider trading may have long-term adverse effects on the economy. The market certainly will operate less efficiently, since insider trading increases market efficiency (Finnerty, 1976). Hostile takeovers will be more difficult to make, so shareholders will lose, since shareholders tend to benefit by hostile takeovers (Jarell et al., 1988).

Having insider trading laws on the books will result in compliance and escape costs. The legal and accounting fees involved in complying with or circumventing the law can be fairly expensive, an expense that would not be incurred in the absence of insider trading laws. Using indirect means to accomplish what could otherwise be accomplished directly also leads to unnecessary costs (Demsetz, 1969; Manne, 1985). The delay in disclosure that results from using indirect means of accomplishing the goal also increases market inefficiency. There may also be other transaction costs, such as using an obscure mutual fund or a foreign bank or broker, when a more direct purchase would be less costly.

Taxpayers are adversely affected by insider trading laws, since enormous resources must be placed at the disposal of the police power to do any kind of policing. The resources used to police the insider trading laws might be better used to prevent some real criminal activity from being committed. For any use of government resources, there is a cost and a benefit. Since insider trading is regarded as a victimless crime (Manne, 1985), if, indeed, it is a crime at all, an argument can be made that the resources government uses to enforce the insider trading laws can be better employed elsewhere. Furthermore, the risk of being caught is small, and the potential gain from using insider information can be enormous, so having an insider trading law on the books will not stop the practice or even reduce it significantly.

Insider Trading in Developing Economies

Insider trading takes place in developing economies, as it does in the rest of the world. One concern is that the OECD "guidelines" restricting the practice may have a detrimental effect on economic growth in these countries.

Table 7.1 shows the extent to which selected developing economies comply with the OECD (2004) guidelines on insider trading.

As can be seen, there is widespread noncompliance at present. However, this situation is likely to change in the future, as companies in developing countries make an attempt with what the OECD considers to be good corporate governance practices.

Table 7.1 Insider trading and abusive self-dealing

Country	O	LO	PO	MNO	NO
Bhutan			X		
Brazil		X			
Chile			X		
Colombia				X	
Egypt			X		
Ghana			X		
India			X		
Indonesia			X		
Jordan		X			
Korea			X		
Malaysia		X			
Mauritius			X		
Mexico		X			
Nepal			X		
Pakistan			X		
Panama		X			
Peru				X	
Philippines			X		
Senegal					X
South Africa	X				
Thailand		X			
Uruguay				X	
Vietnam				X	

O = Observed; LO = Largely Observed; PO = Partially Observed;
MNO = Materially Not Observed; NO = Not Observed.
Source: World Bank

References

Aquinas, St. Thomas. (1920). Summa Theologica, II-II, Q.77. Available at www.newadvent.org/summa.

Bandow, D. (1988). Curbing raiders is bad for business. *The New York Times*, February 7.

Barath, D. (1960). The just price and the costs of production according to St. Thomas Aquinas. *New Scholasticism, 34*, 420.

Bartell, E. (1962). Value, price, and St. Thomas. *The Thomist, 25*(3), 359–360.

Bubb, F. W. (1986). Hostile acquisitions and the restructuring of corporate America. *The Freeman, 36*(5), 166–176.

Buttarazzi, J. E. (1987). Corporate takeovers: What is the federal role? Backgrounder 606, The Heritage Foundation, September 29.

Carlton, D. W., & Fischel, D. R. (1983). The regulation of insider trading. *Stanford Law Review, 35*: 857–895.

Chiarella v. United States, 445 U.S. 222 (1980).

Coffee, J. C., Jr., Grundfest, J. A., Romano, R., & Weidenbaum, M. L. (1988). Corporate takeovers: Who wins; who loses; who should regulate? *Regulation, 88*(1), 23–29, 47–51.

Crisp, R. (1997). *Mill on utilitarianism.* London and New York: Routledge.

Dalcourt, G. J. (1965). *The philosophy and writings of St. Thomas Aquinas* (p. 105). New York: Simon and Schuster/Monarch Press.

Demsetz, H. (1969). Perfect competition, regulation, and the stock market, in Henry G. M. (ed.), *Economic policy and the regulation of corporate securities*. Washington, DC: American Enterprise Institute.

Dirks v. Securities and Exchange Commission, 463 U.S. 646 (1983).

Easterbrook, F. H. (1981). Insider trading, secret agents, evidentiary privileges, and the production of information. *Supreme Court Review, 1981*, 309–365.

Finnerty, J. E. (1976). Insiders and market efficiency. *The Journal of Finance, 31*(4), 1141–1148.

Frey, R.G. (ed.) (1984). *Utility and rights*. Minneapolis, MN: University of Minnesota Press.

Goodin, R.E. (1995). Utilitarianism as a public philosophy. Cambridge, UK and New York: Cambridge University Press.

Herzel, L., & Katz, L. (1987). Insider trading: who loses? *Lloyds Bank Review*, July, 15–26.

Hetherington, J. A. C. (1967). Insider trading and the logic of the law. *Wisconsin Law Review, 1967*: 720–737.

Jarell, G. A., Brickley, J. A., & Netter, J. M. (1988). The market for corporate control: The empirical evidence since 1980. *Journal of Economic Perspectives*, Winter, 49–68.

Jensen, M. C. (1984). Takeovers: Folklore and science. *Harvard Business Review*, November–December, 109–121.

Johnson, J. A. (1986–87). Antitakeover legislation: Not necessary, not wise. *Cleveland State Law Review, 35*, 303–348.

Kelly, W. A., Jr., Nardinelli, C., & Wallace, M. S. (1987). Regulation of insider trading: rethinking SEC policy rules. *The Cato Journal, 7*(2), 441–448.

Macey, J. R. (1988). *The SEC's insider trading proposal: Good politics, bad policy*. Policy Analysis No. 101. Washington, DC: Cato Institute, March 31, 2.

Manne, H. G. (1966a) *Insider trading and the stock market*. JSD dissertation, Yale University, New Heaven, CT.

Manne, H. G. (1966b). *Insider trading and the stock market*. New York: The Free Press.

Manne, H. G. (1966c). In defense of insider trading. *Harvard Business Review*, November/December, 113–122.

Manne, H. G. (1970). Insider trading and the law professors. *Vanderbilt Law Review, 23*: 547–590.

Manne, H. G. (1985). Insider trading and property rights in new information. *The Cato Journal, 4*(3), 933–943, reprinted in J. A. Dorn & H. G. Manne (eds.), *Economic liberties and the judiciary*. Fairfax, VA: George Mason University Press, 1987, 317–327.

Manne, H. G. (1986). The real Boesky-case issue. *The New York Times*, November 25, A-27, column 1.

Martin, J. K. (1986). Insider trading and the misappropriation theory: Has the second circuit gone too far? *St. John's Law Review, 16*(1), 78–112.

McGee, R. W. (1994). The fatal flaw in NAFTA, GATT and All other trade agreements. *Northwestern Journal of International Law & Business, 14*(3), 549–565.

McMenamin, M. (1988, October). Witchhunt. *Reason, 20*(5), 34–40.

Morgan, R. J. (1987). Insider trading and the infringement of property rights. *Ohio State Law Journal, 48*, 79–116.

Organisation for Economic Co-operation and Development (2004). *Principles of Corporate Governance*. Paris: Author.

Padilla, A. (2002). Can agency theory justify the regulation of insider trading? *The Quarterly Journal of Austrian Economics, 5*(1), 3–38.

Prychitko, D. L. (1987).*Corporate takeovers and shareholder interests*. Issue Alert No. 13, Washington, DC: Citizens for a Sound Economy, April 16.

Rider, B. A., & Ffrench, L. (1979). *The regulation of insider trading*. Dobbs Ferry, NY: Oceana.

Romano, R. (1987). The political economy of takeover statutes. *Virginia Law Review, 73*: 111–199.

Rothbard, M. N. (1970). *Man, economy and state*. Los Angeles, Nash Publishing.

Schotland, R. A. (1967). Unsafe at any price: A reply to manne, insider trading and the stock market. *Virginia Law Review, 53*, 1425–1478.

Scott, K. E. (1980, December). Insider trading: rule 10b-5, disclosure and corporate privacy. *Journal of Legal Studies*, 9, 801–818.

Shaw, W. H. (1999). *Contemporary ethics: Taking account of utilitarianism.* Malden, MA and Oxford: Blackwell Publishers.

Webster (1964). Webster's new world dictionary of the American Language (College ed.). Cleveland and New York: World Publishing Co.

Woodward, S. E. (1988). How much Indiana's anti-takeover law cost shareholders. *The Wall Street Journal*, May 5.

World Bank. (2002). *Report on the Observance of Standards and Codes (ROSC), Corporate Governance Country Assessment, Mauritius, October.* World Bank. Retrieved from www.worldbank.org.

World Bank. (2003). *Report on the Observance of Standards and Codes (ROSC), Corporate Governance Country Assessment, Chile, May.* World Bank. Retrieved from www.worldbank.org.

World Bank. (2003). *Report on the Observance of Standards and Codes (ROSC), Corporate Governance Country Assessment, Colombia, August.* World Bank. Retrieved from www.worldbank.org.

World Bank. (2003). *Report on the Observance of Standards and Codes (ROSC), Corporate Governance Country Assessment, Republic of Korea, September.* World Bank. Retrieved from www.worldbank.org.

World Bank. (2003). Report on the Observance of Standards and Codes (ROSC), Corporate Governance Country Assessment, Mexico, September. World Bank. Retrieved from www.worldbank.org.

World Bank. (2003). *Report on the Observance of Standards and Codes (ROSC), Corporate Governance Country Assessment, Republic of South Africa, July.* World Bank. Retrieved from www.worldbank.org.

World Bank. (2004). *Report on the Observance of Standards and Codes (ROSC), Corporate Governance Country Assessment, Egypt, March.* World Bank. Retrieved from www.worldbank.org.

World Bank. (2004). *Report on the Observance of Standards and Codes (ROSC), Corporate Governance Country Assessment, India, April.* World Bank. Retrieved from www.worldbank.org.

World Bank. (2004). *Report on the Observance of Standards and Codes (ROSC), Corporate Governance Country Assessment, Republic of Indonesia, April.* World Bank. Retrieved from www.worldbank.org.

World Bank. (2004). *Report on the Observance of Standards and Codes (ROSC), Corporate Governance Country Assessment, Jordan, June.* World Bank. Retrieved from www.worldbank.org.

World Bank. (2004). *Report on the Observance of Standards and Codes (ROSC), Corporate Governance Country Assessment, Panama, June.* World Bank. Retrieved from www.worldbank.org.

World Bank. (2004). *Report on the Observance of Standards and Codes (ROSC), Corporate Governance Country Assessment, Republic of Peru, June.* World Bank. Retrieved from www.worldbank.org.

World Bank. (2005). *Report on the Observance of Standards and Codes (ROSC), Corporate Governance Country Assessment, Brazil, May.* World Bank. Retrieved from www.worldbank.org.

World Bank. (2005). *Report on the Observance of Standards and Codes (ROSC), Corporate Governance Country Assessment, Ghana, May.* World Bank. Retrieved from www.worldbank.org.

World Bank. (2005). *Report on the Observance of Standards and Codes (ROSC), Corporate Governance Country Assessment, Malaysia, June.* World Bank. Retrieved from www.worldbank.org.

World Bank. (2005). *Report on the Observance of Standards and Codes (ROSC), Corporate Governance Country Assessment, Nepal, April.* World Bank. Retrieved from www.worldbank.org.

World Bank. (2005). *Report on the Observance of Standards and Codes (ROSC), Corporate Governance Country Assessment, Pakistan, June.* World Bank. Retrieved from www.worldbank.org.

World Bank. (2005). *Report on the Observance of Standards and Codes (ROSC), Corporate Governance Country Assessment, Thailand, June.* World Bank. Retrieved from www.worldbank.org.

World Bank. (2005). *Report on the Observance of Standards and Codes (ROSC), Corporate Governance Country Assessment, Uruguay. September.* World Bank. Retrieved from www.worldbank.org.

World Bank. (2006). *Report on the Observance of Standards and Codes (ROSC), Corporate Governance Country Assessment, Bhutan, December.* World Bank. Retrieved from www. worldbank.org.

World Bank. (2006). *Report on the Observance of Standards and Codes (ROSC), Corporate Governance Country Assessment, Philippines, May.* World Bank. Retrieved from www. worldbank.org.

World Bank. (2006). *Report on the Observance of Standards and Codes (ROSC), Corporate Governance Country Assessment, Senegal, June.* World Bank. Retrieved from www.worldbank.org.

World Bank. (2006). *Report on the Observance of Standards and Codes (ROSC), Corporate Governance Country Assessment, Vietnam, June.* World Bank. Retrieved from www. worldbank.org.

World Bank. (n.d.). *Report on the Observance of Standards and Codes (ROSC), Corporate Governance Country Assessment, Turkey.* World Bank. Retrieved from www.worldbank.org.

World Bank. (n.d.). *Report on the Observance of Standards and Codes (ROSC), Corporate Governance Country Assessment, Zimbabwe.* World Bank. Retrieved from www.worldbank.org.

Wu, H.K. (1968, February). An economist looks at section 16 of the securities exchange act of 1934. *Columbia Law Review, 68*: 260–269.

Chapter 8
The Market for Corporate Control in Developing Economies

Robert W. McGee

Introduction

The merger mania of the 1980s put top corporate management on the defensive as predators sought takeover targets. Hostile takeover activity has dissipated in recent years, for a variety of reasons, but the ethical issues surrounding acquisitions and mergers and the ethically questionable conduct that is often involved remain as relevant as ever. Most ethical discussions of acquisitions and mergers focus on the ethical conduct of the predator. The ethical conduct of the target company's top management is often overlooked. This chapter reviews the ethical literature on hostile takeovers and applies ethical theory to some of the defensive tactics that have been used to thwart unwanted takeovers. The focus will be on the fiduciary duties of top management and ethical issues involved with poison pills, greenmail, golden parachutes, and other defensive tactics. Both utilitarian and nonutilitarian approaches will be used as tools of analysis. It also reviews the attitude toward the market for corporate control that exists in 23 developing economies.

There is much evidence to suggest that most acquisitions and mergers result in a net benefit to the economy (Easterbrook & Fischel, 1981; Ginsburg & Robinson, 1986; Halpern, 1973; Jensen & Ruback, 1983, 1985, 1988). There are more winners than losers. Economists would say that it is a positive-sum game. Yet those who initiate such activity, the "predators," are commonly viewed as greedy, immoral, and uncaring.

Greed may be a vice and viewed as an immoral character trait in some religious and philosophical circles. However, those who are greedy and who play within the rules by not resorting to theft, fraud, deception, or murder to achieve their goals actually perform a service for others. This idea is not new by any means. Adam Smith pointed it out in *The Wealth of Nations* in 1776. Those who have no intention of benefiting others often benefit them more than they know. They try to capture market share by either slashing prices or offering better-quality products or services than the competition. Those who are obsessed with driving their competitors out of

R.W. McGee (✉)
Florida International University, Miami, FL, USA
e-mail: bob414@hotmail.com

R.W. McGee (ed.), *Corporate Governance in Developing Economies*,
DOI 10.1007/978-0-387-84833-4_8, © Springer Science+Business Media, LLC 2009

business by resorting to low prices and high-quality products and services do much more good for consumers and the general population than those who try to prevent or regulate such predatory practices. While it might not be considered nice to be an uncaring individual, it should not be a trait that is subject to punishment in a court of law.

Morality is a highly personal thing. Just because an activity may be considered immoral by some people does not mean that it should be declared illegal. Driving an automobile in Jerusalem on a Saturday afternoon can subject one to being the recipient of projectiles (Orthodox Jews throw rocks at cars on Saturday because of their perception that driving on Saturday is against God's law). Victimless crimes such as prostitution, injecting drugs into your body, dwarf tossing, or suicide do not violate anyone's rights and should not be illegal. One might turn this punishment argument on its head by rightfully advocating the punishment of those who attempt to prevent such consensual activities since they must necessarily violate the contract or property rights of others to accomplish their goal.

While it may be true that some predators are greedy, immoral, or uncaring, that is not the topic of discussion for this chapter. This chapter will look at some overlooked – actually ignored – economic and ethical questions. The focus will be on the individuals who attempt to prevent such activities rather than on the predators. But first, let's take a look at the OECD position on the market for corporate control and how closely 23 developing economies follow the OECD (2004) benchmark.

The Market for Corporate Control in Developing Economies

The OECD examined the market for corporate control as part of its study on corporate governance (OECD, 2004). Below is a summary of the OECD position on this issue:

Markets for corporate control should be allowed to function in an efficient and transparent manner.

1. The rules and procedures governing the acquisition of corporate control in the capital markets, and extraordinary transactions such as mergers, and sales of substantial portions of corporate assets, should be clearly articulated and disclosed so that investors understand their rights and recourse. Transactions should occur at transparent prices and under fair conditions that protect the rights of all shareholders according to their class.
2. Antitakeover devices should not be used to shield management and the board from accountability (OECD, 2004, p. 19).

Later in its report the OECD points out that the fiduciary duty of the directors to shareholders and the company "must remain paramount." (OECD, 2004, p. 36).

The OECD has identified a very real problem of corporate governance. Rather than always keeping the interests of the shareholders in mind, corporate boards sometimes violate their fiduciary duties and instead use their authority to protect themselves at the expense of the shareholders. One area where this kind of behavior is prevalent is in the area of the market for corporate control.

The market for corporate control, which can involve hostile takeovers, serves a valuable market function by making it possible to replace inefficient, incompetent, and deadwood managers with people who can better serve the needs of the shareholders and the company. However, all too frequently, the board and top management attempt to thwart this market process by engaging in antitakeover schemes involving poison pills and other antitakeover devices to protect themselves and their jobs. Such practices are highly unethical, although this fact is seldom pointed out. In fact, the press would have us believe that those who instigate hostile takeovers are the evil ones, when in fact it is often corporate management and the board who are acting unethically.

The market for corporate control is a relatively new one in developing economies. But this topic is not so new in the more developed market economies. In fact, corporate boards have been attempting to thwart hostile takeover attempts for decades and they have often enlisted the aid of the legislature to help them do so. In the case of the United States, they have pressured both the federal government and the state legislatures to pass legislation that would make it more difficult and more expensive to engage in hostile takeovers. Hopefully, such conduct will not carry over to the developing economies that are trying to reform their institutions to more fully reflect the needs of a market economy.

The OECD is providing some guidance in this regard, but local and national special interests have their own agendas that sometimes differ markedly from the OECD benchmark position.

The World Bank *Report on the Observance of Standards and Codes* (ROSC), *Corporate Governance Country Assessment* studies that have been completed as of this writing, categorized the extent of compliance with the OECD benchmark on the market for corporate control into the following five categories: (1) Observed (O); (2) Largely observed (LO); (3) Partially observed (PO); (4) Materially not observed (MNO); and (5) Not observed (NO). Table 8.1 shows how closely some countries comply with the OECD benchmark rule on the market for corporate control.

Table 8.1 Market for corporate control

Country	O	LO	PO	MNO	NO
Bhutan					X
Brazil		X			
Chile		X			
Colombia				X	
Egypt		X			
Ghana				X	
India	X				
Indonesia				X	
Jordan			X		
Korea		X			
Malaysia		X			
Mauritius			X		

Table 8.1 (continued)

Country	O	LO	PO	MNO	NO
Mexico		X			
Nepal				X	
Pakistan			X		
Panama		X			
Peru			X		
Philippines			X		
Senegal					X
South Africa		X			
Thailand			X		
Uruguay				X	
Vietnam				X	

Source: World Bank ROSC Reports (www.worldbank.org)

The next few pages examine some ethical issues involved in the market for corporate control, from two different ethical perspectives.

The Utilitarian Ethical Approach

Utilitarian ethics is the ethical system subscribed to by the vast majority of economists as well as many lawyers, politicians (assuming they have any ethical principles), and policy makers, so it is necessary to analyze ethical issues relating to acquisitions and mergers from the utilitarian perspective if for no other reason than to provide the mainstream perspective. Of course, the utilitarian approach is not the only perspective from which ethical issues may be viewed. It may not even be the best approach. But it is the mainstream approach. Thus, we will begin with the utilitarian perspective.

According to utilitarian ethics, an action is considered to be ethical if the result is the greatest good for the greatest number. Jeremy Bentham (1962), an early exponent of utilitarianism, said:

> ... it is the greatest happiness of the greatest number that is the measure of right and wrong (Bentham, 1962).

Bentham's view was that one must consider the happiness or unhappiness of everyone who is affected by an action in order to determine whether the action is right or wrong. John Stuart Mill, another early utilitarian, took a similar position:

> The creed which accepts as the foundation of morals 'utility' or the 'greatest happiness principle' holds that actions are right in proportion as they tend to promote happiness; wrong as they tend to produce the reverse of happiness (Mill, 1979).

Henry Sidgwick, another nineteenth-century British utilitarian, gives a more precise definition:

> By utilitarianism is here meant the ethical theory, that the conduct which, under any given circumstances, is objectively right, is that which will produce the greatest amount of

happiness on the whole; that is, taking into account all whose happiness is affected by the conduct (Sidgwick, 1966).

Shaw would state the utilitarian position as follows:

An action is right if and only if it brings about at least as much net happiness as any other action the agent could have performed; otherwise it is wrong. ... Utilitarianism tells us to sum up the various good, bad, or indifferent consequences for everybody of each possible action we could perform and then to choose the action that brings about the greatest net happiness (Shaw, 1999, pp. 10–11).

Another, slightly different utilitarian approach would be to view an action as good if there are more winners than losers. The problem with this second approach is that there may be a great multitude of people who benefit or lose a little while some concentrated minority gain or lose a lot, which makes it difficult to determine whether an action is ethical when the losers exceed the winners or vice versa. Rothbard (1970) points out the fact that it is impossible to accurately measure gains and losses. Actually, there are at least two fatal flaws in the utilitarian approach to ethics: the inability to measure gains and losses and the total disregard of rights (McGee, 1994; 1997).

Economists get around this problem by taking the position that an activity or policy is good if the result is a positive-sum game, if the good outweighs the bad. A variation of this economist's approach to the utilitarian ethic is that an activity is good if it increases economic efficiency and best if it maximizes economic efficiency. One might question the veracity of this approach, since something that is efficient is not necessarily moral. Hitler was rather efficient at killing gypsies, Jews, and Poles. The Turks were even more efficient at killing Armenians back in 1915 even though they had less efficient weapons to work with than Hitler. However, the mainstream economic view is that there is no conflict between what is efficient and what is moral, at least not for the most part (Posner, 1998).

Dostoevsky (1952) summarized the utilitarian position quite well in *The Brothers Karamazov* when he asked whether it would be acceptable to torture to death a small child if, as a result, the rest of the human race would live in eternal happiness. If a child in nineteenth-century Russia had a life expectancy of 50 years and if the child being tortured to death was one year old at the time of the torture, the perpetrators would be cutting short one life by 49 years, and along with it all the suffering that would otherwise take place during those 49 years.

Of course, they would be torturing the child for awhile, thus increasing unhappiness for awhile, but this temporary unhappiness must be weighed against all the future unhappiness that is being prevented by killing the child 49 years early. One must then weigh the unhappiness prevented against the happiness the child would experience if it were allowed to live its full natural life. But that is not the end of the comparison because the child's net happiness or unhappiness must then be compared to the vast increase in the total happiness that would accrue to the rest of the human race for all eternity.

Thus, applying utilitarian ethics one could easily conclude that the proper thing to do would be to torture to death the small child, since total happiness would increase greatly. Dostoevsky's question highlights one of the major deficiencies in any utilitarian approach to ethics. However, since the vast majority of economists subscribe to utilitarian ethics (perhaps because they have not read Dostoevsky), we need to examine acquisitions and mergers from the utilitarian perspective, at least as a starting point.

From a utilitarian ethical point of view, we would conclude that acquisition and merger activity is ethical if the result is increased efficiency or if the winners exceed the losers in the positive-sum game sense of the term. If such activity meets the utilitarian ethics test, one may logically conclude that acts perpetrated by individuals to prevent such ethical activity must necessarily constitute unethical conduct, since their efforts to thwart an acquisition or merger must necessarily result in reduced efficiency. Bentham, Mill, and Sidgwick would state it somewhat differently. They would say that engaging in acquisition or merger activity is good and right if it increases overall happiness and bad if it decreases overall happiness.

Before we can reach such a conclusion we must first look at the evidence to see whether allowing an acquisition or merger to become finalized results in increased economic efficiency. If it does, then the action is ethical from the utilitarian perspective and actions to thwart such activity are unethical. Such analyses have been made in the past (McGee, 1989) and we will not review them in detail here, although it is worthwhile to make a few points.

A number of groups benefit as a result of merger activity. The old shareholders benefit because they receive a premium for their stock. New shareholders benefit because they are buying stock in a company that is in the process of becoming more efficient and competitive. Those shareholders who do not tender their stock also benefit because the market value of their shares rises as a result of the tender offer. The general public benefits because the more efficient company that results from the merger is able to reduce its prices and/or provide higher-quality products and services. Employees benefit because a healthy company will be less likely to go out of business. There is some evidence to suggest that hostile takeovers have a beneficial effect on wages and employment (Brown & Medoff, 1987).

It seems like the only group that does not benefit from an acquisition or merger is the company's present management, which stands to lose their jobs as a result of the merger. Up to 50 percent of top management loses their jobs within 3 years of a takeover, according to one report (Jensen, 1988). Management is the only group that stands to gain if the merger is thwarted. This causes problems because management has a fiduciary duty to its shareholders to do things that benefit shareholders. If they put their own interests above those of their employer (the shareholders) they are breaching their fiduciary duty and acting unethically. Yet management almost uniformly resorts to such activity whenever there is a hostile takeover in the works.

Management uses a variety of defensive tactics to thwart a takeover. They sometimes run to Washington or the state legislature screaming that the predator has violated some antitrust law (Armentano, 1986; Block, 1994; Boudreaux & DiLorenzo, 1993; Shughart, 1987), some antitakeover law, which tends to place obstacles in the path of tender offers that hinder their success and efficiency (Asquith, Bruner & Mullins, 1983; Jarrell & Bradley, 1980; Jensen & Ruback, 1983; Smiley, 1975), or the Williams Act (Smiley). They may make the company less desirable as a takeover target by adopting a poison pill, selling the company's most attractive assets, going into debt, giving a third party lock-up rights ("a promise to a bidder for the corporation that if the bid is rejected, the corporation will compensate the bidder for his lost opportunity." Posner, 1998, p. 456) that allow it to repurchase in the event of a hostile takeover, paying a large dividend to deplete cash or awarding golden parachute contracts to management. They may resort to greenmail, which is a form of bribery using corporate assets to persuade the predator to go away.

Several studies have tried to measure the amount of the loss to shareholders that results when a corporation's management tries to block a takeover. A Securities and Exchange Commission study found that the announcement of a poison pill plan by a takeover target causes the stock price to drop by an average of 2.4 percent, whereas announcement of such a plan by a company that is not a target has no effect on stock price (Office of the Chief Economist, 1986). It is generally agreed among economists that all shareholders lose in a poison pill situation (Easterbrook & Jarrell, 1984). Yet their use is expanding.

There is ample evidence to suggest that takeover legislation tends to harm, rather than protect shareholders. Several studies confirm this thesis (Bandow, 1988; Labaton, 1988; Woodward, 1988). Government protection of incumbent management in New Jersey caused the stock prices of 87 affected companies to fall by 11.5 percent (Office of Economic Policy, 1987). Stock prices for 74 companies incorporated in Ohio dropped by 3.2 percent, or $1.5 billion, after the legislature passed restrictive legislation, according to a Securities and Exchange Commission study (Office of the Chief Economist, 1987). New York's statute cost stockholders $1.2 billion, or 1 percent of stock value, according to a Federal Trade Commission estimate (Schumann, 1987).

Since takeovers increase efficiency and since attempts to thwart takeovers, whether successful or not, reduce efficiency, individuals who attempt to takeover a company are acting ethically and anyone who attempts to thwart a takeover is acting unethically, according to the utilitarian ethic as described above.

Poison Pills

A poison pill is a

> ... strategic move by a takeover-target company to make its stock less attractive to an acquirer. For instance, a firm may issue a new series of preferred stock that gives shareholders the right to redeem it at a premium price after a takeover. Two variations: a *flip-in poison pill* allows all existing shareholders of target company shares except the acquirer to buy additional shares at a bargain price; a *flip-over poison pill* allows holders of common stock to buy (or holders of preferred stock to convert into) the acquirer's shares at a bargain price in the event of an unwelcome merger. Such measures raise the cost of an acquisition, and cause dilution, hopefully deterring a takeover bid. A third type of poison pill, known as a people pill, is a threat that in the event of a successful takeover, the entire management team will resign at once, leaving the company without experienced leadership (Downes & Goodman, 1998, pp. 452–453).

Poison pills are financial schemes made by management to make the company a less attractive takeover target. Poison pills may take several forms, many of which involve debt restructuring, preferred stock, discriminatory targeted repurchases, or poison pill rights. An important question to ask is who benefits and who loses by the introduction of a poison pill?

The obvious losers are the potential raiders. A raider may decide not to attempt a takeover because of the poison pill. If an attempt is made, it may be unsuccessful and costly. Even if it is successful, the cost of success is higher where there is a poison pill.

The less obvious losers are the target company shareholders. Since the evidence suggests that target company shareholders tend to benefit by a takeover, thwarting a takeover by use of a poison pill (or by any other means) prevents them from earning a premium on their stock. Ironically, it is management, which is supposed to protect shareholder interests, that makes the poison pill.

Another group that stands to lose by poison pills is consumers. Since the raider is prevented from making more efficient use of the assets than present management, the company is unable to upgrade quality and reduce cost, with the result that consumers will have to pay higher prices to purchase goods or services that are of lower quality.

An even less obvious class of losers consists of the thousands of other industries that would get extra business if the target company was taken over and made to run more efficiently. If the target company's sales were $10 billion before the acquisition and the raider was able to cut costs to the point where the company could reduce prices by 10 percent, an extra $1 billion of customer funds would become available to purchase other goods and services even if the number of units sold did not increase. However, if prices were reduced by 10 percent, it is likely that the number of units sold would increase, so sales would be something more than $900 million. Customer A might decide to use the $10,000 it saves to buy an additional machine for its factory. Customer B might use its $15,000 savings to buy another car for the corporate fleet. Customer C might use its $100,000 savings to invest in employee education or training.

Customers A, B, and C all benefit because they are able to buy something they could not have afforded in the absence of the takeover. The company that sold the machine to Customer A, the car to Customer B, and the education and training to Customer C also benefit because of the takeover, as do the Customer C employees who receive the education and training. There is no way to predict what the target company's customers would do with their cost savings, but the fact that they would do something cannot be denied. Even if all they do is let the savings sit in their bank accounts, the fact that the money is there (perhaps earning interest) means that it is available for the bank to use to make loans to businesses or individuals. Since the quantity of money available for loans has increased, there is downward pressure on interest rates, which benefits anyone who might borrow money. The general economic law that "as supply increases, price decreases" applies to the supply of money as well as to the supply of any other commodity.

If all these groups stand to lose by the introduction of a poison pill, why are such pills introduced? Someone must gain by their introduction. Otherwise, the poison pills would never be introduced. An easy way to find who benefits is to look at who introduces them in the first place, since it is usually the advocate that tends to benefit. The advocate of poison pills is management. It does not take long to see how management stands to benefit by the introduction of a poison pill. Poison pills decrease the chances of a successful takeover. If a takeover is successful, a high percentage of managers stand to lose their jobs. Up to 50 percent of top management loses their jobs within 3 years of a takeover, according to one study (Jensen, 1988). Therefore, management takes action to prevent job losses among their own group by introducing a poison pill.

Thus, it appears that management is working against the interest of its shareholders by introducing a poison pill. Yet some courts have upheld the right of management to introduce poison pills (Moran, 1985). In one case, the Delaware Supreme Court upheld the right of management to restrict the right of its shareholders to sell their stock (Moran, 1985), an interesting result in light of the fact that management is supposed to be the agent of the stockholders.

As a result of this case, corporations are adopting poison pills in record numbers. At least two studies found that the mere announcement of such an adoption causes the company's stock price to fall (Malatesta & Walkling, 1989; Ryngaert, 1988), perhaps because of the decreased likelihood of a successful takeover, which would cause the stock price to rise.

However, not all courts have ruled that management may interfere with shareholder voting rights. New York (Ministar, 1985; Unilever, 1985) and New Jersey (Asarco, 1985) have crushed some poison pills, and an Illinois court, while dissolving one poison pill, allowed the same company to adopt a different poison pill a few weeks later (Dynamics, 1986). But the Delaware court has upheld management's right to use poison pills to thwart predators (Velasco, 2002, 2003). The proposal has been made that poison pills could be defeated through the enactment of state shareholder protection statutes (Braendel, 2000). However, enacting such statutes will be difficult in the absence of powerful interest groups that can lobby the legislature.

Greenmail

Greenmail is

Payment of a premium to a raider trying to take over a company through a proxy contest or other means. Also known as bon voyage bonus, it is designed to thwart the takeover. By accepting the payment, the raider agrees not to buy any more shares or pursue the takeover any further for a specified number of years (Downes & Goodman, 1998, p. 246).

Greenmail is seen in the popular press as something that is evil, a bribe that is paid to a raider to prevent a takeover attempt from proceeding. The raider is seen as being unjustly enriched at the expense of the target company and shareholders. Greenmail is a payment top management decides to make to protect shareholders from a corporate raider. It is seen as an evil, but the lesser of two evils.

Greenmail payments do, indeed, stop takeover attempts dead in their tracks. But an economic analysis of greenmail payments raises questions as to their propriety. Since the evidence suggests that target company shareholders (as well as consumers and the economy in general) tend to benefit by takeovers, should management prevent a takeover by making greenmail payments? Rather than protecting shareholders, it appears that making greenmail payments harms shareholders, since it prevents them from obtaining the benefits that go with a takeover – primarily an increase in the price of their stock. Consumers are also harmed, since blocking a takeover prevents the new owners from using the acquired assets more efficiently, which would otherwise lead to offering higher-quality products or services at lower prices. Preventing takeovers tends to protect management, many of whom would lose their jobs if the takeover attempt were successful. Thus, it appears that management, unwittingly or not, makes greenmail payments to protect themselves against job loss, to the detriment of shareholders and consumers. They are thus breaching their fiduciary duty to the shareholders, since they are using their position to benefit themselves at the expense of the shareholders.

Paying greenmail is actually a form of antitakeover, a targeted repurchase. It could be construed as being unfair to a large group of shareholders, since it involves an offer to repurchase the shares of one or a small group of shareholders at a premium, an offer that is not extended to all shareholders. Ironically, it is the greenmailer who is offering the other shareholders the opportunity to sell their shares at a premium, an offer the company's management is trying to prevent from being made or accepted.

Studies indicate that the stock price increases between the initial purchase by the greenmailer and the later repurchase (Holderness & Sheehan, 1985; Mikkelson & Ruback, 1985). Thus, shareholders benefit rather than suffer harm because the price of their stock is bid up. If management buys off the raider, the shareholders lose the premium (Bradley, Desai & Kim, 1983). However, the stock price might not go back to its pre-takeover attempt position, because the market may anticipate that there will be other future attempts that may prove successful. But if the company's financial position is weakened as a result of having to pay a large sum to thwart a takeover, the stock price may slide, since the company is perceived as being in a weakened financial condition, and thus a less desirable investment.

Golden Parachutes

The subject of "golden parachutes" has become a controversial one. As takeovers become more sophisticated and "junk" bond financing makes it possible to take over even the largest companies, top management is no longer protected by working for a very large firm. That, plus the fact that about half (Jensen, 1988) the target company's top management are no longer with the company 3 years after the takeover, creates a tremendous amount of anxiety and gives them a strong incentive to seek ways to protect themselves in the event of a takeover.

Briefly, a golden parachute is a severance contract to compensate high-level corporate officials for losing their jobs if their company is taken over. Most commentators have seen such contracts as shareholder rip-offs because the high-level employee benefits and the shareholders do not get anything for their money. But this analysis is simplistic. There is really much more involved than initially meets the eye. There are circumstances under which shareholders can benefit by having the corporation enter into golden parachute contracts with top management employees.

One beneficial effect of golden parachute contracts is that they can help reduce the conflict of interest that would otherwise exist between top management and shareholders. Management may resist a takeover attempt that would be in the shareholders' interest because they stand to lose their jobs if the takeover is successful. Thus, they are working against the shareholders' interests. Having a properly constructed golden parachute will eliminate or at least reduce this potential conflict of interest because management would be less likely to attempt to thwart a takeover attempt if their incomes were protected by golden parachutes. The evidence suggests that merely having golden parachute contracts raises the company's stock price by about 3 percent when the existence of the golden parachute contracts is announced (Lambert & Larcker, 1985). This price rise might be due to a perception of the investing public that a takeover attempt is more likely than before, but it may also be because the market sees that the potential conflict of interest between management and the corporation has been reduced, thus making the stock a better investment. In all likelihood, both of these factors have somewhat of an effect on the increase in the company's stock price.

Since the evidence suggests that takeovers are good for the stockholders of the target company, as well as for the general consuming public, it seems logical that company and government policy should be to encourage top management to negotiate takeovers that seem to be in the shareholders' best interests. Yet some present policies, such as the Deficit Reduction Act of 1984, penalize companies and managers who enter into golden parachute contracts and state and federal officials are advocating placing further restrictions on golden parachute contracts. Since a properly structured golden parachute contract reduces top management's conflict of interest, legislation that restricts or prohibits such contracts actually works against the shareholders' interests, and the interests of the economy in general, since takeovers tend to be in the consumers' interest, too. The logical solution would be to repeal legislation that restricts companies from entering into golden parachute contracts with their top management.

However, not all golden parachute contracts resolve the conflict-of-interest problem. Depending on how the contract is structured, it may serve to make management more entrenched than before, which tends to work against the shareholders' interest. A well-designed contract will reduce this potential conflict of interest whereas a badly designed contract will do just the opposite. One way to make such contracts work for the benefit of the shareholders is to extend them to the members of top management who would be negotiating the takeover and implementing the later restructuring. However, extending golden parachute contracts to lower level managers who would not be involved in takeover negotiations would be more difficult to justify on shareholder interest grounds. Extending too many golden parachutes raises the cost of the acquisition, thus making it less attractive to potential raiders, while not gaining any corresponding benefits for the corporation.

Another beneficial effect of golden parachute contracts is that they make it easier to attract top management. Golden parachute contracts are a form of compensation, a salary substitute, an insurance policy against job loss, and potentially a supplemental retirement plan. Absence of a golden parachute provision makes a job offer less attractive to a potential top-level manager, and since golden parachutes are a form of compensation, companies that do not have them would probably have to offer higher salaries to entice potential top managers to join the company.

But not all golden parachute contracts are in the best interests of shareholders. While a properly constructed contract reduces the manager's conflict of interest, an improperly structured contract will do just the opposite. If the golden parachute is too "golden," top management might be too willing to sell the company, so they may tend to take the first offer that comes along rather than negotiate a higher price for their shareholders. Managers and board members who hold a great deal of stock in the company will have less incentive to take the first offer than those who own little or no stock, so the company might provide incentives that encourage top management and board members to own stock in the company. Yet present insider trading laws provide a disincentive, and some top managers and board members are selling their stock so that they will not be accused of insider trading. Offering stock options and restricted stock appreciation rights that are exercisable only if control changes is one possible solution.

The Rights Approach

There are at least two basic problems with the utilitarian approach. For one thing, it is impossible to accurately measure gains and losses, although it is often possible to see that a certain action will increase or reduce efficiency. Another defect with the utilitarian ethic is that it totally ignores property and contract rights. For a utilitarian, an action is ethical if the amount of happiness increases, or if the result is a positive-sum game. For a utilitarian, it does not matter if someone's rights are violated as long as the overall result is increased happiness or a positive-sum game.

The rights approach is completely different. It avoids the two pitfalls of the utilitarian ethical approach. The rights approach to ethics would hold that any action that violates anyone's rights is unethical, even if the majority benefit by the action and even if the result is a positive-sum game. However, the rights approach does not hold that any actions between or among consenting adults are moral, since some such actions might be immoral. All that can be said is that any activity that violates someone's rights is automatically unethical, even if some majority benefits by the rights violation.

In the case of an acquisition or merger, the rights of the individuals launching the takeover attempt and the rights of shareholders are violated if they are prevented or hindered from entering into a contract to buy or sell shares. When one takes a rights approach to ethics, there is no need to first measure increases or decreases in efficiency or total happiness against total unhappiness before determining whether an action is ethical. Those who attempt to prevent a takeover attempt are the ones who are acting unethically, not the ones who initiated the takeover attempt. They are using force or the threat of force (government) to prevent one group of individuals from buying shares and another group of individuals from selling their shares. Thus, they are violating both property and contract rights by preventing such transactions from taking place.

Concluding Comments

Very little has been said about the ethics of individuals who attempt to prevent mergers and acquisitions. This chapter is intended to fill that gap. From the perspective of utilitarian ethics, an action is good if it increases happiness or if there are more winners than losers or if it is a positive-sum game or if it increases efficiency. The evidence is clear that acquisitions and mergers do all of these things, at least in cases where the acquisition or merger is successful. Therefore, from a utilitarian ethic perspective, engaging in acquisition and merger activity constitutes ethical conduct, at least in those cases where the acquisition or merger is successful. Conversely, those who attempt to thwart an acquisition or merger are acting unethically because their actions reduce happiness and efficiency.

The result is the same if one takes a rights approach to ethics. Any action that violates someone's rights is automatically unethical. Preventing consenting adults from entering into merger agreements violates contract and property rights. Therefore, anyone who attempts to prevent an acquisition or merger is acting unethically, from a utilitarian perspective, in cases where the acquisition or merger would result in a positive-sum game, and in all cases from the rights perspective, since rights must necessarily be violated if consensual activity is prevented by force or the threat of force.

In cases where the acquisition or merger fails, that is, where the result is a negative-sum game, utilitarian ethics would hold that using force to prevent such acquisitions and mergers would be justifiable. The problem is that it is impossible to know whether a planned acquisition or merger will result in a positive-sum or negative-sum game until after the fact, whereas the decision whether to allow it must take place before the fact. Thus, applying utilitarian ethics to acquisitions and mergers would, in some cases, result in stopping an acquisition or merger that would have resulted in a positive-sum game, while in other cases, applying utilitarian ethics would result in allowing an acquisition or merger to go through when the final result is a negative-sum game. It is impossible to know in advance whether a particular acquisition or merger will be successful. One can only guess, although the presumption is that it will be successful, since participants would not enter into such an activity if they suspected that they would be making themselves worse off as a result.

Applying rights theory avoids all these uncertainties. Applying rights theory merely allows consenting adults to trade what they have (cash) for what they want (shares), provided no one's rights are violated. Thus, the rights approach to ethics is superior to the utilitarian approach, since making the decision whether to allow or disallow a particular acquisition or merger can be made a priori, before the event, merely by determining whether anyone's rights would be violated if the activity were allowed to proceed.

Developing economies should keep these ethical analyses in mind as they decide what kind of benchmark they want to have.

References

Armentano, D.T. (1986). *Antitrust policy: The case for repeal.* Washington, DC: Cato Institute,
Asarco Inc. v. M.R.H. Holmes a Court (1985). 611 F.Supp. 468 (DCNJ).
Asquith, P., Bruner, R. F., & Mullins, D. W., Jr. (1983). The gains to bidding firms from merger. *Journal of Financial Economics, 11.*
Bandow, D. (1988). Delaware's takeover law: Curbing raiders is bad for business. *The New York Times,* February 7.
Bentham, J. (1962). A fragment on government. In J. Bowring (ed.), *The works of jeremy bentham* (Vol. 1, p. 227), quoted in W. H. Shaw, *Contemporary ethics: Taking account of utilitarianism.* Malden, MA and Oxford: Blackwell, 1999, p. 8.
Block, W. (1994). Total repeal of sntitrust legislation: A critique of bork, brozen, and posner. *Review of Austrian Economics, 8,* 35–70.
Boudreaux, D. J., & DiLorenzo, T. J. (1993). The protectionist roots of antitrust. *Review of Austrian Economics, 6,* 81–96.
Bradley, M., Desai, A., & Kim, E. (1983, April). The rationale behind interfirm tender offers: Information or synergy? *Journal of Financial Economics,* 11, 183–206.
Braendel, A. D. (2000). Defeating poison pills through enactment of a state shareholder protection statute. *Delaware Journal of Corporate Law, 25,* 651–682.
Brown, C., & Medoff, J. L. (1987). *The impact of firm acquisitions on labor.* Washington, DC: National Bureau of Economic Research, May.
Dostoevsky, F. (1952). The brothers Karamazov. Great books of the western world (Vol. 52). Chicago: Encyclopedia Britannica.
Downes, J., & Goodman, J. E. (eds). (1998). Dictionary of finance and investment terms. Barrons Educational Series.
Dynamics Corp. of America v. CTS Corp., et al., (1986, April 17) U.S.D.C., N.D.Ill., Eastern Division, No. 86 C 1624, aff'd. CA-7, Nos. 86–1601, 86–1608, and Dynamics Corp. of America v. CTS Corp., et al. (May 3, 1986).
Easterbrook, F. H., & Fischel, D. R. (1981, April). The proper role of a target's management in responding to a tender offer. *Harvard Law Review, 94,* 1161–1204.
Easterbrook, F. H., & Jarrell, G. A.(1984). Do targets gain from defeating tender offers? *New York University Law Review, 59,* 277, cited in R. A. Posner, (1998). *Economic analysis of law* (5th ed., p. 455). New York: Aspen.
Ginsburg, D. H., & Robinson, J. F. (1986). The case against federal intervention in the market for corporate control. *Brookings Review,* Winter/Spring, , 9–14.
Halpern, P. J., (1973, October). Empirical estimates of the amount and distribution of gains to companies in mergers. *Journal of Business, 46,* 554–575.
Holderness, C., & Sheehan, D. (1985, December). Raiders or saviors? The evidence of six controversial investors. *Journal of Financial Economics, 14,* 555–579.

Jarrell, G. A., & Bradley, M. (1980). The economic effects of federal and state regulations on cash tender offers. *Journal of Law & Economics, 23*, 371, as cited in R. A. Posner, (1998). *Economic Analysis of Law* (5th ed. p. 454), New York: Aspen.

Jensen, M. C. (1988). Takeovers: Their causes and consequences. *Journal of Economic Perspectives, 2*, 21–48.

Jensen, M. C. (1985). The efficiency of takeovers. *The Corporate Board*, September–October, 16–22.

Jensen, M. C., & Ruback, R. S. (1983). The market for corporate control: The scientific evidence. *Journal of Financial Economics, 11*, 5–50.

Labaton, S. A. (1988). Debate over the impact of Delaware takeover law. *The New York Times*, February 1, D1.

Lambert, R., & Larcker, D. (1985, April). Golden parachutes, executive decision-making, and shareholder wealth, *Journal of Accounting and Economics, 7*, 179–204.

Malatesta, P., & Walkling, R. (1989) The impact of poison pill securities on shareholder wealth. *Journal of Financial Economics, 20*(1, 2), 347–376.

McGee, R. W. (1997). The fatal flaw in the methodology of law & economics. *Commentaries on Law & Economics, 1*, 209–223.

McGee, R. W. (1994). The fatal flaw in NAFTA, GATT and all other trade agreements. *Northwestern Journal of International Law & Business, 14*, 549–565.

McGee, R. W. (1989, February). The economics of mergers and acquisitions. *Mid-Atlantic Journal of Business, 25*, 45–55.

Mikkelson, W., & Ruback, R. (1985, December). An empirical analysis of the interfirm equity investment process. *Journal of Financial Economics, 14*, 523–553.

Mill, J. S., (1979). Utilitarianism. In G., Sher, (ed.) *Indianapolis: Hackett*, as quoted in W. H. Shaw, *Contemporary ethics: Taking account of utilitarianism* (p. 9). Malden, MA and Oxford: Blackwell, 1999, p. 9.

Ministar Acquiring Corp. v. AMF, Inc. (1985). 621 F.Supp. 1252 (NY).

Moran v. Household International, Inc. (1985). 490 A.2d 1059, aff'd. 500 A.2d 1346.

OECD. (2004). *OECD Principles of Corporate Governance.* Paris: Author.

Office of the Chief Economist (1986). *The economics of poison pills.* Securities and Exchange Commission, March 5.

Office of the Chief Economist (1987). *Shareholder wealth effects of Ohio legislation affecting takeovers.* Securities and Exchange Commission, May 18.

Office of Economic Policy (1987). New Jersey shareholders protection act: An economic evaluation. Trenton, NJ: State of New Jersey, August.

Posner, R. A. (1998). Economic analysis of law (5th ed., pp. 284–285). New York: Aspen.

Rothbard, M. N. (1970). Man, economy and state (pp. 260–268). Los Angeles: Nash Publishing.

Ryngaert, M. (1988). The effect of poison pill securities on shareholder wealth. *Journal of Financial Economics, 20*, 377–417.

Schumann, L. (1987). *State regulation of takeovers and shareholder wealth: The effects of New York's 1985 takeover statutes.* Bureau of Economics Staff Report to the Federal Trade Commission, March.

Shaw, W. H. (1999). Contemporary ethics: Taking account of utilitarianism. Malden, MA and Oxford: Blackwell.

Shughart, W. F., II. (1987, Winter). Don't revise the Clayton act, scrap it! *Cato Journal, 6*, 925–932.

Sidgwick, H. (1966). The methods of ethics, New York: Dover, , as quoted in W. H. Shaw, (1999). *Contemporary ethics: Taking account of utilitarianism* (pp. 9–10). Malden, MA and Oxford: Blackwell.

Smiley, R. (1975). The effect of the Williams amendment and other factors on transactions costs in tender offers. *Industrial Organization Review, 3*, 138–145.

Unilever Acquisition Corp. v. Richardson-Vicks, Inc. (1985). 618 F.Supp. 407 (SDNY).

Velasco, J. (2003, Spring). Just do it: An antidote to the poison pill. *Emory Law Journal, 52*, 849–908.

Velasco, J. (2002, Spring). The enduring illegitimacy of the poison pill. *Iowa Journal of Corporation Law, 27*, 381–423.

Williams Act. 15 U.S.C. §§78m(d)–(e), 78n(d)(f).

Woodward, S. E. (1988). How much Indiana's anti-takeover law cost shareholders. *Wall Street Journal*, May 5.

World Bank. (2002). *Report on the Observance of Standards and Codes (ROSC), Corporate Governance Country Assessment, Mauritius, October.* World Bank. Retrieved from www.worldbank.org.

World Bank. (2003a). *Report on the Observance of Standards and Codes (ROSC), Corporate Governance Country Assessment, Chile, May.* World Bank. Retrieved from www.worldbank.org.

World Bank. (2003b). *Report on the Observance of Standards and Codes (ROSC), Corporate Governance Country Assessment, Colombia, August.* World Bank. Retrieved from www.worldbank.org.

World Bank. (2003c). *Report on the Observance of Standards and Codes (ROSC), Corporate Governance Country Assessment, Republic of Korea, September.* World Bank. Retrieved from www.worldbank.org.

World Bank. (2003d). *Report on the Observance of Standards and Codes (ROSC), Corporate Governance Country Assessment, Mexico, September.* World Bank. Retrieved from www.worldbank.org.

World Bank. (2003e). *Report on the Observance of Standards and Codes (ROSC), Corporate Governance Country Assessment, Republic of South Africa, July.* World Bank. Retrieved from www.worldbank.org.

World Bank. (2004a). *Report on the Observance of Standards and Codes (ROSC), Corporate Governance Country Assessment, Egypt, March.* World Bank. Retrieved from www.worldbank.org.

World Bank. (2004b). *Report on the Observance of Standards and Codes (ROSC), Corporate Governance Country Assessment, India, April.* World Bank. Retrieved from www.worldbank.org.

World Bank. (2004c). *Report on the Observance of Standards and Codes (ROSC), Corporate Governance Country Assessment, Republic of Indonesia, April.* World Bank. Retrieved from www.worldbank.org.

World Bank. (2004d). *Report on the Observance of Standards and Codes (ROSC), Corporate Governance Country Assessment, Jordan, June.* World Bank. Retrieved from www.worldbank.org.

World Bank. (2004e). *Report on the Observance of Standards and Codes (ROSC), Corporate Governance Country Assessment, Panama, June.* World Bank. Retrieved from www.worldbank.org.

World Bank. (2004f). *Report on the Observance of Standards and Codes (ROSC), Corporate Governance Country Assessment, Republic of Peru, June.* World Bank. Retrieved from www.worldbank.org.

World Bank. (2005a). *Report on the Observance of Standards and Codes (ROSC), Corporate Governance Country Assessment, Brazil, May.* World Bank. Retrieved from www.worldbank.org.

World Bank. (2005b). Report on the Observance of Standards and Codes (ROSC), Corporate Governance Country Assessment, Ghana, May. World Bank. www.worldbank.org.

World Bank. (2005c). *Report on the Observance of Standards and Codes (ROSC), Corporate Governance Country Assessment, Malaysia, June.* World Bank. Retrieved from www.worldbank.org.

World Bank. (2005d). *Report on the Observance of Standards and Codes (ROSC), Corporate Governance Country Assessment, Nepal, April.* World Bank. Retrieved from www.worldbank.org.

World Bank. (2005e). *Report on the Observance of Standards and Codes (ROSC), Corporate Governance Country Assessment, Pakistan, June.* World Bank. Retrieved from www.worldbank.org.

World Bank. (2005f), *Report on the Observance of Standards and Codes (ROSC), Corporate Governance Country Assessment, Thailand, June.* World Bank. Retrieved from www. worldbank.org.

World Bank. (2005g). *Report on the Observance of Standards and Codes (ROSC), Corporate Governance Country Assessment, Uruguay. September.* World Bank. Retrieved from www. worldbank.org.

World Bank. (2006a). *Report on the Observance of Standards and Codes (ROSC), Corporate Governance Country Assessment, Bhutan, December.* World Bank. Retrieved from www. worldbank.org.

World Bank. (2006b), *Report on the Observance of Standards and Codes (ROSC), Corporate Governance Country Assessment, Philippines, May.* World Bank. Retrieved from www. worldbank.org.

World Bank. (2006c). *Report on the Observance of Standards and Codes (ROSC), Corporate Governance Country Assessment, Senegal, June.* World Bank. Retrieved from www. worldbank.org.

World Bank. (2006d). *Report on the Observance of Standards and Codes (ROSC), Corporate Governance Country Assessment, Vietnam, June.* World Bank. Retrieved from www. worldbank.org.

World Bank. (n.d.). *Report on the Observance of Standards and Codes (ROSC), Corporate Governance Country Assessment, Turkey.* World Bank. Retrieved from www.worldbank.org.

World Bank. (n.d.). *Report on the Observance of Standards and Codes (ROSC), Corporate Governance Country Assessment, Zimbabwe.* World Bank. Retrieved from www.worldbank.org.

Part II
Case Studies and Comparative Studies

Chapter 9
The Timeliness of Financial Reporting in Developing Countries: An Overview

Robert W. McGee

Introduction

Transparency is one of those terms that have many facets. It is used in different ways. It can refer to the openness of governmental functions. It can also refer to a country's economy. Or it can refer to various aspects of corporate governance and financial reporting. The Organisation for Economic Co-operation and Development (OECD, 1998) lists transparency as one element of good corporate governance. Kulzick (2004) and others (Blanchet, 2002; Prickett, 2002) view transparency from a user perspective. According to their view, transparency includes the following eight concepts: accuracy, consistency, appropriateness, completeness, clarity, timeliness, convenience, and governance and enforcement. This chapter focuses on just one aspect of transparency – timeliness.

The International Accounting Standards Board considers timeliness to be an essential aspect of financial reporting. In Accounting Principles Board (APB) Statement No. 4, the APB (1970) in the USA listed timeliness as one of the qualitative objectives of financial reporting disclosure. APB Statement No. 4 was later superseded but the Financial Accounting Standards Board continued to recognize the importance of timeliness in its *Statement of Financial Accounting Concepts No. 2* (1980). The U.S. Securities and Exchange Commission also recognizes the importance of timeliness and requires that listed companies file their annual 10-K reports by a certain deadline. The OECD (2004) lists timeliness as a principle of good corporate governance.

The issue of timeliness has several facets. There is an inverse relationship between the quality of financial information and the timeliness with which it is reported (Kenley & Staubus, 1974). Accounting information becomes less relevant with the passage of time (Atiase, Bamber, & Tse, 1989; Hendriksen & van Breda, 1992; Lawrence & Glover, 1998).

R.W. McGee (✉)
Florida International University, Miami, FL, USA
e-mail: bob414@hotmail.com

R.W. McGee (ed.), *Corporate Governance in Developing Economies*,
DOI 10.1007/978-0-387-84833-4_9, © Springer Science+Business Media, LLC 2009

Review of the Literature

Studies show mixed conclusions regarding the relationship of quickness of reporting and the nature of the information being reported. Some studies show that good news is reported before bad news, whereas other studies show that bad news is reported before good news.

There is some evidence to suggest that it takes more time to report bad news than good news (Bates, 1968; Beaver, 1968), both because companies hesitate to report bad news and because companies take more time to massage the numbers or resort to creative accounting techniques when they have to report bad news (Givoli & Palmon, 1982; Chai & Tung, 2002; Trueman, 1990). Stated differently, there seems to be a tendency to rush good news to press, such as better-than-expected earnings, and delay the reporting of bad news or less-than-expected earnings (Chambers & Penman, 1984; Kross & Schroeder, 1984). Dwyer and Wilson (1989) found this relationship to hold true for municipalities. Haw, Qi, and Wu (2000) found it to be the case with Chinese companies. Leventis and Weetman (2004) found it to be the case for Greek firms.

However, Annaert, DeCeuster, Polfliet, and Campenhout (2002) found that this was not the case for Belgian companies, and Han and Wang (1998) found that this was not the case for petroleum refining companies, which delayed reporting extraordinarily high profits during the Gulf crisis of the 1990s, perhaps because political repercussions outweighed what would otherwise have been a good market reaction. Rees and Giner (2001) found that companies in France, Germany, and the UK tended to report bad news sooner than good news.

A study by Basu (1997) found that companies tend to report bad news quicker than good news, presumably because of conservatism. Gigler and Hemmer (2001) discuss this point in their study, which finds that firms with more conservative accounting systems are less likely to make timely voluntary disclosures than are firms with less conservative accounting systems.

Building upon the Basu study (1997), Pope and Walker (1999) found that there were cross-jurisdictional effects when extraordinary items were either included or excluded, using US and UK firms for comparison. Han and Wild (1997) examined the potential relationship between earnings timeliness and the share price reactions of competing firms. But Jindrichovska and Mcleay (2005) found that there was no evidence of conservatism in the Czech accounting system when it came to reporting bad news earlier than good news, presumably because the Czech tax system offers little incentive to do so. Ball, Kothari, and Robin (2000) found that companies in jurisdictions that have a strong shareholder orientation tend to disclose earnings information sooner than companies in countries operating under a legal code system.

There is also a relationship between the speed with which financial results are announced and the effect the announcement has on stock prices. If information is released sooner, the effect on stock prices is more pronounced. The longer the time lapse between year-end and the release of the financial information, the less effect there is on stock price, all other things being equal (Ball & Brown, 1968; Brown & Kennelly, 1972). This phenomenon can be explained by the fact that financial information seems to seep into the stock price over time, so the more time that elapses between year-end and the release of the financial reports, the more such information is already included in the stock price.

Some countries report financial results faster than other countries (Mc Gee & Preobragenskaya, 1005; 2006). DeCeuster and Trappers (1993) found that Belgian companies take longer to report their financial results than do Anglo-Saxon countries. Annaert et al. (2002) found this to be the case for interim information as well. Companies can report financial results faster on the internet and the information can be more widely disbursed but posting 2-year-old annual reports does nothing to improve timeliness (Ashbaugh, Johnstone, & Warfield, 1999).

Atiase et al. (1989) found that large companies report earnings faster than small companies and that the reporting of earnings has a more significant market reaction for small firms than for large firms. In a study of Australian firms, Davies and Whittred (1980) found that small firms and large firms made significantly more timely reports than did medium-size firms and that profitability was not a significant variable.

Whittred (1980) found that the release of financial information for Australian companies is delayed the first time an audit firm issues a qualified report and that the extent of the delay is longer in cases where the qualification is more serious. Keller (1986) replicated that study for US companies and found the same thing to be true. Whittred and Zimmer (1984) found that it took Australian firms in financial distress a significantly longer time to publish their financial information. A study of more than 5,000 annual reports of French companies found that it took longer to release audit reports where there had been a qualified opinion, and that the more serious the qualification, the greater the delay in releasing the report (Soltani, 2002; also see Ashton, Graul & Newton, 1989).

Krishnan (2005) found that the audit firm's degree of expertise has an effect on the timeliness of the publication of bad earnings news. Audit firms that specialize in the industry in which the company operates are timelier in reporting bad financial news than are audit firms that have less industry expertise.

The OECD (2004) lists timeliness as a principle of good corporate governance. The World Bank conducted more than 40 studies of various aspects of corporate governance in various countries. More than 20 of those studies examined corporate governance practices in developing economies. One item looked at the timeliness and accuracy of financial disclosure. It ranked timeliness and accuracy into the following five categories:

O = Observed
LO = Largely Observed
PO = Partially Observed
MNO = Materially Not Observed
NO = Not Observed

Table 9.1 summarizes the results of those more than 20 studies.

If one were to assign points based on how close each country came to achieving the OECD benchmark, where O = 5 and NO = 1, the graph of the relative scores would look like the following:

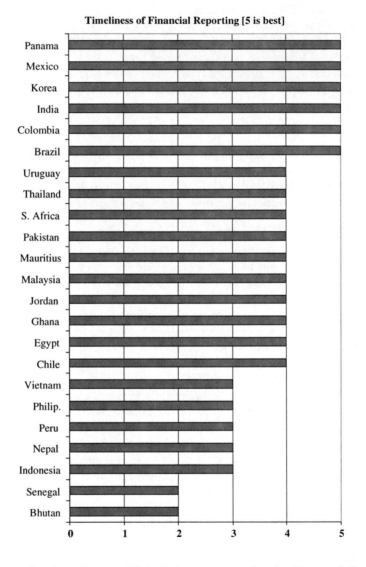

Timeliness of Financial Reporting [5 is best]

A few studies have been published that compare the timeliness of financial reporting in transition economies and in the more developed market economies. McGee (2006, 2007b) found that companies in the Russian energy sector take a significantly longer amount of time to report financial results than do non-Russian companies in the energy sector. Another study found the same thing to be true of

Table 9.1 Timeliness and accuracy of financial reporting practices in developing economies

Country	O	LO	PO	MNO	NO
Bhutan				X	
Brazil	X				
Chile		X			
Colombia	X				
Egypt		X			
Ghana		X			
India	X				
Indonesia			X		
Jordan		X			
Korea	X				
Malaysia		X			
Mauritius		X			
Mexico	X				
Nepal			X		
Pakistan		X			
Panama	X				
Peru			X		
Philippines			X		
Senegal				X	
South Africa		X			
Thailand		X			
Uruguay		X			
Vietnam			X		

Source: World Bank

the Russian telecom industry (McGee, 2007a). A comparative study of Chinese and non-Chinese companies found that Chinese companies took significantly longer to report than non-Chinese companies (McGee & Yuan, 2008). But a study comparing new European Union (EU) countries that are also transition economies to EU countries that are not transition economies found no difference in timeliness (McGee & Igoe, 2008). Table 9.2 shows the number of days delay in reporting results from the studies that have been done on this topic.

Table 9.2 Days delay findings from prior studies

Rank	Sample	Days delay
1	Non-Russian telecom (McGee, 2007a)	63.2
2	Non-Chinese companies (McGee & Yuan, 2008)	65.5
3	Non-Russian energy (McGee, 2007b)	70.2
4	New EU countries (McGee & Igoe, 2008)	84.7
5	Old EU countries (McGee & Igoe, 2008)	85.6
6	Chinese companies (McGee & Yuan, 2008)	92.1
7	Russian banks (McGee & Tarangelo, 2008)	98.8
8	Russian companies (McGee, 2007c)	136.6
9	Russian telecom (McGee, 2007a)	138.3
10	Russian energy (McGee, 2007b)	145.5

The following chart shows how these time delays compare graphically.

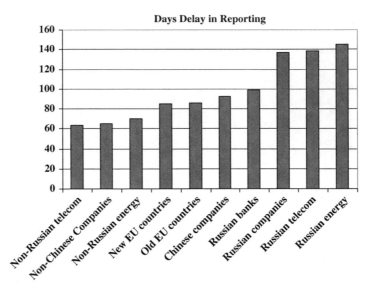

As can be seen, the Russian companies in these studies tend to take more time to report financial results than do non-Russian companies (Demos, 2006). The next few chapters of this book expand on this research by comparing data taken from the Kenya Stock Exchange with data from companies in China, the EU, Russia, and the USA.

References

Accounting Principles Board. (1970). *Basic concepts and accounting principles underlying financial statements of business enterprises – statement no. 4.* New York: American Institute of Certified Public Accountants.

Annaert, J., DeCeuster, M. J. K., Polfliet, R., & Campenhout, G. V. (2002). To be or not be ... 'too late': The case of the Belgian semi-annual earnings announcements. *Journal of Business Finance & Accounting, 29*(3 & 4), 477–495.

Ashbaugh, H., Johnstone, K. M., & Warfield, T. D. (1999). Corporate reporting on the internet. *Accounting Horizons, 13*(3), 241–257.

Ashton, R. H., Graul, P. R., & Newton, J. D. (1989). Audit delay and the timeliness of corporate reporting. *Contemporary Accounting Research, 5*(2), 657–673.

Atiase, R. K., Bamber, L. S., & Tse, S. (1989). Timeliness of financial reporting, the firm size effect, and stock price reactions to annual earnings announcements. *Contemporary Accounting Research, 5*(2), 526–552.

Ball, R., & Brown, P. (1968). An empirical evaluation of accounting income numbers. *Journal of Accounting Research, 6*, 159–178.

Ball, R., Kothari, S.P., & Robin, A. (2000). The effect of international institutional factors on properties of accounting earnings. *Journal of Accounting and Economics, 29*(1), 1–51.

Basu, S. (1997). The conservatism principle and the asymmetric timeliness of earnings. *Journal of Accounting & Economics, 24*, 3–37.

Bates, R. J. (1968). Discussion of the information content of annual earnings announcements. *Journal of Accounting Research, 6*(Supp.), 93–95.

Beaver, W.H. (1968). The information content of annual earnings announcements. *Journal of Accounting Research, 6*(Supp), 67–92.

Blanchet, J. (2002). Global standards offer opportunity. *Financial Executive* (March/April), 28–30.

Brown, P., & Kennelly, J. W. (1972). The information content of quarterly earnings: An extension and some further evidence. *Journal of Business, 45*, 403–415.

Chai, M. L., & Tung, S. (2002). The effect of earnings-announcement timing on earnings management. *Journal of Business Finance & Accounting, 29*(9 & 10), 1337–1354.

Chambers, A. E., & Penman, S. H. (1984). Timeliness of reporting and the stock price reaction to earnings announcements. *Journal of Accounting Research, 22*(1), 21–47.

Davies, B., & Whittred. G. P. (1980). The association between selected corporate attributes and timeliness in corporate reporting: Further analysis. *Abacus, 16*(1), 48–60.

DeCeuster, M., & Trappers, D. (1993). *Determinants of the timeliness of Belgian financial statements.* Working Paper, University of Antwerp, cited in Annaert et al, 2002.

Demos, T. (2006, February 6). The Russia 50: The country's largest public companies. *Fortune, 153*(2), 70–71.

Dwyer, P. D., & Wilson, E. R. (1989). An empirical investigation of factors affecting the timeliness of reporting by municipalities. *Journal of Accounting and Public Policy, 8*(1), 29–55.

Financial Accounting Standards Board. (1980). *Statement of financial accounting concepts no. 2, qualitative characteristics of accounting information.* Stamford, CT: Author.

Gigler, F. B., & Hemmer, T. (2001). Conservatism, optimal disclosure policy, and the timeliness of financial reports. *The Accounting Review, 76*(4), 471–493.

Givoli, D., & Palmon, D. (1982). Timeliness of annual earnings announcements: Some empirical evidence. *The Accounting Review, 57*(3), 486–508.

Han, J. C.Y., & Wang, S.-W. (1998). Political costs and earnings management of oil companies during the 1990 Persian Gulf crises. *The Accounting Review, 73*, 103–117.

Han, J. C.Y., & Wild, J. J. (1997). Timeliness of reporting and earnings information transfers. *Journal of Business Finance & Accounting, 24*(3&4), 527–540.

Haw, I.-M., Qi, D., & Wu, W. (2000). Timeliness of annual report releases and market reaction to earnings announcements in an emerging capital market: The case of China. *Journal of International Financial Management and Accounting, 11*(2), 108–131.

Hendriksen, E. S., & van Breda, M. F. (1992). *Accounting theory* (5th ed.). Burr Ridge, IL: Irwin.

Jindrichovska, I., & Mcleay, S. (2005). Accounting for good news and accounting for bad news: Some empirical evidence from the Czech Republic. *European Accounting Review, 14*(3): 635–655.

Keller, S. B. (1986). Reporting timeliness in the presence of subject to audit qualifications. *Journal of Business Finance & Accounting, 13*(1), 117–124.

Kenley, W. J., & Staubus, G. J. (1974). Objectives and concepts of financial statements. *Accounting Review, 49*(4), 888–889.

Krishnan, G. V. (2005). The association between big 6 auditor industry expertise and the asymmetric timeliness of earnings. *Journal of Accounting, Auditing & Finance, 20*(3), 209–228.

Kross, W., & Schroeder, D.A. (1984). An empirical investigation of the effect of quarterly earnings announcement timing on stock returns. *Journal of Accounting Research, 22*(1), 153–176.

Kulzick, R. S. (2004). Sarbanes-Oxley: Effects on financial transparency. *S.A.M. Advanced Management Journal, 69*(1), 43–49.

Lawrence, J. E., & Glover, H. D. (1998). The effect of audit firm mergers on audit delay. *Journal of Managerial Issues, 10*(2), 151–164.

Leventis, S., & Weetman, P. (2004). Timeliness of financial reporting: Applicability of disclosure theories in an emerging capital market. *Accounting and Business Research, 34*(1), 43–56.

McGee, R. W. (2006). Timeliness of financial reporting in the energy sector. *Russian/CIS Energy & Mining Law Journal, 4*(2), 6–10.

McGee, R. W. (2007a). Corporate governance in Russia: A case study of timeliness of financial reporting in the telecom industry, *International Finance Review, 7*, 365–390.

McGee, R. W. (2007b). *Corporate governance and the timeliness of financial reporting: A case study of the Russian energy sector.* Fifth International Conference on Accounting and Finance in Transition. London, July 12–14.

McGee, R. W. (2007c). Transparency and disclosure in Russia. In T. M. Mickiewicz (ed.), Corporate governance and finance in Poland and Russia (pp. 278–295). London: Palgrave Macmillan.

McGee, R. W., & Igoe, D. N. (2008). Corporate governance and the timeliness of financial reporting: A comparative study of selected EU and Transition countries. *Proceedings of the 43rd Annual Western Regional Meeting of the American Accounting Association, San Francisco, May 1–3*, pp. 74–87.

McGee, R. W., & Preobragenskaya, G. G. (2005). *Accounting and financial system reform in a transition economy: A case study of Russia.* New York: Springer.

McGee, R. W., & Preobragenskaya, G. G. (2006). *Accounting and financial system reform in Eastern Europe and Asia.* New York: Springer.

McGee, R. W., & Tarangelo, T. (2008). The timeliness of financial reporting and the Russian banking system: An empirical study. In R. W. McGee (ed.), *Accounting reform in transition and developing economies.* New York: Springer.

McGee, R. W., & Yuan, X. (2008). Corporate governance and the timeliness of financial reporting: An empirical study of the People's Republic of China. *International Journal of Business, Accounting and Finance*, forthcoming.

Organisation for Economic Co-operation and Development. (1998). *Global Corporate Governance Principles.* Paris: Author.

OECD (2004). *OECD Principles of Corporate Governance.* Paris: Author.

Pope, P. F., & Walker, M. (1999). International differences in the timeliness, conservatism, and classification of earnings. *Journal of Accounting Research, 37*(Supp.), 53–87.

Prickett, R. (2002). Sweet clarity. *Financial Management* (September), 18–20.

Rees, W. P., & Giner. B. (2001). On the asymmetric recognition of good and bad news in France, Germany and the UK. *Journal of Business Finance & Accounting, 28*(9&10), 1285–1332.

Soltani, B. (2002). Timeliness of corporate and audit reports: Some empirical evidence in the French context. *The International Journal of Accounting, 37*, 215–246.

Trueman, B. (1990). Theories of earnings-announcement timing. *Journal of Accounting & Economics, 13*, 285–301.

Whittred, G., & Zimmer, I. (1984). Timeliness of financial reporting and financial distress. *The Accounting Review, 59*(2), 287–295.

Whittred, G. P. (1980). Audit qualification and the timeliness of corporate annual reports. *The Accounting Review, 55*(4), 563–577.

World Bank. (2001). *Report on the Observance of Standards and Codes (ROSC), Corporate Governance Country Assessment, Republic of Croatia, September.* World Bank. Retrieved from www.worldbank.org.

World Bank. (2002a). *Report on the Observance of Standards and Codes (ROSC), Corporate Governance Country Assessment, Bulgaria, September.* Washington, DC: World Bank. Retrieved from www.worldbank.org.

World Bank. (2002b). *Report on the Observance of Standards and Codes (ROSC), Corporate Governance Country Assessment, Czech Republic, July.* Washington, DC: World Bank. Retrieved from www.worldbank.org.

World Bank. (2002c). *Report on the Observance of Standards and Codes (ROSC), Corporate Governance Country Assessment, Georgia, March.* Washington, DC: World Bank. Retrieved from www.worldbank.org.

World Bank. (2002d). *Report on the Observance of Standards and Codes (ROSC), Corporate Governance Country Assessment, Latvia, December.* Washington, DC: World Bank. Retrieved from www.worldbank.org.

World Bank. (2002e). *Report on the Observance of Standards and Codes (ROSC), Corporate Governance Country Assessment, Republic of Lithuania, July.* Washington, DC: World Bank. Retrieved from www.worldbank.org.

World Bank. (2003a). *Report on the Observance of Standards and Codes (ROSC), Corporate Governance Country Assessment, Hungary, February.* Washington, DC: World Bank. Retrieved from www.worldbank.org.

World Bank. (2003b). *Report on the Observance of Standards and Codes (ROSC), Corporate Governance Country Assessment, Slovak Republic, October.* Washington, DC: World Bank. Retrieved from www.worldbank.org.

World Bank. (2004a). *Report on the Observance of Standards and Codes (ROSC), Corporate Governance Country Assessment, Moldova, May.* Washington, DC: World Bank. Retrieved from www.worldbank.org.

World Bank. (2004b). *Report on the Observance of Standards and Codes (ROSC), Corporate Governance Country Assessment, Romania, April.* Washington, DC: World Bank. Retrieved from www.worldbank.org.

World Bank. (2004c). *Report on the Observance of Standards and Codes (ROSC), Corporate Governance Country Assessment, Slovenia, May.* Washington, DC: World Bank. Retrieved from www.worldbank.org.

World Bank. (2005a), *Report on the Observance of Standards and Codes (ROSC), Corporate Governance Country Assessment, Armenia, April.* Washington, DC: World Bank. Retrieved from www.worldbank.org.

World Bank. (2005b). *Report on the Observance of Standards and Codes (ROSC), Corporate Governance Country Assessment, Azerbaijan, July.* Washington, DC: World Bank. Retrieved from www.worldbank.org.

World Bank. (2005c). *Report on the Observance of Standards and Codes (ROSC), Corporate Governance Country Assessment, Macedonia, June.* Washington, DC: World Bank. Retrieved from www.worldbank.org.

World Bank. (2005d). *Report on the Observance of Standards and Codes (ROSC), Corporate Governance Country Assessment, Poland, June.* Washington, DC: World Bank. Retrieved from www.worldbank.org.

World Bank. (2006a). *Report on the Observance of Standards and Codes (ROSC), Corporate Governance Country Assessment, Bosnia and Herzegovina, June.* Washington, DC: World Bank. Retrieved from www.worldbank.org.

World Bank. (2006b). *Report on the Observance of Standards and Codes (ROSC), Corporate Governance Country Assessment, Ukraine, October.* Washington, DC: World Bank. Retrieved from www.worldbank.org.

Chapter 10
Corporate Governance and the Timeliness of Financial Reporting: A Case Study of Kenya

Judith Muhoro and Robert W. McGee

Introduction

It is important to report financial information in a timely fashion. The longer a company waits to release its annual report and accompanying financial statements, the more stale the information is and the less useful it is.

A number of studies have been done on various aspects of timeliness in financial reporting. Those studies will not be summarized here but a listing is provided in the reference section for further research.

Various organizations have cited the importance of timely financial reporting. The Accounting Principles Board (1970) addressed the issue in one of its statements. The Organisation for Economic Co-operation and Development (OECD, 2004) lists it as an important principle of corporate governance. The World Bank has conducted more than 40 studies on corporate governance in various countries that have included a look at their financial reporting practices, including timeliness. However, Kenya was not among the countries studied.

The present study replicates studies that have measured the timeliness of financial reporting in Russia (McGee, 2006, 2007a, 2007b, 2007c, 2008; McGee & Gunn, 2008; McGee, & Tarangelo, 2008; McGee & Tyler, 2008; McGee, Tarangelo, & Tyler, 2008; McGee, Tyler, Tarangelo, & Igoe, 2008; McGee, Yuan, Tyler, & Tarangelo, 2008), China (McGee, & Yuan, 2008a, 2008b; McGee et al., 2008; McGee, Igoe, Yuan, Tarangelo, & Tyler, 2008), and the European Union (EU) (McGee & Igoe, 2008; McGee et al., 2008; McGee et al., 2008). Those studies found that Russia and China take longer to report financial information than do either the USA or the EU, but that there is no statistical difference between the time it takes for new EU members to report financial information and the time it takes old EU members to do so.

J. Muhoro (✉)
St. Paul's University, Limuru, Kenya
e-mail: nduturas@yahoo.com

R.W. Mc Gee (✉)
Florida International University, Miami, FL, USA
e-mail: bob414@hotmail.com

R.W. McGee (ed.), *Corporate Governance in Developing Economies*,
DOI 10.1007/978-0-387-84833-4_10, © Springer Science+Business Media, LLC 2009

This is the first empirical study, to our knowledge, that has been conducted on the timeliness of financial reporting in an African country. Thus, there is a gap in the literature that needs to be filled. The purpose of the present study is to partially fill that gap.

Methodology

Timeliness was determined by counting the number of days that elapsed between year-end and the date of the auditor's report. Data was gathered from the financial statements of 46 companies that are listed on the Kenya Stock Exchange. In some cases, data was available for 5 or more years. In other cases, companies only reported a year or two worth of data. In some cases the authors were not able to obtain the necessary information for some companies.

Such a methodology is less than perfect for several reasons. For one, the date on the audit report might not be the same as the date the information was released to the general public. However, there is no way to obtain the date the information was released to the general public, so the date on the audit report acted as a surrogate for the actual release date.

Another possible criticism of the present study is that some companies report only 1 or 2 years worth of data while others publish 10 or more years of data. Analyzing data where the sample population differs by year is not as desirable as analyzing data where the sample sizes by year are about the same. However, the sample population was small to begin with, so the authors decided that it was better to enlarge the sample size even if that meant having sample sizes that differed by year. The alternative would have been to be forced to work with a much smaller sample size.

Findings

Table 10.1 shows the sample size, mean, median, and range for each year included in the study.

The total sample size for all years combined was 556. The mean and median for all years combined were 97.1 and 82 days, respectively. What that means is that the average Kenyan company that has a December 31 year-end had an audit opinion dated April 8 if the mean were used or March 23 if the median were used. Whether that is good or bad depends on a number of factors, including the national and regional financial reporting culture. Data was not available for other African countries, so comparisons could not be made.

The sample sizes varied by year. In the earlier years the sample sizes tended to be smaller. In the more recent years they tended to be larger.

Both the means and medians were computed. Computing medians eliminated the possible distortion that could occur in the event that there are some outliers.

Ranges were also computed so that the reader could get an idea of the minimum and maximum time delays for each of the years under study.

Table 10.1 Full sample data

Year	Sample size	Mean	Median	Range
1988	10	103.5	83	32–216
1989	15	102.0	112.9	47–234
1990	12	119.8	110.5	46–244
1991	15	122.2	107.0	37–262
1992	25	115.7	88.0	28–245
1993	22	102.5	83.0	27–211
1994	31	108.1	82.0	32–273
1995	33	116.0	88.0	43–336
1996	32	111.0	96.0	46–327
1997	30	99.6	87.5	39–357
1998	31	96.4	86.0	27–268
1999	36	96.9	88.0	40–243
2000	38	94.8	78.0	25–251
2001	40	89.3	71.0	35–318
2002	37	87.5	78.0	42–243
2003	36	80.1	75.5	37–170
2004	44	81.8	78.0	16–153
2005	34	84.4	74.0	33–281
2006	27	78.8	77.0	32–123
All years	556	97.1	82	16–357

Chart 1 shows the number of days delay in issuing the audit opinion for each year from 1988 to 2006. Visually, it appears to be a downward trend. It took more time to issue an audit opinion in the earlier years and less time in the more recent years. Medians were charted rather than means in order to avoid distortions caused by outliers in a small sample.

Chart 1
Days Delay - medians

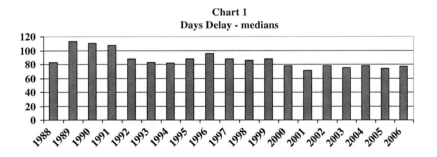

We decided to test this tentative conclusion that was arrived at by visual inspection by conducting a few Wilcoxon tests to see if the differences between certain years were statistically significant. Table 10.2 shows the comparisons and the results. The tests might not prove conclusive due to the small annual sample sizes but it was thought that an attempt should at least be made to determine whether the differences were significant.

Table 10.2 Wilcoxon tests
of statistical significance

Years compared	p-values
1989 vs. 1994	0.5193
1996 vs. 2006	0.08018*
1996 vs. 2001	0.1289
1996 vs. 2002	0.2266

*Significant at the 10% level

The tests revealed that the only significant difference is for the 1996 vs. 2006 comparison ($p<=0.08018$). No significant difference was found for the other comparisons, although the 1996 versus 2001 comparison came close ($p<=0.1289$).

Chart 2 shows the range of dates for four periods that are 5 years apart. Visual inspection reveals that the range seems to have decreased if one compares the most recent year to the other 3 years selected.

Chart 2
Ranges

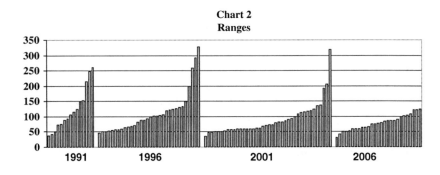

Concluding Comments

The present study found that the average Kenyan company takes about 97 or 82 days to report financial information after year-end, depending on whether the mean or median is used. The trend seems to be toward quicker disclosure of financial results and the range seems to have narrowed.

There are several areas for possible further research. Comparisons could be made between Kenya and some other African countries to see how Kenya compares in terms of timeliness. Comparisons could also be made with countries on other continents to see how Kenya fares in terms of timeliness with countries in North America, the EU, various transition or developing countries in Latin America or Asia.

References

Accounting Principles Board. (1970). *Basic concepts and accounting principles underlying financial statements of business enterprises – statement no. 4.* New York: American Institute of Certified Public Accountants.

Annaert, J., DeCeuster, M. J. K., Polfliet, R., & Campenhout, G. V. (2002). To be or not be ...
'too late': The case of the Belgian semi-annual earnings announcements. *Journal of Business Finance & Accounting, 29*(3 & 4), 477–495.

Ashbaugh, H., Johnstone, K. M., & Warfield, T. D. (1999). Corporate reporting on the internet. *Accounting Horizons, 13*(3), 241–257.

Ashton, R. H., Graul, P. R., & Newton, J. D. (1989). Audit delay and the timeliness of corporate reporting. *Contemporary Accounting Research, 5*(2), 657–673.

Atiase, R. K., Bamber, L. S., & Tse, S. (1989). Timeliness of financial reporting, the firm size effect, and stock price reactions to annual earnings announcements. *Contemporary Accounting Research, 5*(2), 526–552.

Ball, R., Kothari, S. P., & Robin, A. (2000). The effect of international institutional factors on properties of accounting earnings. *Journal of Accounting and Economics, 29*(1), 1–51.

Ball, R., & Brown, P. (1968). An empirical evaluation of accounting income numbers. *Journal of Accounting Research, 6*, 159–178.

Basu, S. (1997). The conservatism principle and the asymmetric timeliness of earnings. *Journal of Accounting & Economics, 24*, 3–37.

Bates, R.J. (1968). Discussion of the information content of annual earnings announcements. *Journal of Accounting Research, 6*(Supp.), 93–95.

Beaver, W. H. (1968). The information content of annual earnings announcements. *Journal of Accounting Research, 6* (Supp), 67–92.

Blanchet, J. (2002). Global standards offer opportunity. *Financial Executive* (March/April), 28–30.

Brown, P., & Kennelly, J. W. (1972). The information content of quarterly earnings: An extension and some further evidence. *Journal of Business, 45*, 403–415.

Chai, M. L., & Tung, S. (2002). The effect of earnings-announcement timing on earnings management. *Journal of Business Finance & Accounting, 29* (9 & 10), 1337–1354.

Chambers, A. E., & Penman, S. H. (1984). Timeliness of reporting and the stock price reaction to earnings announcements. *Journal of Accounting Research, 22*(1), 21–47.

Davies, B., & Whittred, G. P. (1980). The association between selected corporate attributes and timeliness in corporate reporting: Further analysis. *Abacus, 16*(1), 48–60.

DeCeuster, M., & Trappers, D. (1993). *Determinants of the timeliness of belgian financial statements.* Working Paper, University of Antwerp, cited in Annaert et al, 2002.

Demos, T.. (2006, February 6). The Russia 50: The country's largest public companies. *Fortune 153*(2), 70–71.

Dwyer, P. D. & Wilson, E. R. (1989). An empirical investigation of factors affecting the timeliness of reporting by municipalities. *Journal of Accounting and Public Policy, 8*(1), 29–55.

Financial Accounting Standards Board. (1980). *Statement of financial accounting concepts no. 2, qualitative characteristics of accounting information.* Stamford, CT: Author.

Gigler, F. B., & Hemmer, T. (2001). Conservatism, optimal disclosure policy, and the timeliness of financial reports. *The Accounting Review, 76*(4), 471–493.

Givoli, D., & Palmon, D. (1982). Timeliness of annual earnings announcements: Some empirical evidence. *The Accounting Review, 57*(3), 486–508.

Han, J. C. Y., & Wang, S.-W. (1998). Political co sts and earnings management of oil companies during the 1990 Persian Gulf crises. *The Accounting Review, 73*, 103–117.

Han, J. C. Y., & Wild, J. J. (1997). Timeliness of reporting and earnings information transfers. *Journal of Business Finance & Accounting, 24*(3&4), 527–540.

Haw, I.-M., Qi, D., & Wu, W. (2000). Timeliness of annual report releases and market reaction to earnings announcements in an emerging capital market: The case of China. *Journal of International Financial Management and Accounting, 11*(2), 108–131.

Hendriksen, E. S., & van Breda, M. F. (1992). Accounting theory (5th ed.). Burr Ridge, IL: Irwin.

Hoover's Most Viewed Company Directory by Country Retrieved from www.hoovers.com/free/mvc/country.xhtml

Jindrichovska, I., & Mcleay, S. (2005). Accounting for good news and accounting for bad news: Some empirical evidence from the Czech Republic. European *Accounting Review, 14*(3), 635–655.

Keller, S. B. (1986). Reporting timeliness in the presence of subject to audit qualifications. *Journal of Business Finance & Accounting, 13*(1), 117–124.

Kenley, W. J., & Staubus, G. J. (1974). Objectives and concepts of financial statements. *Accounting Review, 49*(4), 888–889.

Krishnan, G. V. (2005). The association between big 6 auditor industry expertise and the asymmetric timeliness of earnings. *Journal of Accounting, Auditing & Finance, 20*(3), 209–228.

Kross, W., & Schroeder, D.A. (1984). An empirical investigation of the effect of quarterly earnings announcement timing on stock returns. *Journal of Accounting Research, 22*(1), 153–176.

Kulzick, R. S. (2004). Sarbanes-Oxley: Effects on financial transparency. *S.A.M. Advanced Management Journal, 69*(1), 43–49.

Lawrence, J. E., & Glover, H. D. (1998). The effect of audit firm mergers on audit delay. *Journal of Managerial Issues, 10*(2), 151–164.

Leventis, S., & Weetman, P. (2004). Timeliness of financial reporting: Applicability of disclosure theories in an emerging capital market. *Accounting and Business Research 34*(1), 43–56.

McGee, R. W. (2006). Timeliness of financial reporting in the energy sector. *Russian/CIS Energy & Mining Law Journal, 4*(2), 6–10.

McGee, R. W. (2007a). Corporate governance in Russia: A case study of timeliness of financial reporting in the telecom industry, *International Finance Review, 7*, 365–390.

McGee, R. W. (2007b). *Corporate governance and the timeliness of financial reporting: A case study of the Russian energy sector.* Fifth International Conference on Accounting and Finance in Transition. London, July 12–14.

McGee, R. W. (2007c). Transparency and disclosure in Russia. In T. M. Mickiewicz (ed.), *Corporate governance and finance in Poland and Russia* (pp. 278–295). London: Palgrave Macmillan.

McGee, R. W. (2008). The timeliness of financial reporting: The Russian oil, gas and power industries. In R. W. McGee (ed.), *Accounting reform in transition and developing economies.* New York: Springer.

McGee, R. W., & Gunn, R. (2008). The timeliness of financial reporting: A comparative study of Russian and Non-Russian companies in the transportation industry. In R. W. McGee (ed.), *Accounting reform in transition and developing economies.* New York: Springer.

McGee, R. W., & Igoe, D. N. (2008). Corporate governance and the timeliness of financial reporting: A comparative study of selected EU and transition countries. *Proceedings of the 43rd Annual Western Regional Meeting of the American Accounting Association, San Francisco, May 1–3*, pp. 74–87. Reprinted in Robert W. McGee (ed.), *Accounting reform in transition and developing economies.* New York: Springer.

McGee, R. W., Igoe, D. N., Yuan, X., Tarangelo, T., & Tyler, M. (2008). The timeliness of financial reporting: A comparative study of the People's Republic of China and the European Union. In R. W. McGee (ed), *Accounting reform in transition and developing economies.* New York: Springer.

McGee, R. W., & Preobragenskaya, G. G. (2005). *Accounting and financial system reform in a transition economy: A case study of Russia.* New York: Springer.

McGee, R W., & Preobragenskaya, G. G. (2006). *Accounting and financial system reform in Eastern Europe and Asia.* New York: Springer.

McGee, R. W., & Tarangelo, T. (2008). The timeliness of financial reporting and the Russian banking system: An empirical study. In R. W. McGee (ed.), *Accounting reform in transition and developing economies.* New York: Springer.

McGee, R. W., Tarangelo, T., & Tyler, M. (2008). The timeliness of financial reporting: A comparative study of companies in Russian and the USA. In R. W. McGee (ed.), *Accounting reform in transition and developing economies.* New York: Springer.

McGee, R. W., & Tyler, M. (2008). The timeliness of financial reporting: A comparative study of Russian and Non-Russian Companies. In R. W. McGee (ed.), *Accounting reform in transition and developing economies.* New York: Springer.

McGee, R. W., Tyler, M., Tarangelo, T., & Igoe, D. N. (2008). The timeliness of financial reporting: A comparative study of companies in Russia and the European Union. In

R. W. McGee (ed.), *Accounting reform in transition and developing economies*. New York: Springer.

McGee, R. W., & Yuan, X. (2008a). Corporate governance and the timeliness of financial reporting: An empirical study of the People's Republic of China. *International Journal of Business, Accounting and Finance*, forthcoming.

McGee, R. W., & Yuan, X. (2008b). The timeliness of financial reporting: A comparative study of the People's Republic of China and the USA. In R. W. McGee (ed.), *Accounting reform in transition and developing economies*. New York: Springer.

McGee, R. W., Yuan, X. Tyler, M., & Tarangelo, T. (2008). The timeliness of financial reporting: A comparative study of the People's republic of China and Russia. In R. W. McGee (ed.), *Accounting reform in transition and developing economies*. New York: Springer.

Organisation for Economic Co-operation and Development. (1998). *Global Corporate Governance Principles*. Paris: Author.

OECD (2004). *OECD Principles of Corporate Governance*. Paris: Author.

Pope, P. F., & Walker, M. (1999). International differences in the timeliness, conservatism, and classification of earnings. *Journal of Accounting Research, 37* (Supp), 53–87.

Prickett, R. (2002). Sweet clarity. *Financial Management* (September): 18–20.

Rees, W. P., & Giner, B.. (2001). On the asymmetric recognition of good and bad news in France, Germany and the UK. *Journal of Business Finance & Accounting, 28*(9&10), 1285–1332.

Soltani, B.. (2002). Timeliness of corporate and audit reports: Some empirical evidence in the French context. *The International Journal of Accounting, 37*, 215–246.

Trueman, B. (1990). Theories of earnings-announcement timing. *Journal of Accounting & Economics, 13*, 285–301.

Whittred, G., & Zimmer, I. (1984). Timeliness of financial reporting and financial distress. *The Accounting Review, 59*(2), 287–295.

Whittred, G.P. (1980). Audit qualification and the timeliness of corporate annual reports. *The Accounting Review, 55*(4), 563–577.

World Bank. (2001). *Report on the Observance of Standards and Codes (ROSC), Corporate Governance Country Assessment, Republic of Croatia, September.* World Bank. Retrieved from www.worldbank.org.

World Bank. (2002a). *Report on the Observance of Standards and Codes (ROSC), Corporate Governance Country Assessment, Bulgaria, September.* Washington, DC: World Bank. Retrieved from www.worldbank.org.

World Bank. (2002b). *Report on the Observance of Standards and Codes (ROSC), Corporate Governance Country Assessment, Czech Republic, July.* Washington, DC: World Bank. Retrieved from www.worldbank.org.

World Bank. (2002c). *Report on the Observance of Standards and Codes (ROSC), Corporate Governance Country Assessment, Georgia, March.* Washington, DC: World Bank. Retrieved from www.worldbank.org.

World Bank. (2002d). *Report on the Observance of Standards and Codes (ROSC), Corporate Governance Country Assessment, Latvia, December.* Washington, DC: World Bank. Retrieved from www.worldbank.org.

World Bank. (2002e). *Report on the Observance of Standards and Codes (ROSC), Corporate Governance Country Assessment, Republic of Lithuania, July.* Washington, DC: World Bank. Retrieved from www.worldbank.org.

World Bank. (2003a). *Report on the Observance of Standards and Codes (ROSC), Corporate Governance Country Assessment, Hungary, February.* Washington, DC: World Bank. Retrieved from www.worldbank.org.

World Bank. (2003b). *Report on the Observance of Standards and Codes (ROSC), Corporate Governance Country Assessment, Slovak Republic, October.* Washington, DC: World Bank. Retrieved from www.worldbank.org.

World Bank. (2004a), *Report on the Observance of Standards and Codes (ROSC), Corporate Governance Country Assessment, Moldova, May.* Washington, DC: World Bank. Retrieved from www.worldbank.org.

World Bank. (2004b). *Report on the Observance of Standards and Codes (ROSC), Corporate Governance Country Assessment, Romania, April.* Washington, DC: World Bank. Retrieved from www.worldbank.org.

World Bank. (2004c). *Report on the Observance of Standards and Codes (ROSC), Corporate Governance Country Assessment, Slovenia, May.* Washington, DC: World Bank. Retrieved from www.worldbank.org.

World Bank. (2005a). *Report on the Observance of Standards and Codes (ROSC), Corporate Governance Country Assessment, Armenia, April.* Washington, DC: World Bank. Retrieved from www.worldbank.org.

World Bank. (2005b). *Report on the Observance of Standards and Codes (ROSC), Corporate Governance Country Assessment, Azerbaijan, July.* Washington, DC: World Bank. Retrieved from www.worldbank.org.

World Bank. (2005c). *Report on the Observance of Standards and Codes (ROSC), Corporate Governance Country Assessment, Macedonia, June.* Washington, DC: World Bank. Retrieved from www.worldbank.org.

World Bank. (2005d). *Report on the Observance of Standards and Codes (ROSC), Corporate Governance Country Assessment, Poland, June.* Washington, DC: World Bank. Retrieved from www.worldbank.org.

World Bank. (2006a). *Report on the Observance of Standards and Codes (ROSC), Corporate Governance Country Assessment, Bosnia and Herzegovina, June.* Washington, DC: World Bank. Retrieved from www.worldbank.org.

World Bank. (2006b). *Report on the Observance of Standards and Codes (ROSC), Corporate Governance Country Assessment, Ukraine, October.* Washington, DC: World Bank. Retrieved from www.worldbank.org.

Chapter 11
Corporate Governance and the Timeliness of Financial Reporting: A Comparative Study of Kenya and the European Union

Judith Muhoro, Robert W. McGee, Danielle N. Igoe, Thomas Tarangelo, and Michael Tyler

Introduction

It is important to report financial information in a timely fashion. The longer a company waits to release its annual report and accompanying financial statements, the more stale the information is and the less useful it is.

A number of studies have been done on various aspects of timeliness in financial reporting. Those studies will not be summarized here but a listing is provided in the reference section for further research.

Various organizations have cited the importance of timely financial reporting. The Accounting Principles Board (1970) addressed the issue in one of its statements. The Organisation for Economic Co-operation and Development (OECD, 2004) lists it as an important principle of corporate governance. The World Bank has conducted more than 40 studies on corporate governance in various countries that have included a look at their financial reporting practices, including timeliness. However, Kenya was not among the countries studied.

The present study replicates studies that have measured the timeliness of financial reporting in Russia (McGee, 2006, 2007a, 2007b, 2007c, 2008; McGee & Gunn, 2008;

J. Muhoro (✉)
St. Paul's University, Limuru, Kenya
e-mail: nduturas@yahoo.com

R.W. McGee (✉)
Florida International University, Miami, FL, USA
e-mail: bob414@hotmail.com

D.N. Igoe (✉)
University of Florida, Gainesville, FL, USA
e-mail: dingoe@gmail.com

T. Tarangelo (✉)
Florida International University, Miami, FL, USA
e-mail: tarangel@fiu.edu

M. Tyler (✉)
Barry University, Miami Shores, FL, USA
e-mail: mtyler@mail.barry.edu

R.W. McGee (ed.), *Corporate Governance in Developing Economies*,
DOI 10.1007/978-0-387-84833-4_11, © Springer Science+Business Media, LLC 2009

McGee & Tarangelo, 2008; McGee & Tyler, 2008; McGee, Tarangelo & Tyler, 2008; McGee, Tyler, Tarangelo & Igoe, 2008; McGee, Yuan, Tyler & Tarangelo, 2008), China (McGee & Yuan, 2008a, 2008b, McGee, et al., 2008; McGee, Igoe, Yuan, Tarangelo & Tyler, 2008), and the European Union (EU) (McGee & Igoe, 2008; McGee et al., 2008; McGee et al., 2008). These studies found that Russia and China take longer to report financial information than do either the USA or the EU, but that there is no statistical difference between the time it takes for new EU members to report financial information and the time it takes old EU members to do so.

This is one of the first empirical studies, to our knowledge, that has been conducted on the timeliness of financial reporting in an African country. Thus, there is a gap in the literature that needs to be filled. The purpose of the present study is to partially fill that gap.

Methodology

Timeliness was determined by counting the number of days that elapsed between year-end and the date of the auditor's report. Data for Kenya was gathered from the financial statements of 46 companies that are listed on the Kenya Stock Exchange. Data for EU companies was collected from the websites of large EU companies.

Such a methodology is less than perfect. The date on the audit report might not be the same as the date the information was released to the general public. However, there is no way to obtain the date the information was released to the general public, so the date on the audit report acted as a surrogate for the actual release date.

Findings

Table 11.1 shows the sample size, range, median, mean, and p-value for both samples. Kenyan companies took an average of 97.1 days after year-end to report financial results. The EU companies took an average of 78.7 days after year-end to report financial results. The medians for Kenya and China were 82 and 69 days, respectively. Using the median data, it appears that the average Kenyan company takes about 13 days longer to report financial results.

Table 11.1 Full sample data

	Sample size (years)	Mean (days)	Median (days)	Range (days)	p-value
Kenyan companies	556	97.1	82.0	16–357	2.944e–09
EU companies	439	78.7	69	23–354	

*Significant at 1%

A Wilcoxon test found the differences in time delay to be significant at the one percent level ($p <= 2.944e-09$). Kenyan companies take an average of 2 additional weeks to report financial data. The chart below shows the median days delay for Kenyan and EU companies.

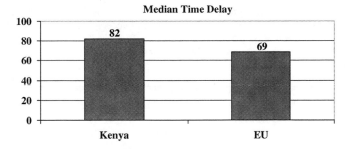

Median Time Delay

The chart below shows the range of days delay for all the companies included in the study. As can be seen, the shapes of the graphs are similar, although the Kenyan graph is thicker at the high end.

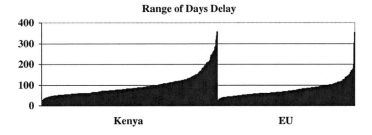

Range of Days Delay

Concluding Comments

The present study compared the delay in issuing an audit report for a sample of companies in Kenya and the EU. The finding was that it takes Kenyan companies about 2 more weeks to report their annual results. The difference was found to be significant at the 1 percent level.

References

Accounting Principles Board. (1970). *Basic concepts and accounting principles underlying financial statements of business enterprises – statement no. 4.* New York: American Institute of Certified Public Accountants.

Annaert, J., DeCeuster, M. J. K., Polfliet, R., & Campenhout, G. V. (2002). To be or not be … 'too late': The case of the Belgian semi-annual earnings announcements. *Journal of Business Finance & Accounting, 29*(3 & 4): 477–495.

Ashbaugh, H., Johnstone, K. M., & Warfield, T. D. (1999). Corporate reporting on the internet. *Accounting Horizons 13*(3), 241–257.

Ashton, R. H., Graul, P. R., & Newton, J. D. (1989). Audit delay and the timeliness of corporate reporting. *Contemporary Accounting Research, 5*(2), 657–673.

Atiase, R. K., Bamber, L. S., & Tse, S. (1989). Timeliness of financial reporting, the firm size effect, and stock price reactions to annual earnings announcements. *Contemporary Accounting Research, 5*(2), 526–552.

Ball, R., Kothari, S. P., & Robin, A. (2000). The effect of international institutional factors on properties of accounting earnings. *Journal of Accounting and Economics, 29*(1), 1–51.

Ball, R., & Brown, P. (1968). An empirical evaluation of accounting income numbers. *Journal of Accounting Research, 6,* 159–178.

Basu, S. (1997). The conservatism principle and the asymmetric timeliness of earnings. *Journal of Accounting & Economics, 24,* 3–37.

Bates, R. J. (1968). Discussion of the information content of annual earnings announcements. *Journal of Accounting Research, 6*(Supp.), 93–95.

Beaver, W. H. (1968). The information content of annual earnings announcements. *Journal of Accounting Research, 6*(Supp), 67–92.

Blanchet, J. (2002). Global standards offer opportunity. *Financial Executive* (March/April), 28–30.

Brown, P., & Kennelly, J. W. (1972). The information content of quarterly earnings: An extension and some further evidence. *Journal of Business, 45,* 403–415.

Chai, M. L., & Tung, S. (2002). The effect of earnings-announcement timing on earnings management. *Journal of Business Finance & Accounting, 29*(9 & 10), 1337–1354.

Chambers, A. E., & Penman, S. H. (1984). Timeliness of reporting and the stock price reaction to earnings announcements. *Journal of Accounting Research, 22*(1), 21–47.

Davies, B., & Whittred, G. P. (1980). The association between selected corporate attributes and timeliness in corporate reporting: Further analysis. *Abacus, 16*(1), 48–60.

DeCeuster, M., & Trappers, D. (1993). *Determinants of the timeliness of Belgian financial statements.* Working Paper, University of Antwerp, cited in Annaert et al, 2002.

Demos, T. (2006, February 6). The Russia 50: The country's largest public companies. *Fortune, 153*(2), 70–71.

Dwyer, P. D., & Wilson, E. R. (1989). An empirical investigation of factors affecting the timeliness of reporting by municipalities. *Journal of Accounting and Public Policy, 8*(1), 29–55.

Financial Accounting Standards Board. (1980). Statement of financial accounting concepts no. 2, qualitative characteristics of accounting information. Stamford, CT: Author.

Gigler, F. B., & Hemmer, T. (2001). Conservatism, optimal disclosure policy, and the timeliness of financial reports. *The Accounting Review, 76*(4), 471–493.

Givoli, D., & Palmon, D. (1982). Timeliness of annual earnings announcements: Some empirical evidence. *The Accounting Review, 57*(3), 486–508.

Han, J. C. Y., & Wang, S.-W. (1998). Political costs and earnings management of oil companies during the 1990 Persian Gulf crises. *The Accounting Review, 73,* 103–117.

Han, J. C. Y., & Wild, J. J. (1997). Timeliness of reporting and earnings information transfers. *Journal of Business Finance & Accounting, 24*(3&4), 527–540.

Haw, I.-M., Qi, D., & Wu, W. (2000). Timeliness of annual report releases and market reaction to earnings announcements in an emerging capital market: The case of China. *Journal of International Financial Management and Accounting, 11*(2), 108–131.

Hendriksen, E. S. & van Breda, M. F. (1992). Accounting theory (5th ed.), Burr Ridge, IL: Irwin.

Hoover's Most Viewed Company Directory by Country Retrieved from www.hoovers.com/free/mvc/country.xhtml

Jindrichovska, I., & Mcleay, S. (2005). Accounting for good news and accounting for bad news: Some empirical evidence from the Czech Republic. *European Accounting Review 14*(3), 635–655.

Keller, S. B. (1986). Reporting timeliness in the presence of subject to audit qualifications. *Journal of Business Finance & Accounting, 13*(1), 117–124.

Kenley, W. J., & Staubus, G. J. (1974). Objectives and concepts of financial statements. *Accounting Review, 49*(4), 888–889.

Krishnan, G. V., (2005). The association between big 6 auditor industry expertise and the asymmetric timeliness of earnings. *Journal of Accounting, Auditing & Finance, 20*(3), 209–228.

Kross, W., & Schroeder, D. A. (1984). An empirical investigation of the effect of quarterly earnings announcement timing on stock returns. *Journal of Accounting Research, 22*(1), 153–176.

Kulzick, R. S., (2004). Sarbanes-Oxley: Effects on financial transparency. *S.A.M. Advanced Management Journal, 69*(1), 43–49.

Lawrence, J. E., & Glover, H. D. (1998). The effect of audit firm mergers on audit delay. *Journal of Managerial Issues, 10*(2), 151–164.

Leventis, S., & Weetman, P. (2004). Timeliness of financial reporting: applicability of disclosure theories in an emerging capital market. *Accounting and Business Research, 34*(1), 43–56.

McGee, R. W. (2006). Timeliness of financial reporting in the energy sector. *Russian/CIS Energy & Mining Law Journal, 4*(2), 6–10.

McGee, R. W. (2007a). Corporate governance in Russia: A case study of timeliness of financial reporting in the telecom industry. *International Finance Review, 7*, 365–390.

McGee, R. W. (2007b). *Corporate governance and the timeliness of financial reporting: A case study of the Russian energy sector.* Fifth International Conference on Accounting and Finance in Transition. London, July 12–14, 2007.

McGee, R. W. (2007c). Transparency and disclosure in Russia. In T. M. Mickiewicz (ed.), *Corporate governance and finance in Poland and Russia* (pp. 278–295). London: Palgrave Macmillan.

McGee, R. W. (2008). The timeliness of financial reporting: The Russian oil, gas and power industries. In R. W. McGee (ed.), *Accounting reform in transition and developing economies.* New York: Springer.

McGee, R. W., & Gunn, R. (2008). The timeliness of financial reporting: A comparative study of Russian and Non-Russian companies in the transportation industry. In R. W. McGee (ed.), *Accounting reform in transition and developing economies.* New York: Springer.

McGee, R. W., & Igoe, D. N. (2008). Corporate governance and the timeliness of financial reporting: A comparative study of selected EU and transition countries. *Proceedings of the 43rd Annual Western Regional Meeting of the American Accounting Association, San Francisco, May 1–3,* pp. 74–87. Reprinted in R. W. McGee (ed.), Accounting reform in transition and developing economies. New York: Springer.

McGee, R. W., Igoe, D. N., Yuan, X., Tarangelo, T., & Tyler, M. (2008). The timeliness of financial reporting: A comparative study of the People's Republic of China and the European Union. In R. W. McGee (ed.), *Accounting reform in transition and developing economies.* New York: Springer.

McGee, R. W., & Preobragenskaya, G. G. (2005). *Accounting and financial system reform in a transition economy: A case study of Russia.* New York: Springer.

McGee, R. W., & Preobragenskaya, G. G. (2006). *Accounting and financial system reform in Eastern Europe and Asia.* New York: Springer.

McGee, R. W., & Tarangelo, T. (2008). The timeliness of financial reporting and the Russian banking system: An empirical study. In R. W. McGee (ed.), *Accounting reform in transition and developing economies.* New York: Springer.

McGee, R. W., Tarangelo, T., & Tyler, M. (2008). The timeliness of financial reporting: A comparative study of companies in Russian and the USA. In R. W. McGee (ed.), *Accounting reform in transition and developing economies.* New York: Springer.

McGee, R. W., & Tyler, M. (2008). The timeliness of financial reporting: A comparative study of Russian and Non-Russian companies. In R. W. McGee (ed.), Accounting reform in transition and developing economies. New York: Springer.

McGee, R. W., Tyler, M., Tarangelo, T., & Igoe, D. N. (2008). The timeliness of financial reporting: A comparative study of companies in Russia and the European Union. In R. W. McGee (ed.), *Accounting reform in transition and developing economies.* New York: Springer.

McGee, R. W., & Yuan, X. (2008a). Corporate governance and the timeliness of financial reporting: An empirical study of the People's Republic of China. *International Journal of Business, Accounting and Finance*, forthcoming.

McGee, R. W., & Yuan, X. (2008b). The timeliness of financial reporting: A comparative study of the People's Republic of China and the USA. In R. W. McGee (ed.), *Accounting reform in transition and developing economies.* New York: Springer.

McGee, R. W., Yuan, X., Tyler, M., & Tarangelo, T. (2008). The timeliness of financial reporting: A comparative study of the People's republic of China and Russia. In R. W. McGee (ed.), *Accounting reform in transition and developing economies.* New York: Springer.

Organisation for Economic Co-operation and Development. (1998). *Global Corporate Governance Principles.* Paris: Author.

OECD (2004). *OECD Principles of Corporate Governance.* Paris: Author.

Pope, P. F., & Walker, M. (1999). International differences in the timeliness, conservatism, and classification of earnings. *Journal of Accounting Research, 37*(Supp), 53–87.

Prickett, R. (2002). Sweet clarity. *Financial Management* (September), 18–20.

Rees, W. P., & Giner, B. (2001). On the asymmetric recognition of good and bad news in France, Germany and the UK. *Journal of Business Finance & Accounting, 28*(9&10), 1285–1332.

Soltani, B. (2002). Timeliness of corporate and audit reports: Some empirical evidence in the French context. *The International Journal of Accounting, 37,* 215–246.

Trueman, B. (1990). Theories of earnings-announcement timing. *Journal of Accounting & Economics, 13,* 285–301.

Whittred, G., & Zimmer, I. (1984). Timeliness of financial reporting and financial distress. *The Accounting Review, 59*(2), 287–295.

Whittred, G. P. (1980). Audit qualification and the timeliness of corporate annual reports. *The Accounting Review, 55*(4), 563–577.

World Bank. (2001). *Report on the Observance of Standards and Codes (ROSC), Corporate Governance Country Assessment, Republic of Croatia, September.* World Bank. Retrieved from www.worldbank.org.

World Bank. (2002a). *Report on the Observance of Standards and Codes (ROSC), Corporate Governance Country Assessment, Bulgaria, September.* Washington, DC: World Bank. Retrieved from www.worldbank.org.

World Bank. (2002b). *Report on the Observance of Standards and Codes (ROSC), Corporate Governance Country Assessment, Czech Republic, July.* Washington, DC: World Bank. Retrieved from www.worldbank.org.

World Bank. (2002c). *Report on the Observance of Standards and Codes (ROSC), Corporate Governance Country Assessment, Georgia, March.* Washington, DC: World Bank. Retrieved from www.worldbank.org.

World Bank. (2002d). *Report on the Observance of Standards and Codes (ROSC), Corporate Governance Country Assessment, Latvia, December.* Washington, DC: World Bank. Retrieved from www.worldbank.org.

World Bank. (2002e). *Report on the Observance of Standards and Codes (ROSC), Corporate Governance Country Assessment, Republic of Lithuania, July.* Washington, DC: World Bank. Retrieved from www.worldbank.org.

World Bank. (2003a). *Report on the Observance of Standards and Codes (ROSC), Corporate Governance Country Assessment, Hungary, February.* Washington, DC: World Bank. Retrieved from www.worldbank.org.

World Bank. (2003b). *Report on the Observance of Standards and Codes (ROSC), Corporate Governance Country Assessment, Slovak Republic, October.* Washington, DC: World Bank. Retrieved from www.worldbank.org.

World Bank. (2004a). *Report on the Observance of Standards and Codes (ROSC), Corporate Governance Country Assessment, Moldova, May.* Washington, DC: World Bank. Retrieved from www.worldbank.org.

World Bank. (2004b). *Report on the Observance of Standards and Codes (ROSC), Corporate Governance Country Assessment, Romania, April.* Washington, DC: World Bank. Retrieved from www.worldbank.org.

World Bank. (2004c). *Report on the Observance of Standards and Codes (ROSC), Corporate Governance Country Assessment, Slovenia, May.* Washington, DC: World Bank. Retrieved from www.worldbank.org.

World Bank. (2005a). *Report on the Observance of Standards and Codes (ROSC), Corporate Governance Country Assessment, Armenia, April.* Washington, DC: World Bank. Retrieved from www.worldbank.org.

World Bank. (2005b). *Report on the Observance of Standards and Codes (ROSC), Corporate Governance Country Assessment, Azerbaijan, July.* Washington, DC: World Bank. Retrieved from www.worldbank.org.

World Bank. (2005c). *Report on the Observance of Standards and Codes (ROSC), Corporate Governance Country Assessment, Macedonia, June.* Washington, DC: World Bank. Retrieved from www.worldbank.org.

World Bank. (2005d). *Report on the Observance of Standards and Codes (ROSC), Corporate Governance Country Assessment, Poland, June.* Washington, DC: World Bank. Retrieved from www.worldbank.org.

World Bank. (2006a). *Report on the Observance of Standards and Codes (ROSC), Corporate Governance Country Assessment, Bosnia and Herzegovina, June.* Washington, DC: World Bank. Retrieved from www.worldbank.org.

World Bank. (2006b). *Report on the Observance of Standards and Codes (ROSC), Corporate Governance Country Assessment, Ukraine, October.* Washington, DC: World Bank. Retrieved from www.worldbank.org.

Chapter 12
Corporate Governance and the Timeliness of Financial Reporting: A Comparative Study of Kenya and the United States of America

Judith Muhoro and Robert W. McGee

Introduction

It is important to report financial information in a timely fashion. The longer a company waits to release its annual report and accompanying financial statements, the more stale the information is and the less useful it is.

A number of studies have been done on various aspects of timeliness in financial reporting. Those studies will not be summarized here but a listing is provided in the reference section for further research.

Various organizations have cited the importance of timely financial reporting. The Accounting Principles Board (1970) addressed the issue in one of its statements. The Organisation for Economic Co-operation and Development (OECD, 2004) lists it as an important principle of corporate governance. The World Bank has conducted more than 40 studies on corporate governance in various countries that have included a look at their financial reporting practices, including timeliness. However, Kenya was not among the countries studied.

The present study replicates studies that have measured the timeliness of financial reporting in Russia (McGee, 2006, 2007a, 2007b, 2007c, 2008; McGee & Gunn, 2008; McGee & Tarangelo, 2008; McGee & Tyler, 2008; McGee, Tarangelo, & Tyler, 2008; McGee, Tyler, Tarangelo, & Igoe, 2008; McGee, Yuan, Tyler, & Tarangelo, 2008), China (McGee & Yuan, 2008a. 2008b; McGee et al., 2008; McGee, Igoe, Yuan, Tarangelo, & Tyler, 2008), and the European Union (EU) (McGee & Igoe, 2008; McGee et al., 2008; McGee et al., 2008). Those studies found that Russia and China take longer to report financial information than do either the USA or the EU, but that there is no statistical difference between the time it takes for new EU members to report financial information and the time it takes old EU members to do so.

J. Muhoro (✉)
St. Paul's University, Limuru, Kenya
e-mail: nduturas@yahoo.com

R.W. McGee (✉)
Florida International University, Miami, FL, USA
e-mail: bob414@hotmail.com

R.W. McGee (ed.), *Corporate Governance in Developing Economies*,
DOI 10.1007/978-0-387-84833-4_12, © Springer Science+Business Media, LLC 2009

This is one of the first empirical studies, to our knowledge, that has been conducted on the timeliness of financial reporting in an African country. Thus, there is a gap in the literature that needs to be filled. The purpose of the present study is to partially fill that gap.

Methodology

Timeliness was determined by counting the number of days that elapsed between year-end and the date of the auditor's report. Data for Kenya was gathered from the financial statements of 46 companies that are listed on the Kenya Stock Exchange. Data for the U.S. companies was collected from the websites of large U.S. companies.

Such a methodology is less than perfect. The date on the audit report might not be the same as the date the information was released to the general public. However, there is no way to obtain the date the information was released to the general public, so the date on the audit report acted as a surrogate for the actual release date.

Findings

Table 12.1 shows the sample size, range, median, mean, and p-value for both samples. Kenyan companies took an average of 97.1 days after year-end to report financial results. The U.S. companies took an average of 65.8 days after year-end to report financial results. The medians for Kenya and the USA were 82 and 53 days, respectively. Using the median data, it appears that the average Kenyan company takes about 29 days longer to report financial results.

A Wilcoxon test found the differences in time delay to be significant at the 1 percent level ($p \leq 2.077\text{e}{-}27$). The chart below shows the median days delay for Kenyan and U.S. companies.

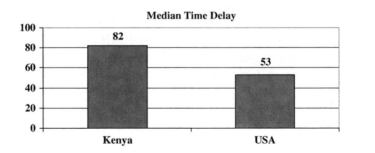

Table 12.1 Full sample data

	Sample size (years)	Mean (days)	Median (days)	Range (days)	p-value
Kenyan companies	556	97.1	82.0	16–357	2.077e–27*
U.S. companies	107	65.8	53.0	8–100	

*Significant at 1%

The chart below shows the range of days delay for all the companies included in the study. As can be seen, many Kenyan companies take significantly longer to report their financial results.

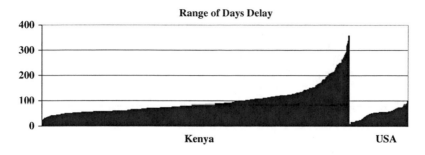

Range of Days Delay

Kenya   USA

Concluding Comments

The present study compared the time it takes Kenyan companies to report financial information with the time it takes companies in the USA. The study found it takes Kenyan companies about a month longer to report. The difference was found to be significant at the 1 percent level.

References

Accounting Principles Board. (1970). *Basic concepts and accounting principles underlying financial statements of business enterprises – statement no. 4*. New York: American Institute of Certified Public Accountants.

Annaert, J., DeCeuster, M. J. K., Polfliet, R., & Campenhout, G. V. (2002). To be or not be ... 'too late': The case of the Belgian semi-annual earnings announcements. *Journal of Business Finance & Accounting, 29*(3 & 4): 477–495.

Ashbaugh, H., Johnstone, K. M., & Warfield, T. D. (1999). Corporate reporting on the internet. *Accounting Horizons 13*(3), 241–257.

Ashton, R. H., Graul, P. R., & Newton, J. D. (1989). Audit delay and the timeliness of corporate reporting. *Contemporary Accounting Research, 5*(2), 657–673.

Atiase, R. K., Bamber, L. S., & Tse, S. (1989). Timeliness of financial reporting, the firm size effect, and stock price reactions to annual earnings announcements. *Contemporary Accounting Research, 5*(2), 526–552.

Ball, R., Kothari, S. P., & Robin, A. (2000). The effect of international institutional factors on properties of accounting earnings. *Journal of Accounting and Economics, 29*(1), 1–51.

Ball, R., & Brown, P. (1968). An empirical evaluation of accounting income numbers. *Journal of Accounting Research, 6*, 159–178.

Basu, S. (1997). The conservatism principle and the asymmetric timeliness of earnings. *Journal of Accounting & Economics, 24*, 3–37.

Bates, R. J. (1968). Discussion of the information content of annual earnings announcements. *Journal of Accounting Research, 6*(Supp.), 93–95.

Beaver, W. H. (1968). The information content of annual earnings announcements. *Journal of Accounting Research, 6*(Supp), 67–92.

Blanchet, J. (2002). Global standards offer opportunity. *Financial Executive* (March/April), 28–30.

Brown, P., & Kennelly, J. W. (1972). The information content of quarterly earnings: An extension and some further evidence. *Journal of Business, 45*, 403–415.

Chai, M. L., & Tung, S. (2002). The effect of earnings-announcement timing on earnings management. *Journal of Business Finance & Accounting, 29*(9 & 10), 1337–1354.

Chambers, A. E., & Penman, S. H. (1984). Timeliness of reporting and the stock price reaction to earnings announcements. *Journal of Accounting Research, 22*(1), 21–47.

Davies, B., & Whittred, G. P. (1980). The association between selected corporate attributes and timeliness in corporate reporting: Further analysis. *Abacus, 16*(1), 48–60.

DeCeuster, M., & Trappers, D. (1993). *Determinants of the timeliness of Belgian financial statements.* Working Paper, University of Antwerp, cited in Annaert et al, 2002.

Demos, T. (2006, February 6). The Russia 50: The country's largest public companies. *Fortune, 153*(2), 70–71.

Dwyer, P. D., & Wilson, E. R. (1989). An empirical investigation of factors affecting the timeliness of reporting by municipalities. *Journal of Accounting and Public Policy, 8*(1), 29–55.

Financial Accounting Standards Board. (1980). Statement of financial accounting concepts no. 2, qualitative characteristics of accounting information. Stamford, CT: Author.

Gigler, F. B., & Hemmer, T. (2001). Conservatism, optimal disclosure policy, and the timeliness of financial reports. *The Accounting Review, 76*(4), 471–493.

Givoli, D., & Palmon, D. (1982). Timeliness of annual earnings announcements: Some empirical evidence. *The Accounting Review, 57*(3), 486–508.

Han, J. C. Y., & Wang, S.-W. (1998). Political costs and earnings management of oil companies during the 1990 Persian Gulf crises. *The Accounting Review, 73*, 103–117.

Han, J. C. Y., & Wild, J. J. (1997). Timeliness of reporting and earnings information transfers. *Journal of Business Finance & Accounting, 24*(3&4), 527–540.

Haw, I.-M., Qi, D., & Wu, W. (2000). Timeliness of annual report releases and market reaction to earnings announcements in an emerging capital market: The case of China. *Journal of International Financial Management and Accounting, 11*(2), 108–131.

Hendriksen, E. S. & van Breda, M. F. (1992). Accounting theory (5th ed.), Burr Ridge, IL: Irwin.

Hoover's Most Viewed Company Directory by Country Retrieved from www.hoovers.com/free/mvc/country.xhtml

Jindrichovska, I., & Mcleay, S. (2005). Accounting for good news and accounting for bad news: Some empirical evidence from the Czech Republic. *European Accounting Review 14*(3), 635–655.

Keller, S. B. (1986). Reporting timeliness in the presence of subject to audit qualifications. *Journal of Business Finance & Accounting, 13*(1), 117–124.

Kenley, W. J., & Staubus, G. J. (1974).Objectives and concepts of financial statements. *Accounting Review, 49*(4), 888–889.

Krishnan, G. V., (2005). The association between big 6 auditor industry expertise and the asymmetric timeliness of earnings. *Journal of Accounting, Auditing & Finance, 20*(3), 209–228.

Kross, W., & Schroeder, D. A. (1984). An empirical investigation of the effect of quarterly earnings announcement timing on stock returns. *Journal of Accounting Research, 22*(1), 153–176.

Kulzick, R. S., (2004). Sarbanes-Oxley: Effects on financial transparency. *S.A.M. Advanced Management Journal, 69*(1), 43–49.

Lawrence, J. E., & Glover, H. D. (1998). The effect of audit firm mergers on audit delay. *Journal of Managerial Issues, 10*(2), 151–164.

Leventis, S., & Weetman, P. (2004). Timeliness of financial reporting: applicability of disclosure theories in an emerging capital market. *Accounting and Business Research, 34*(1), 43–56.

McGee, R. W. (2006). Timeliness of financial reporting in the energy sector. *Russian/CIS Energy & Mining Law Journal, 4*(2), 6–10.

McGee, R. W. (2007a). Corporate governance in Russia: A case study of timeliness of financial reporting in the telecom industry. *International Finance Review, 7*, 365–390.

McGee, R. W. (2007b). *Corporate governance and the timeliness of financial reporting: A case study of the Russian energy sector.* Fifth International Conference on Accounting and Finance in Transition. London, July 12–14, 2007.

McGee, R. W. (2007c). Transparency and disclosure in Russia. In T. M. Mickiewicz (ed.), *Corporate governance and finance in Poland and Russia* (pp. 278–295). London: Palgrave Macmillan.

McGee, R. W. (2008). The timeliness of financial reporting: The Russian oil, gas and power industries. In R. W. McGee (ed.), *Accounting reform in transition and developing economies.* New York: Springer.

McGee, R. W., & Gunn, R. (2008). The timeliness of financial reporting: A comparative study of Russian and Non-Russian companies in the transportation industry. In R. W. McGee (ed.), *Accounting reform in transition and developing economies.* New York: Springer.

McGee, R. W., & Igoe, D. N. (2008). Corporate governance and the timeliness of financial reporting: A comparative study of selected EU and transition countries. *Proceedings of the 43rd Annual Western Regional Meeting of the American Accounting Association, San Francisco, May 1–3,* pp. 74–87. Reprinted in R. W. McGee (ed.), Accounting reform in transition and developing economies. New York: Springer.

McGee, R. W., Igoe, D. N., Yuan, X., Tarangelo, T., & Tyler, M. (2008). The timeliness of financial reporting: A comparative study of the People's Republic of China and the European Union. In R. W. McGee (ed.), *Accounting reform in transition and developing economies.* New York: Springer.

McGee, R. W., & Preobragenskaya, G. G. (2005). *Accounting and financial system reform in a transition economy: A case study of Russia.* New York: Springer.

McGee, R. W., & Preobragenskaya, G. G. (2006). *Accounting and financial system reform in Eastern Europe and Asia.* New York: Springer.

McGee, R. W., & Tarangelo, T. (2008). The timeliness of financial reporting and the Russian banking system: An empirical study. In R. W. McGee (ed.), *Accounting reform in transition and developing economies.* New York: Springer.

McGee, R. W., Tarangelo, T., & Tyler, M. (2008). The timeliness of financial reporting: A comparative study of companies in Russian and the USA. In R. W. McGee (ed.), *Accounting reform in transition and developing economies.* New York: Springer.

McGee, R. W., & Tyler, M. (2008). The timeliness of financial reporting: A comparative study of Russian and Non-Russian companies. In R. W. McGee (ed.), Accounting reform in transition and developing economies. New York: Springer.

McGee, R. W., Tyler, M., Tarangelo, T., & Igoe, D. N. (2008). The timeliness of financial reporting: A comparative study of companies in Russia and the European Union. In R. W. McGee (ed.), *Accounting reform in transition and developing economies.* New York: Springer.

McGee, R. W., & Yuan, X. (2008a). Corporate governance and the timeliness of financial reporting: An empirical study of the People's Republic of China. *International Journal of Business, Accounting and Finance,* forthcoming.

McGee, R. W., & Yuan, X. (2008b). The timeliness of financial reporting: A comparative study of the People's Republic of China and the USA. In R. W. McGee (ed.), *Accounting reform in transition and developing economies.* New York: Springer.

McGee, R. W., Yuan, X., Tyler, M., & Tarangelo, T. (2008). The timeliness of financial reporting: A comparative study of the People's republic of China and Russia. In R. W. McGee (ed.), *Accounting reform in transition and developing economies.* New York: Springer.

Organisation for Economic Co-operation and Development. (1998). *Global Corporate Governance Principles.* Paris: Author.

OECD (2004). *OECD Principles of Corporate Governance.* Paris: Author.

Pope, P. F., & Walker, M. (1999). International differences in the timeliness, conservatism, and classification of earnings. *Journal of Accounting Research, 37*(Supp), 53–87.

Prickett, R. (2002). Sweet clarity. *Financial Management* (September), 18–20.

Rees, W. P., & Giner, B. (2001). On the asymmetric recognition of good and bad news in France, Germany and the UK. *Journal of Business Finance & Accounting, 28*(9&10), 1285–1332.

Soltani, B. (2002). Timeliness of corporate and audit reports: Some empirical evidence in the French context. *The International Journal of Accounting, 37,* 215–246.

Trueman, B. (1990). Theories of earnings-announcement timing. *Journal of Accounting & Economics, 13,* 285–301.

Whittred, G., & Zimmer, I. (1984). Timeliness of financial reporting and financial distress. *The Accounting Review, 59*(2), 287–295.

Whittred, G. P. (1980). Audit qualification and the timeliness of corporate annual reports. *The Accounting Review, 55*(4), 563–577.

World Bank. (2001). *Report on the Observance of Standards and Codes (ROSC), Corporate Governance Country Assessment, Republic of Croatia, September.* World Bank. Retrieved from www.worldbank.org.

World Bank. (2002a). *Report on the Observance of Standards and Codes (ROSC), Corporate Governance Country Assessment, Bulgaria, September.* Washington, DC: World Bank. Retrieved from www.worldbank.org.

World Bank. (2002b). *Report on the Observance of Standards and Codes (ROSC), Corporate Governance Country Assessment, Czech Republic, July.* Washington, DC: World Bank. Retrieved from www.worldbank.org.

World Bank. (2002c). *Report on the Observance of Standards and Codes (ROSC), Corporate Governance Country Assessment, Georgia, March.* Washington, DC: World Bank. Retrieved from www.worldbank.org.

World Bank. (2002d). *Report on the Observance of Standards and Codes (ROSC), Corporate Governance Country Assessment, Latvia, December.* Washington, DC: World Bank. Retrieved from www.worldbank.org.

World Bank. (2002e). *Report on the Observance of Standards and Codes (ROSC), Corporate Governance Country Assessment, Republic of Lithuania, July.* Washington, DC: World Bank. Retrieved from www.worldbank.org.

World Bank. (2003a). *Report on the Observance of Standards and Codes (ROSC), Corporate Governance Country Assessment, Hungary, February.* Washington, DC: World Bank. Retrieved from www.worldbank.org.

World Bank. (2003b). *Report on the Observance of Standards and Codes (ROSC), Corporate Governance Country Assessment, Slovak Republic, October.* Washington, DC: World Bank. Retrieved from www.worldbank.org.

World Bank. (2004a). *Report on the Observance of Standards and Codes (ROSC), Corporate Governance Country Assessment, Moldova, May.* Washington, DC: World Bank. Retrieved from www.worldbank.org.

World Bank. (2004b). *Report on the Observance of Standards and Codes (ROSC), Corporate Governance Country Assessment, Romania, April.* Washington, DC: World Bank. Retrieved from www.worldbank.org.

World Bank. (2004c). *Report on the Observance of Standards and Codes (ROSC), Corporate Governance Country Assessment, Slovenia, May.* Washington, DC: World Bank. Retrieved from www.worldbank.org.

World Bank. (2005a). *Report on the Observance of Standards and Codes (ROSC), Corporate Governance Country Assessment, Armenia, April.* Washington, DC: World Bank. Retrieved from www.worldbank.org.

World Bank. (2005b). *Report on the Observance of Standards and Codes (ROSC), Corporate Governance Country Assessment, Azerbaijan, July.* Washington, DC: World Bank. Retrieved from www.worldbank.org.

World Bank. (2005c). *Report on the Observance of Standards and Codes (ROSC), Corporate Governance Country Assessment, Macedonia, June.* Washington, DC: World Bank. Retrieved from www.worldbank.org.

World Bank. (2005d). *Report on the Observance of Standards and Codes (ROSC), Corporate Governance Country Assessment, Poland, June.* Washington, DC: World Bank. Retrieved from www.worldbank.org.

World Bank. (2006a). *Report on the Observance of Standards and Codes (ROSC), Corporate Governance Country Assessment, Bosnia and Herzegovina, June.* Washington, DC: World Bank. Retrieved from www.worldbank.org.

World Bank. (2006b). *Report on the Observance of Standards and Codes (ROSC), Corporate Governance Country Assessment, Ukraine, October.* Washington, DC: World Bank. Retrieved from www.worldbank.org.

Chapter 13
Corporate Governance and the Timeliness of Financial Reporting: A Comparative Study of Kenya and Russia

Judith Muhoro, Robert W. McGee, Michael Tyler and Thomas Tarangelo

Introduction

It is important to report financial information in a timely fashion. The longer a company waits to release its annual report and accompanying financial statements, the more stale the information is and the less useful it is.

A number of studies have been done on various aspects of timeliness in financial reporting. Those studies will not be summarized here but a listing is provided in the reference section for further research.

Various organizations have cited the importance of timely financial reporting. The Accounting Principles Board (1970) addressed the issue in one of its statements. The Organisation for Economic Co-operation and Development (OECD, 2004) lists it as an important principle of corporate governance. The World Bank has conducted more than 40 studies on corporate governance in various countries that have included a look at their financial reporting practices, including timeliness. However, Kenya was not among the countries studied.

The present study replicates studies that have measured the timeliness of financial reporting in Russia (McGee, 2006, 2007a, 2007b, 2007c, 2008; McGee & Gunn, 2008; McGee & Tarangelo, 2008; McGee & Tyler, 2008; McGee, Tarangelo, & Tyler, 2008; McGee, Tyler, Tarangelo, & Igoe, 2008; McGee, Yuan, Tyler, &

J. Muhoro (✉)
St. Paul's University, Limuru, Kenya
e-mail: nduturas@yahoo.com

R.W. McGee (✉)
Florida International University, Miami, FL, USA
e-mail: bob414@hotmail.com

M. Tyler (✉)
Barry University. Miami Shores, FL, USA
e-mail: bob414@hotmail.com

T. Tarangelo (✉)
Florida International University, Miami, FL, USA
e-mail: tarangel@fiu.edu

R.W. McGee (ed.), *Corporate Governance in Developing Economies*,
DOI 10.1007/978-0-387-84833-4_13, © Springer Science+Business Media, LLC 2009

Tarangelo, 2008), China (McGee & Yuan, 2008a, 2008b; McGee et al., 2008; McGee, Igoe, Yuan, Tarangelo, & Tyler, 2008), and the European Union (EU) (McGee & Igoe, 2008; McGee et al., 2008; McGee et al., 2008). Those studies found that Russia and China take longer to report financial information than do either the USA or the EU, but that there is no statistical difference between the time it takes for new EU members to report financial information and the time it takes old EU members to do so.

This is one of the first empirical studies, to our knowledge, that has been conducted on the timeliness of financial reporting in an African country. Thus, there is a gap in the literature that needs to be filled. The purpose of the present study is to partially fill that gap.

Methodology

Timeliness was determined by counting the number of days that elapsed between year-end and the date of the auditor's report. Data for Kenya was gathered from the financial statements of 46 companies that are listed on the Kenya Stock Exchange. Data for Russian companies was collected from Russtocks.com and the websites of some Russian companies.

Such a methodology is less than perfect. The date on the audit report might not be the same as the date the information was released to the general public. However, there is no way to obtain the date the information was released to the general public, so the date on the audit report acted as a surrogate for the actual release date. The Russian data is skewed toward more recent years. Some Russian companies publish only 1 or 2 years of data on their websites while others publish 10 or more years of data.

Findings

Table 13.1 shows the sample size, range, median, mean, and p-value for both samples. Kenyan companies took an average of 97.1 days after year-end to report financial results. Russian companies took an average of 101.7 days after year-end to report financial results. The medians for Kenya and Russia were 82 and 100 days,

Table 13.1 Full sample data

	Sample size (years)	Mean (days)	Median (days)	Range (days)	p-value
Kenya companies	556	97.1	82.0	16–357	5.402e–09*
Russian companies	433	101.7	100	18–159	

*Significant at 1%

respectively. Using the median data, it appears that the average Russian company takes about 18 days longer to report financial results. But if the mean data are compared, it appears that the average Russian company takes only 4.6 days longer to report. The reason for the difference might be explained by the fact that Kenya has some outliers, which beef up its mean score.

A Wilcoxon test found the differences in time delay to be significant at the 1 percent level ($p <= 5.402e–09$). The chart below shows the median days delay for Kenyan and EU companies.

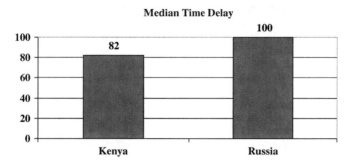

The chart below shows the range of days delay for all the companies included in the study. As can be seen, the shape of the graphs are somewhat similar at the left end, but the Kenyan graph shoots up on the right end, which indicates there are some outliers.

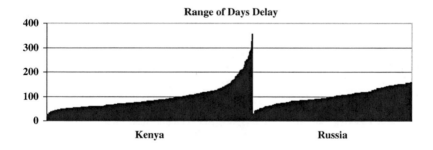

Concluding Comments

The present study examined the extent of the time delay between year-end and the issuance of the auditor's report for companies in Russia and Kenya. The study found that Russian companies that issue English language financial statement take significantly longer to report financial results than do Kenyan countries.

References

Accounting Principles Board. (1970). *Basic concepts and accounting principles underlying financial statements of business enterprises – statement no. 4.* New York: American Institute of Certified Public Accountants.

Annaert, J., DeCeuster, M. J. K., Polfliet, R., & Campenhout, G. V. (2002). To be or not be … 'too late': The case of the Belgian semi-annual earnings announcements. *Journal of Business Finance & Accounting, 29*(3 & 4): 477–495.

Ashbaugh, H., Johnstone, K. M., & Warfield, T. D. (1999). Corporate reporting on the internet. *Accounting Horizons 13*(3), 241–257.

Ashton, R. H., Graul, P. R., & Newton, J. D. (1989). Audit delay and the timeliness of corporate reporting. *Contemporary Accounting Research, 5*(2), 657–673.

Atiase, R. K., Bamber, L. S., & Tse, S. (1989). Timeliness of financial reporting, the firm size effect, and stock price reactions to annual earnings announcements. *Contemporary Accounting Research, 5*(2), 526–552.

Ball, R., Kothari, S. P., & Robin, A. (2000). The effect of international institutional factors on properties of accounting earnings. *Journal of Accounting and Economics, 29*(1), 1–51.

Ball, R., & Brown, P. (1968). An empirical evaluation of accounting income numbers. *Journal of Accounting Research, 6*, 159–178.

Basu, S. (1997). The conservatism principle and the asymmetric timeliness of earnings. *Journal of Accounting & Economics, 24*, 3–37.

Bates, R. J. (1968). Discussion of the information content of annual earnings announcements. *Journal of Accounting Research, 6*(Supp.), 93–95.

Beaver, W. H. (1968). The information content of annual earnings announcements. *Journal of Accounting Research, 6*(Supp), 67–92.

Blanchet, J. (2002). Global standards offer opportunity. *Financial Executive* (March/April), 28–30.

Brown, P., & Kennelly, J. W. (1972). The information content of quarterly earnings: An extension and some further evidence. *Journal of Business, 45*, 403–415.

Chai, M. L., & Tung, S. (2002). The effect of earnings-announcement timing on earnings management. *Journal of Business Finance & Accounting, 29*(9 & 10), 1337–1354.

Chambers, A. E., & Penman, S. H. (1984). Timeliness of reporting and the stock price reaction to earnings announcements. *Journal of Accounting Research, 22*(1), 21–47.

Davies, B., & Whittred, G. P. (1980). The association between selected corporate attributes and timeliness in corporate reporting: Further analysis. *Abacus, 16*(1), 48–60.

DeCeuster, M., & Trappers, D. (1993). *Determinants of the timeliness of Belgian financial statements.* Working Paper, University of Antwerp, cited in Annaert et al, 2002.

Demos, T. (2006, February 6). The Russia 50: The country's largest public companies. *Fortune, 153*(2), 70–71.

Dwyer, P. D., & Wilson, E. R. (1989). An empirical investigation of factors affecting the timeliness of reporting by municipalities. *Journal of Accounting and Public Policy, 8*(1), 29–55.

Financial Accounting Standards Board. (1980). Statement of financial accounting concepts no. 2, qualitative characteristics of accounting information. Stamford, CT: Author.

Gigler, F. B., & Hemmer, T. (2001). Conservatism, optimal disclosure policy, and the timeliness of financial reports. *The Accounting Review, 76*(4), 471–493.

Givoli, D., & Palmon, D. (1982). Timeliness of annual earnings announcements: Some empirical evidence. *The Accounting Review, 57*(3), 486–508.

Han, J. C. Y., & Wang, S.-W. (1998). Political costs and earnings management of oil companies during the 1990 Persian Gulf crises. *The Accounting Review, 73*, 103–117.

Han, J. C. Y., & Wild, J. J. (1997). Timeliness of reporting and earnings information transfers. *Journal of Business Finance & Accounting, 24*(3&4), 527–540.

Haw, I.-M., Qi, D., & Wu, W. (2000). Timeliness of annual report releases and market reaction to earnings announcements in an emerging capital market: The case of China. *Journal of International Financial Management and Accounting, 11*(2), 108–131.

Hendriksen, E. S. & van Breda, M. F. (1992). Accounting theory (5th ed.), Burr Ridge, IL: Irwin.
Hoover's Most Viewed Company Directory by Country Retrieved from www.hoovers.com/free/mvc/country.xhtml
Jindrichovska, I., & Mcleay, S. (2005). Accounting for good news and accounting for bad news: Some empirical evidence from the Czech Republic. *European Accounting Review 14*(3), 635–655.
Keller, S. B. (1986). Reporting timeliness in the presence of subject to audit qualifications. *Journal of Business Finance & Accounting, 13*(1), 117–124.
Kenley, W. J., & Staubus, G. J. (1974). Objectives and concepts of financial statements. *Accounting Review, 49*(4), 888–889.
Krishnan, G. V., (2005). The association between big 6 auditor industry expertise and the asymmetric timeliness of earnings. *Journal of Accounting, Auditing & Finance, 20*(3), 209–228.
Kross, W., & Schroeder, D. A. (1984). An empirical investigation of the effect of quarterly earnings announcement timing on stock returns. *Journal of Accounting Research, 22*(1), 153–176.
Kulzick, R. S., (2004). Sarbanes-Oxley: Effects on financial transparency. *S.A.M. Advanced Management Journal, 69*(1), 43–49.
Lawrence, J. E., & Glover, H. D. (1998). The effect of audit firm mergers on audit delay. *Journal of Managerial Issues, 10*(2), 151–164.
Leventis, S., & Weetman, P. (2004). Timeliness of financial reporting: applicability of disclosure theories in an emerging capital market. *Accounting and Business Research, 34*(1), 43–56.
McGee, R. W. (2006). Timeliness of financial reporting in the energy sector. *Russian/CIS Energy & Mining Law Journal, 4*(2), 6–10.
McGee, R. W. (2007a). Corporate governance in Russia: A case study of timeliness of financial reporting in the telecom industry. *International Finance Review, 7*, 365–390.
McGee, R. W. (2007b). *Corporate governance and the timeliness of financial reporting: A case study of the Russian energy sector.* Fifth International Conference on Accounting and Finance in Transition. London, July 12–14, 2007.
McGee, R. W. (2007c). Transparency and disclosure in Russia. In T. M. Mickiewicz (ed.), *Corporate governance and finance in Poland and Russia* (pp. 278–295). London: Palgrave Macmillan.
McGee, R. W. (2008). The timeliness of financial reporting: The Russian oil, gas and power industries. In R. W. McGee (ed.), *Accounting reform in transition and developing economies.* New York: Springer.
McGee, R. W., & Gunn, R. (2008). The timeliness of financial reporting: A comparative study of Russian and Non-Russian companies in the transportation industry. In R. W. McGee (ed.), *Accounting reform in transition and developing economies.* New York: Springer.
McGee, R. W., & Igoe, D. N. (2008). Corporate governance and the timeliness of financial reporting: A comparative study of selected EU and transition countries. *Proceedings of the 43rd Annual Western Regional Meeting of the American Accounting Association, San Francisco, May 1–3*, pp. 74–87. Reprinted in R. W. McGee (ed.), Accounting reform in transition and developing economies. New York: Springer.
McGee, R. W., Igoe, D. N., Yuan, X., Tarangelo, T., & Tyler, M. (2008). The timeliness of financial reporting: A comparative study of the People's Republic of China and the European Union. In R. W. McGee (ed.), *Accounting reform in transition and developing economies.* New York: Springer.
McGee, R. W., & Preobragenskaya, G. G. (2005). *Accounting and financial system reform in a transition economy: A case study of Russia.* New York: Springer.
McGee, R. W., & Preobragenskaya, G. G. (2006). *Accounting and financial system reform in Eastern Europe and Asia.* New York: Springer.
McGee, R. W., & Tarangelo, T. (2008). The timeliness of financial reporting and the Russian banking system: An empirical study. In R. W. McGee (ed.), *Accounting reform in transition and developing economies.* New York: Springer.
McGee, R. W., Tarangelo, T., & Tyler, M. (2008). The timeliness of financial reporting: A comparative study of companies in Russian and the USA. In R. W. McGee (ed.), *Accounting reform in transition and developing economies.* New York: Springer.

McGee, R. W., & Tyler, M. (2008). The timeliness of financial reporting: A comparative study of Russian and Non-Russian companies. In R. W. McGee (ed.), Accounting reform in transition and developing economies. New York: Springer.

McGee, R. W., Tyler, M., Tarangelo, T., & Igoe, D. N. (2008). The timeliness of financial reporting: A comparative study of companies in Russia and the European Union. In R. W. McGee (ed.), Accounting reform in transition and developing economies. New York: Springer.

McGee, R. W., & Yuan, X. (2008a). Corporate governance and the timeliness of financial reporting: An empirical study of the People's Republic of China. International Journal of Business, Accounting and Finance, forthcoming.

McGee, R. W., & Yuan, X. (2008b). The timeliness of financial reporting: A comparative study of the People's Republic of China and the USA. In R. W. McGee (ed.), Accounting reform in transition and developing economies. New York: Springer.

McGee, R. W., Yuan, X., Tyler, M., & Tarangelo, T. (2008). The timeliness of financial reporting: A comparative study of the People's republic of China and Russia. In R. W. McGee (ed.), Accounting reform in transition and developing economies. New York: Springer.

Organisation for Economic Co-operation and Development. (1998). Global Corporate Governance Principles. Paris: Author.

OECD (2004). OECD Principles of Corporate Governance. Paris: Author.

Pope, P. F., & Walker, M. (1999). International differences in the timeliness, conservatism, and classification of earnings. Journal of Accounting Research, 37(Supp), 53–87.

Prickett, R. (2002). Sweet clarity. Financial Management (September), 18–20.

Rees, W. P., & Giner, B. (2001). On the asymmetric recognition of good and bad news in France, Germany and the UK. Journal of Business Finance & Accounting, 28(9&10), 1285–1332.

Soltani, B. (2002). Timeliness of corporate and audit reports: Some empirical evidence in the French context. The International Journal of Accounting, 37, 215–246.

Trueman, B. (1990). Theories of earnings-announcement timing. Journal of Accounting & Economics, 13, 285–301.

Whittred, G., & Zimmer, I. (1984). Timeliness of financial reporting and financial distress. The Accounting Review, 59(2), 287–295.

Whittred, G. P. (1980). Audit qualification and the timeliness of corporate annual reports. The Accounting Review, 55(4), 563–577.

World Bank. (2001). Report on the Observance of Standards and Codes (ROSC), Corporate Governance Country Assessment, Republic of Croatia, September. World Bank. Retrieved from www.worldbank.org.

World Bank. (2002a). Report on the Observance of Standards and Codes (ROSC), Corporate Governance Country Assessment, Bulgaria, September. Washington, DC: World Bank. Retrieved from www.worldbank.org.

World Bank. (2002b). Report on the Observance of Standards and Codes (ROSC), Corporate Governance Country Assessment, Czech Republic, July. Washington, DC: World Bank. Retrieved from www.worldbank.org.

World Bank. (2002c). Report on the Observance of Standards and Codes (ROSC), Corporate Governance Country Assessment, Georgia, March. Washington, DC: World Bank. Retrieved from www.worldbank.org.

World Bank. (2002d). Report on the Observance of Standards and Codes (ROSC), Corporate Governance Country Assessment, Latvia, December. Washington, DC: World Bank. Retrieved from www.worldbank.org.

World Bank. (2002e). Report on the Observance of Standards and Codes (ROSC), Corporate Governance Country Assessment, Republic of Lithuania, July. Washington, DC: World Bank. Retrieved from www.worldbank.org.

World Bank. (2003a). Report on the Observance of Standards and Codes (ROSC), Corporate Governance Country Assessment, Hungary, February. Washington, DC: World Bank. Retrieved from www.worldbank.org.

World Bank. (2003b). *Report on the Observance of Standards and Codes (ROSC), Corporate Governance Country Assessment, Slovak Republic, October.* Washington, DC: World Bank. Retrieved from www.worldbank.org.

World Bank. (2004a). *Report on the Observance of Standards and Codes (ROSC), Corporate Governance Country Assessment, Moldova, May.* Washington, DC: World Bank. Retrieved from www.worldbank.org.

World Bank. (2004b). *Report on the Observance of Standards and Codes (ROSC), Corporate Governance Country Assessment, Romania, April.* Washington, DC: World Bank. Retrieved from www.worldbank.org.

World Bank. (2004c). *Report on the Observance of Standards and Codes (ROSC), Corporate Governance Country Assessment, Slovenia, May.* Washington, DC: World Bank. Retrieved from www.worldbank.org.

World Bank. (2005a). *Report on the Observance of Standards and Codes (ROSC), Corporate Governance Country Assessment, Armenia, April.* Washington, DC: World Bank. Retrieved from www.worldbank.org.

World Bank. (2005b). *Report on the Observance of Standards and Codes (ROSC), Corporate Governance Country Assessment, Azerbaijan, July.* Washington, DC: World Bank. Retrieved from www.worldbank.org.

World Bank. (2005c). *Report on the Observance of Standards and Codes (ROSC), Corporate Governance Country Assessment, Macedonia, June.* Washington, DC: World Bank. Retrieved from www.worldbank.org.

World Bank. (2005d). *Report on the Observance of Standards and Codes (ROSC), Corporate Governance Country Assessment, Poland, June.* Washington, DC: World Bank. Retrieved from www.worldbank.org.

World Bank. (2006a). *Report on the Observance of Standards and Codes (ROSC), Corporate Governance Country Assessment, Bosnia and Herzegovina, June.* Washington, DC: World Bank. Retrieved from www.worldbank.org.

World Bank. (2006b). *Report on the Observance of Standards and Codes (ROSC), Corporate Governance Country Assessment, Ukraine, October.* Washington, DC: World Bank. Retrieved from www.worldbank.org.

Chapter 14
Corporate Governance and the Timeliness of Financial Reporting: A Comparative Study of Kenya and the People's Republic of China

Judith Muhoro, Robert W. McGee, and Xiaoli Yuan

Introduction

It is important to report financial information in a timely fashion. The longer a company waits to release its annual report and accompanying financial statements, the more stale the information is and the less useful it is.

A number of studies have been done on various aspects of timeliness in financial reporting. Those studies will not be summarized here but a listing is provided in the reference section for further research.

Various organizations have cited the importance of timely financial reporting. The Accounting Principles Board (1970) addressed the issue in one of its statements. The Organisation for Economic Co-operation and Development (OECD, 2004) lists it as an important principle of corporate governance. The World Bank has conducted more than 40 studies on corporate governance in various countries that have included a look at their financial reporting practices, including timeliness. However, Kenya was not among the countries studied.

The present study replicates studies that have measured the timeliness of financial reporting in Russia (McGee, 2006, 2007a, 2007b, 2007c, 2008; McGee & Gunn, 2008; McGee & Tarangelo, 2008; McGee & Tyler, 2008; McGee, Tarangelo, & Tyler, 2008; McGee, Tyler, Tarangelo, & Igoe, 2008; McGee, Yuan, Tyler, & Tarangelo, 2008), China (McGee & Yuan 2008a, 2008b; McGee et al., 2008; McGee, Igoe, Yuan, Tarangelo, & Tyler, 2008), and the European Union (EU) (McGee & Igoe, 2008; McGee et al., 2008; McGee et al., 2008). Those studies found

J. Muhoro (✉)
St. Paul's University, Limuru, Kenya
e-mail: nduturas@yahoo.com

R.W. McGee (✉)
Florida International University, Miami, FL, USA
e-mail: bob414@hotmail.com

X. Yuan (✉)
California State University-East Bay, Hayward, CA, USA
e-mail: acg2021@gmail.com

R.W. McGee (ed.), *Corporate Governance in Developing Economies*,
DOI 10.1007/978-0-387-84833-4_14, © Springer Science+Business Media, LLC 2009

that Russia and China take longer to report financial information than do either the USA or the EU, but that there is no statistical difference between the time it takes for new EU members to report financial information and the time it takes old EU members to do so.

This is one of the first empirical studies, to our knowledge, that has been conducted on the timeliness of financial reporting in an African country. Thus, there is a gap in the literature that needs to be filled. The purpose of the present study is to partially fill that gap.

Methodology

Timeliness was determined by counting the number of days that elapsed between year-end and the date of the auditor's report. Data for Kenya was gathered from the financial statements of 46 companies that are listed on the Kenya Stock Exchange. In some cases, data was available for 5 or more years. In other cases, companies only reported a year or two worth of data. In some cases the authors were not able to obtain the necessary information for some companies. Data for China was gathered randomly from companies listed on the Shanghai Stock Exchange.

Such a methodology is less than perfect. The date on the audit report might not be the same as the date the information was released to the general public. However, there is no way to obtain the date the information was released to the general public, so the date on the audit report acted as a surrogate for the actual release date.

Findings

Table 14.1 shows the sample size, range, median, mean, and p-value for both samples. Kenyan companies took an average of 97.1 days after year-end to report financial results. Chinese companies took an average of 89.7 days after year-end to report financial results. The medians for Kenya and China were 82 and 86 days, respectively. Using the median data, it appears that the average Chinese company takes about 4 days longer to report financial results. But using the mean data, it would appear that Kenyan companies take about a week longer than Chinese companies to report financial data. The differences in results can be attributed to some outliers in the Kenya sample.

Table 14.1 Full sample data

	Sample size (years)	Mean (days)	Median (days)	Range (days)	p-value
Kenyan companies	556	97.1	82.0	16–357	0.2407
PRC companies	211	89.7	86.0	28–181	

A Wilcoxon test found the differences in time delay to be insignificant ($p <= 0.2407$), so even though the Kenyan mean was larger than the Chinese mean score, the difference was not significant. The chart below shows the median days delay for Kenyan and Chinese companies.

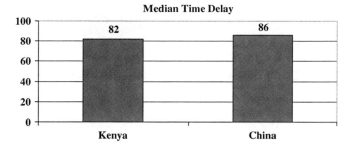

The chart below shows the range of days delay for all the companies included in the study. As can be seen, at the upper end of the scale, Kenyan companies take longer to report than do Chinese companies.

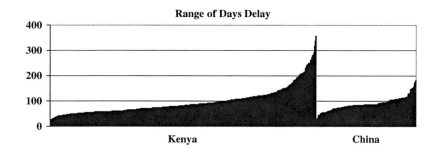

Concluding Comments

The present study compared the timeliness of financial reporting for a group of Chinese and Kenyan companies in an attempt to determine whether one country reports significantly faster than the other. The results show that the reporting difference between Chinese and Kenyan companies is insignificant.

References

Accounting Principles Board. (1970). *Basic concepts and accounting principles underlying financial statements of business enterprises – statement no. 4.* New York: American Institute of Certified Public Accountants.

Annaert, J., DeCeuster, M. J. K., Polfliet, R., & Campenhout, G. V. (2002). To be or not be...'too late': The case of the Belgian semi-annual earnings announcements. *Journal of Business Finance & Accounting, 29*(3 & 4): 477–495.

Ashbaugh, H., Johnstone, K. M., & Warfield, T. D. (1999). Corporate reporting on the internet. *Accounting Horizons 13*(3), 241–257.

Ashton, R. H., Graul, P. R., & Newton, J. D. (1989). Audit delay and the timeliness of corporate reporting. *Contemporary Accounting Research, 5*(2), 657–673.

Atiase, R. K., Bamber, L. S., & Tse, S. (1989). Timeliness of financial reporting, the firm size effect, and stock price reactions to annual earnings announcements. *Contemporary Accounting Research, 5*(2), 526–552.

Ball, R., Kothari, S. P., & Robin, A. (2000). The effect of international institutional factors on properties of accounting earnings. *Journal of Accounting and Economics, 29*(1), 1–51.

Ball, R., & Brown, P. (1968). An empirical evaluation of accounting income numbers. *Journal of Accounting Research, 6,* 159–178.

Basu, S. (1997). The conservatism principle and the asymmetric timeliness of earnings. *Journal of Accounting & Economics, 24,* 3–37.

Bates, R. J. (1968). Discussion of the information content of annual earnings announcements. *Journal of Accounting Research, 6*(Supp.), 93–95.

Beaver, W. H. (1968). The information content of annual earnings announcements. *Journal of Accounting Research, 6*(Supp), 67–92.

Blanchet, J. (2002). Global standards offer opportunity. *Financial Executive* (March/April), 28–30.

Brown, P., & Kennelly, J. W. (1972). The information content of quarterly earnings: An extension and some further evidence. *Journal of Business, 45,* 403–415.

Chai, M. L., & Tung, S. (2002). The effect of earnings-announcement timing on earnings management. *Journal of Business Finance & Accounting, 29*(9 & 10), 1337–1354.

Chambers, A. E., & Penman, S. H. (1984). Timeliness of reporting and the stock price reaction to earnings announcements. *Journal of Accounting Research, 22*(1), 21–47.

Davies, B., & Whittred, G. P. (1980). The association between selected corporate attributes and timeliness in corporate reporting: Further analysis. *Abacus, 16*(1), 48–60.

DeCeuster, M., & Trappers, D. (1993). *Determinants of the timeliness of Belgian financial statements.* Working Paper, University of Antwerp, cited in Annaert et al., 2002.

Demos, T. (2006, February 6). The Russia 50: The country's largest public companies. *Fortune, 153*(2), 70–71.

Dwyer, P. D., & Wilson, E. R. (1989). An empirical investigation of factors affecting the timeliness of reporting by municipalities. *Journal of Accounting and Public Policy, 8*(1), 29–55.

Financial Accounting Standards Board. (1980). Statement of financial accounting concepts no. 2, qualitative characteristics of accounting information. Stamford, CT: Author.

Gigler, F. B., & Hemmer, T. (2001). Conservatism, optimal disclosure policy, and the timeliness of financial reports. *The Accounting Review, 76*(4), 471–493.

Givoli, D., & Palmon, D. (1982). Timeliness of annual earnings announcements: Some empirical evidence. *The Accounting Review, 57*(3), 486–508.

Han, J. C. Y., & Wang, S.-W. (1998). Political costs and earnings management of oil companies during the 1990 Persian Gulf crises. *The Accounting Review, 73,* 103–117.

Han, J. C. Y., & Wild, J. J. (1997). Timeliness of reporting and earnings information transfers. *Journal of Business Finance & Accounting, 24*(3&4), 527–540.

Haw, I.-M., Qi, D., & Wu, W. (2000). Timeliness of annual report releases and market reaction to earnings announcements in an emerging capital market: The case of China. *Journal of International Financial Management and Accounting, 11*(2), 108–131.

Hendriksen, E. S. & van Breda, M. F. (1992). Accounting theory (5th ed.), Burr Ridge, IL: Irwin.

Hoover's Most Viewed Company Directory by Country Retrieved from www.hoovers.com/free/mvc/country.xhtml

Jindrichovska, I., & Mcleay, S. (2005). Accounting for good news and accounting for bad news: Some empirical evidence from the Czech Republic. *European Accounting Review 14*(3), 635–655.

Keller, S. B. (1986). Reporting timeliness in the presence of subject to audit qualifications. *Journal of Business Finance & Accounting, 13*(1), 117–124.

Kenley, W. J., & Staubus, G. J. (1974). Objectives and concepts of financial statements. *Accounting Review, 49*(4), 888–889.

Krishnan, G. V., (2005). The association between big 6 auditor industry expertise and the asymmetric timeliness of earnings. *Journal of Accounting, Auditing & Finance, 20*(3), 209–228.

Kross, W., & Schroeder, D. A. (1984). An empirical investigation of the effect of quarterly earnings announcement timing on stock returns. *Journal of Accounting Research, 22*(1), 153–176.

Kulzick, R. S., (2004). Sarbanes-Oxley: Effects on financial transparency. *S.A.M. Advanced Management Journal, 69*(1), 43–49.

Lawrence, J. E., & Glover, H. D. (1998). The effect of audit firm mergers on audit delay. *Journal of Managerial Issues, 10*(2), 151–164.

Leventis, S., & Weetman, P. (2004). Timeliness of financial reporting: applicability of disclosure theories in an emerging capital market. *Accounting and Business Research, 34*(1), 43–56.

McGee, R. W. (2006). Timeliness of financial reporting in the energy sector. *Russian/CIS Energy & Mining Law Journal, 4*(2), 6–10.

McGee, R. W. (2007a). Corporate governance in Russia: A case study of timeliness of financial reporting in the telecom industry. *International Finance Review, 7*, 365–390.

McGee, R. W. (2007b). *Corporate governance and the timeliness of financial reporting: A case study of the Russian energy sector.* Fifth International Conference on Accounting and Finance in Transition. London, July 12–14, 2007.

McGee, R. W. (2007c). Transparency and disclosure in Russia. In T. M. Mickiewicz (ed.), *Corporate governance and finance in Poland and Russia* (pp. 278–295). London: Palgrave Macmillan.

McGee, R. W. (2008). The timeliness of financial reporting: The Russian oil, gas and power industries. In R. W. McGee (ed.), *Accounting reform in transition and developing economies.* New York: Springer.

McGee, R. W., & Gunn, R. (2008). The timeliness of financial reporting: A comparative study of Russian and Non-Russian companies in the transportation industry. In R. W. McGee (ed.), *Accounting reform in transition and developing economies.* New York: Springer.

McGee, R. W., & Igoe, D. N. (2008). Corporate governance and the timeliness of financial reporting: A comparative study of selected EU and transition countries. *Proceedings of the 43rd Annual Western Regional Meeting of the American Accounting Association, San Francisco, May 1–3*, pp. 74–87. Reprinted in R. W. McGee (ed.), Accounting reform in transition and developing economies. New York: Springer.

McGee, R. W., Igoe, D. N., Yuan, X., Tarangelo, T., & Tyler, M. (2008). The timeliness of financial reporting: A comparative study of the People's Republic of China and the European Union. In R. W. McGee (ed.), *Accounting reform in transition and developing economies.* New York: Springer.

McGee, R. W., & Preobragenskaya, G. G. (2005). *Accounting and financial system reform in a transition economy: A case study of Russia.* New York: Springer.

McGee, R. W., & Preobragenskaya, G. G. (2006). *Accounting and financial system reform in Eastern Europe and Asia.* New York: Springer.

McGee, R. W., & Tarangelo, T. (2008). The timeliness of financial reporting and the Russian banking system: An empirical study. In R. W. McGee (ed.), *Accounting reform in transition and developing economies.* New York: Springer.

McGee, R. W., Tarangelo, T., & Tyler, M. (2008). The timeliness of financial reporting: A comparative study of companies in Russian and the USA. In R. W. McGee (ed.), *Accounting reform in transition and developing economies.* New York: Springer.

McGee, R. W., & Tyler, M. (2008). The timeliness of financial reporting: A comparative study of Russian and Non-Russian companies. In R. W. McGee (ed.), *Accounting reform in transition and developing economies.* New York: Springer.

McGee, R. W., Tyler, M., Tarangelo, T., & Igoe, D. N. (2008). The timeliness of financial reporting: A comparative study of companies in Russia and the European Union. In R. W. McGee (ed.), *Accounting reform in transition and developing economies.* New York: Springer.

McGee, R. W., & Yuan, X. (2008a). Corporate governance and the timeliness of financial reporting: An empirical study of the People's Republic of China. *International Journal of Business, Accounting and Finance*, forthcoming.

McGee, R. W., & Yuan, X. (2008b). The timeliness of financial reporting: A comparative study of the People's Republic of China and the USA. In R. W. McGee (ed.), *Accounting reform in transition and developing economies*. New York: Springer.

McGee, R. W., Yuan, X., Tyler, M., & Tarangelo, T. (2008). The timeliness of financial reporting: A comparative study of the People's republic of China and Russia. In R. W. McGee (ed.), *Accounting reform in transition and developing economies*. New York: Springer.

Organisation for Economic Co-operation and Development. (1998). *Global Corporate Governance Principles*. Paris: Author.

OECD (2004). *OECD Principles of Corporate Governance*. Paris: Author.

Pope, P. F., & Walker, M. (1999). International differences in the timeliness, conservatism, and classification of earnings. *Journal of Accounting Research, 37*(Supp), 53–87.

Prickett, R. (2002). Sweet clarity. *Financial Management* (September), 18–20.

Rees, W. P., & Giner, B. (2001). On the asymmetric recognition of good and bad news in France, Germany and the UK. *Journal of Business Finance & Accounting, 28*(9&10), 1285–1332.

Soltani, B. (2002). Timeliness of corporate and audit reports: Some empirical evidence in the French context. *The International Journal of Accounting, 37*, 215–246.

Trueman, B. (1990). Theories of earnings-announcement timing. *Journal of Accounting & Economics, 13*, 285–301.

Whittred, G., & Zimmer, I. (1984). Timeliness of financial reporting and financial distress. *The Accounting Review, 59*(2), 287–295.

Whittred, G. P. (1980). Audit qualification and the timeliness of corporate annual reports. *The Accounting Review, 55*(4), 563–577.

World Bank. (2001). *Report on the Observance of Standards and Codes (ROSC), Corporate Governance Country Assessment, Republic of Croatia, September.* World Bank. Retrieved from www.worldbank.org.

World Bank. (2002a). *Report on the Observance of Standards and Codes (ROSC), Corporate Governance Country Assessment, Bulgaria, September.* Washington, DC: World Bank. Retrieved from www.worldbank.org.

World Bank. (2002b). *Report on the Observance of Standards and Codes (ROSC), Corporate Governance Country Assessment, Czech Republic, July.* Washington, DC: World Bank. Retrieved from www.worldbank.org.

World Bank. (2002c). *Report on the Observance of Standards and Codes (ROSC), Corporate Governance Country Assessment, Georgia, March.* Washington, DC: World Bank. Retrieved from www.worldbank.org.

World Bank. (2002d). *Report on the Observance of Standards and Codes (ROSC), Corporate Governance Country Assessment, Latvia, December.* Washington, DC: World Bank. Retrieved from www.worldbank.org.

World Bank. (2002e). *Report on the Observance of Standards and Codes (ROSC), Corporate Governance Country Assessment, Republic of Lithuania, July.* Washington, DC: World Bank. Retrieved from www.worldbank.org.

World Bank. (2003a). *Report on the Observance of Standards and Codes (ROSC), Corporate Governance Country Assessment, Hungary, February.* Washington, DC: World Bank. Retrieved from www.worldbank.org.

World Bank. (2003b). *Report on the Observance of Standards and Codes (ROSC), Corporate Governance Country Assessment, Slovak Republic, October.* Washington, DC: World Bank. Retrieved from www.worldbank.org.

World Bank. (2004a). *Report on the Observance of Standards and Codes (ROSC), Corporate Governance Country Assessment, Moldova, May.* Washington, DC: World Bank. Retrieved from www.worldbank.org.

World Bank. (2004b). *Report on the Observance of Standards and Codes (ROSC), Corporate Governance Country Assessment, Romania, April.* Washington, DC: World Bank. Retrieved from www.worldbank.org.

World Bank. (2004c). *Report on the Observance of Standards and Codes (ROSC), Corporate Governance Country Assessment, Slovenia, May.* Washington, DC: World Bank. Retrieved from www.worldbank.org.

World Bank. (2005a). *Report on the Observance of Standards and Codes (ROSC), Corporate Governance Country Assessment, Armenia, April.* Washington, DC: World Bank. Retrieved from www.worldbank.org.

World Bank. (2005b). *Report on the Observance of Standards and Codes (ROSC), Corporate Governance Country Assessment, Azerbaijan, July.* Washington, DC: World Bank. Retrieved from www.worldbank.org.

World Bank. (2005c). *Report on the Observance of Standards and Codes (ROSC), Corporate Governance Country Assessment, Macedonia, June.* Washington, DC: World Bank. Retrieved from www.worldbank.org.

World Bank. (2005d). *Report on the Observance of Standards and Codes (ROSC), Corporate Governance Country Assessment, Poland, June.* Washington, DC: World Bank. Retrieved from www.worldbank.org.

World Bank. (2006a). *Report on the Observance of Standards and Codes (ROSC), Corporate Governance Country Assessment, Bosnia and Herzegovina, June.* Washington, DC: World Bank. Retrieved from www.worldbank.org.

World Bank. (2006b). *Report on the Observance of Standards and Codes (ROSC), Corporate Governance Country Assessment, Ukraine, October.* Washington, DC: World Bank. Retrieved from www.worldbank.org.

Chapter 15
Corporate Governance in Asia: A Comparative Study

Robert W. McGee

Introduction

The World Bank has done 10 *Report on the Observance of Standards and Codes* (ROSC) studies of corporate governance for Asian countries. The template it used was based on the categories used in an Organisation for Economic Co-operation and Development publication (OECD, 2004).

The following pages summarize the findings of those studies and do a comparative analysis.

Methodology

The World Bank studies used a template to evaluate various corporate governance categories. It classified various aspects of corporate governance into five categories. The present study assigned weights to those categories, which makes it possible to quantify the various rankings that the World Bank studies assigned to each country. The categories and points assigned to each category are as follows:

O = Observed (5 points)
LO = Largely Observed (4 points)
PO = Partially Observed (3 points)
MNO = Materially Not Observed (2 points)
NO = Not Observed (1 point)

Findings

The findings are subdivided into five categories and are also combined into a single corporate governance score.

R.W. McGee (✉)
Florida International University, Miami, FL, USA
e-mail: bob414@hotmail.com

R.W. McGee (ed.), *Corporate Governance in Developing Economies,*
DOI 10.1007/978-0-387-84833-4_15, © Springer Science+Business Media, LLC 2009

Table 15.1 Rights of
shareholders
(30 points = maximum
score)

Country	Points	Percentage of possible
Bhutan	15	50.0
India	26	86.7
Indonesia	17	56.7
Korea	24	80.0
Malaysia	22	73.3
Nepal	15	50.0
Pakistan	20	66.7
Philippines	20	66.7
Thailand	22	73.3
Vietnam1	65	3.3

Rights of Shareholders

Table 15.1 shows the scores for the 10 Asian countries in the category of Rights of
Shareholders. There are separate columns for points (30 points maximum) and percentage of possible points. India and Korea were the only countries to score at the
80 percent level. Korea was included in the study even though it is not technically a
developing country because (1) the World Bank did a study of Korea and (2) it was
thought that including Korea would serve as a good benchmark against which the
other countries could be measured.

The bar chart below shows the relative ranking for the various countries. Bhutan
and Nepal are at the bottom, followed closely by Vietnam and Indonesia. India and
Korea are at the other end of the spectrum, although not with perfect scores.

Equitable Treatment of Shareholders

Table 15.2 shows the scores for the category Equitable Treatment of Shareholders.
None of the countries scored at or above 80 percent for this category. Malaysia,
Pakistan, and Thailand came the closest, at 73.3 percent.

Table 15.2 Equitable treatment of shareholders (15 points = maximum score)

Country	Points	Percentage of possible
Bhutan	9	60.0
India	9	60.0
Indonesia	9	60.0
Korea	10	66.7
Malaysia	11	73.3
Nepal	7	46.7
Pakistan	11	73.3
Philippines	9	60.0
Thailand	11	73.3
Vietnam	6	40.0

The bar chart below shows the relative ranking. Malaysia, Pakistan, and Thailand are in a tie for first place. Vietnam and Nepal lag behind.

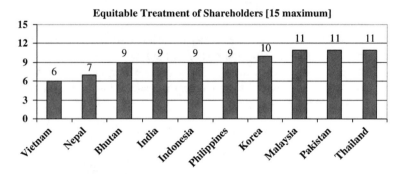

Role of Stakeholders in Corporate Governance

Table 15.3 shows the scores in the category of Role of Stakeholders in corporate governance. India scored an impressive 90 percent in this category and four other countries scored 80 percent or above.

Table 15.3 Role of stakeholders in corporate governance (20 points = maximum score)

Country	Points	Percentage of possible
Bhutan	11	55.0
India	18	90.0
Indonesia	12	60.0
Korea	17	85.0
Malaysia	16	80.0
Nepal	13	65.0
Pakistan	17	85.0
Philippines	13	65.0
Thailand	16	80.0
Vietnam	11	55.0

The bar chart below shows the relative ranking. India is in first place, followed closely by Korea and Pakistan. Bhutan and Vietnam are at the other end of the scale.

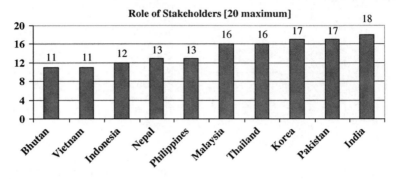

Disclosure and Transparency

Table 15.4 shows the scores in the category of Disclosure and Transparency. Only three countries scored at or above the 80 percent level.

The bar chart below shows the relative scores. Malaysia had the best score, followed closely by Korea and Pakistan. Nepal was at the low end of the scale, followed by Bhutan and Vietnam.

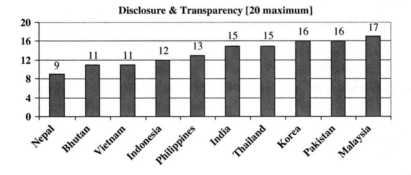

Table 15.4 Disclosure and transparency (20 points = maximum score)

Country	Points	Percentage of possible
Bhutan	11	55.0
India	15	75.0
Indonesia	12	60.0
Korea	16	80.0
Malaysia	17	85.0
Nepal	9	45.0
Pakistan	16	80.0
Philippines	13	65.0
Thailand	15	75.0
Vietnam	11	55.0

Table 15.5 Responsibilities
of the board (30 points =
maximum score)

Country	Points	Percentage of possible
Bhutan	18	60.0
India	25	83.3
Indonesia	18	60.0
Korea	20	66.7
Malaysia	22	73.3
Nepal	21	70.0
Pakistan	21	70.0
Philippines	19	63.3
Thailand	20	66.7
Vietnam	14	46.7

Responsibilities of the Board

Table 15.5 shows the scores in the category Responsibilities of the Board. Only
India scored at or above 80 percent.

The bar chart below shows the relative scores. India had the best score, followed
by Malaysia. Vietnam was at the low end of the scale.

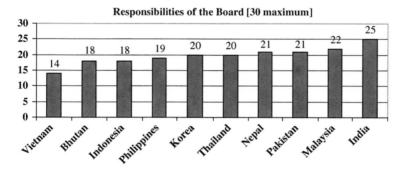

Overall Scores

Table 15.6 shows the combined scores for all categories. India was the only country
to reach the 80 percent level, followed by Malaysia and Korea. The Vietnamese
score was only slightly above 50 percent. Bhutan, Indonesia and Nepal were also
less than 60 percent.

The bar chart below shows the relative rankings. Although India was in first
place with 93 points, it is still below the 115-point maximum. Vietnam has a long
way to go before achieving a respectable score.

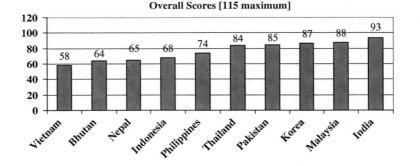

Overall Scores [115 maximum]

Table 15.6 Overall scores (115 points = maximum score)

Country	Points	Percentage of possible
Bhutan	64	55.7
India	93	80.9
Indonesia	68	59.1
Korea	87	75.7
Malaysia	88	76.5
Nepal	65	56.5
Pakistan	85	73.9
Philippines	74	64.3
Thailand	84	73.0
Vietnam	58	50.4

References

Organisation for Economic Co-operation and Development (2004). *Principles of Corporate Governance.* Paris: Author.

World Bank (2005). *Corporate Governance Country Assessment: Nepal. Report on the Observance of Standards and Codes (ROSC).*

World Bank and International Monetary Fund (2003). *Report on the Observance of Standards and Codes (ROSC), Corporate Governance Country Assessment: Republic of Korea.* Washington, DC: Author (September).

World Bank and International Monetary Fund (2004a). *Report on the Observance of Standards and Codes (ROSC), Corporate Governance Country Assessment: India.* Washington, DC: Author (April).

World Bank and International Monetary Fund (2004b). *Report on the Observance of Standards and Codes (ROSC), Corporate Governance Country Assessment: Republic of Indonesia.* Washington, DC: Author (August).

World Bank and International Monetary Fund (2005a). *Report on the Observance of Standards and Codes (ROSC), Corporate Governance Country Assessment: Malaysia.* Washington, DC: Author (June).

World Bank and International Monetary Fund (2005b). *Report on the Observance of Standards and Codes (ROSC), Corporate Governance Country Assessment: Pakistan.* Washington, DC: Author (June).

World Bank and International Monetary Fund (2005c). *Report on the Observance of Standards and Codes (ROSC), Corporate Governance Country Assessment: Thailand.* Washington, DC: Author (June).

World Bank and International Monetary Fund (2006a). *Report on the Observance of Standards and Codes (ROSC), Corporate Governance Country Assessment: Philippines.* Washington, DC: Author (May).

World Bank and International Monetary Fund (2006b). *Report on the Observance of Standards and Codes (ROSC), Corporate Governance Country Assessment: Vietnam.* Washington, DC: Author (June).

World Bank and International Monetary Fund. (2006c). Report on the Observance of Standards and Codes (ROSC), Corporate Governance Country Assessment: Bhutan.. December.

Chapter 16
Corporate Governance in Latin America:
A Comparative Study

Robert W. McGee

Introduction

The World Bank has done seven *Report on the Observance of Standards and Codes* (ROSC) studies of corporate governance for Latin American countries. The template it used was based on the categories used in an Organisation for Economic Co-operation and Development publication (OECD, 2004).

The following pages summarize the findings of those studies and do a comparative analysis.

Methodology

The World Bank studies used a template to evaluate various corporate governance categories. It classified various aspects of corporate governance into five categories. The present study assigned weights to those categories, which makes it possible to quantify the various rankings that the World Bank studies assigned to each country. The categories and points assigned to each category are as follows:

O=Observed (5 points)
LO=Largely Observed (4 points)
PO=Partially Observed (3 points)
MNO=Materially Not Observed (2 points)
NO=Not Observed (1 point)

Findings

The findings are subdivided into five categories and are also combined into a single corporate governance score.

R.W. McGee (✉)
Florida International University, Miami, FL, USA
e-mail: bob414@hotmail.com

R.W. McGee (ed.), *Corporate Governance in Developing Economies*,
DOI 10.1007/978-0-387-84833-4_16, © Springer Science+Business Media, LLC 2009

Table 16.1 Rights of
shareholders (30 points=
maximum score)

Country	Points	Percentage of possible
Brazil	22	73.3
Chile	24	80.0
Colombia	15	50.0
Mexico	18	60.0
Panama	18	60.0
Peru	20	66.7
Uruguay	15	50.0

Rights of Shareholders

Table 16.1 shows the scores in the category Rights of Shareholders. Only Chile achieved a score of 80 percent or higher. Colombia and Uruguay barely got it to the halfway point.

The bar chart below shows the relative scores. Chile did the best, followed by Brazil. Colombia and Uruguay were at the other end of the scale.

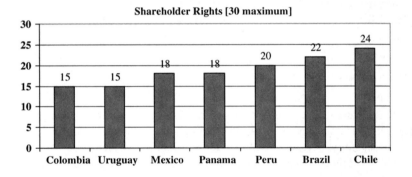

Equitable Treatment of Shareholders

Table 16.2 shows the scores in the category Equitable Treatment of Shareholders. None of the countries broke the 80 percent barrier and only Chile broke into the 70 percent plus range. Uruguay barely made it past the 50 percent mark.

Table 16.2 Equitable
treatment of shareholders
(15 points=maximum score)

Country	Points	Percentage of possible
Brazil	10	66.7
Chile	11	73.3
Colombia	6	40.0
Mexico	10	66.7
Panama	10	66.7
Peru	7	46.7
Uruguay	8	53.3

The bar chart below shows how the countries ranked in comparative terms. Chile did the best, followed closely by Brazil, Mexico, and Panama. Colombia was at the other end of the spectrum.

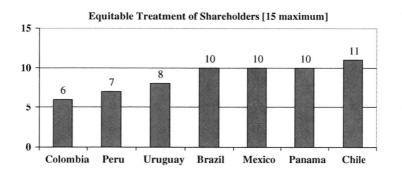

Role of Stakeholders in Corporate Governance

Table 16.3 shows the scores for the category Role of Stakeholders in Corporate Governance. Panama showed a respectable 95 percent, followed by Brazil at 90 percent. Five of the seven countries scored at 80 percent or higher. Uruguay was at the low end.

The bar chart below shows the relative position of the countries. Panama is in first place, followed closely by Brazil. Uruguay had the lowest score in this category.

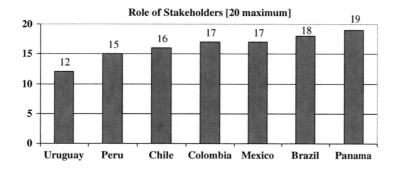

Table 16.3 Role of stakeholders in corporate governance (20 points= maximum score)

Country	Points	Percentage of possible
Brazil	18	90.0
Chile	16	80.0
Colombia	17	85.0
Mexico	17	85.0
Panama	19	95.0
Peru	15	75.0
Uruguay	12	60.0

Table 16.4 Disclosure and transparency (20 points = maximum score)

Country	Points	Percentage of possible
Brazil	14	70.0
Chile	13	65.0
Colombia	12	60.0
Mexico	15	75.0
Panama	14	70.0
Peru	11	55.0
Uruguay	12	60.0

Disclosure and Transparency

Table 16.4 shows the scores in the category of Disclosure and Transparency. None of the countries had a score of 80 or above. Mexico came the closest, with a score of 75. Peru had the lowest score at 55 percent.

The bar chart below shows how the countries compared graphically. Mexico had the highest score, followed closely by Brazil and Panama.

Responsibilities of the Board

Table 16.5 shows the results for the category Responsibilities of the Board. None of the countries scored 80 percent or better. Mexico came the closest, with a score of 70 percent. Uruguay had the lowest score, 46.7 percent.

Table 16.5 Responsibilities of the board (30 points = maximum score)

Country	Points	Percentage of possible
Brazil	19	63.3
Chile	20	66.7
Colombia	19	63.3
Mexico	21	70.0
Panama	20	66.7
Peru	17	56.7
Uruguay	14	46.7

The bar chart shows the relative scores graphically. None of the countries came close to the top score of 30. Uruguay had only 14 points, out of a possible 30.

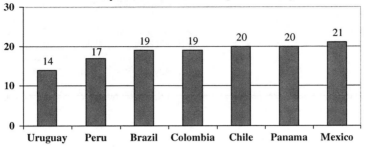

Responsibilities of the Board [30 maximum]

Overall Scores

Table 16.6 shows the overall scores. None of the countries had an average of 80 percent or better. The country that came closest was Chile, with a score of 73.0 percent, followed closely by Brazil at 72.2 percent. Uruguay had the lowest score, 53.0 percent.

The bar chart shows how the scores compare graphically. Chile had the most points (84), out of a total possible of 115. Brazil was close behind at 83, followed by Mexico and Panama. Uruguay had the lowest point total at 61.

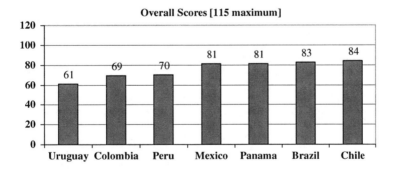

Overall Scores [115 maximum]

Table 16.6 Overall scores
(115 points = maximum score)

Country	Points	Percentage of possible
Brazil	83	72.2
Chile	84	73.0
Colombia	69	60.0
Mexico	81	70.4
Panama	81	70.4
Peru	70	60.9
Uruguay	61	53.0

References

OECD (2004). *Principles of Corporate Governance*. Paris: Author.

World Bank. (2002). *Report on the Observance of Standards and Codes (ROSC), Corporate Governance Country Assessment, Mauritius, October.* World Bank. Retrieved from www.worldbank.org.

World Bank. (2003a). *Report on the Observance of Standards and Codes (ROSC), Corporate Governance Country Assessment, Chile, May.* World Bank. Retrieved from www.worldbank.org.

World Bank. (2003b). *Report on the Observance of Standards and Codes (ROSC), Corporate Governance Country Assessment, Colombia, August.* World Bank. Retrieved from www.worldbank.org.

World Bank. (2003c). *Report on the Observance of Standards and Codes (ROSC), Corporate Governance Country Assessment, Republic of Korea, September.* World Bank. Retrieved from www.worldbank.org.

World Bank. (2003d). *Report on the Observance of Standards and Codes (ROSC), Corporate Governance Country Assessment, Mexico, September.* World Bank. Retrieved from www.worldbank.org.

World Bank. (2003e). *Report on the Observance of Standards and Codes (ROSC), Corporate Governance Country Assessment, Republic of South Africa, July.* World Bank. Retrieved from www.worldbank.org.

World Bank. (2004a). *Report on the Observance of Standards and Codes (ROSC), Corporate Governance Country Assessment, Egypt, March.* World Bank. Retrieved from www.worldbank.org.

World Bank. (2004b). *Report on the Observance of Standards and Codes (ROSC), Corporate Governance Country Assessment, India, April.* World Bank. Retrieved from www.worldbank.org.

World Bank. (2004c). *Report on the Observance of Standards and Codes (ROSC), Corporate Governance Country Assessment, Republic of Indonesia, April.* World Bank. Retrieved from www.worldbank.org.

World Bank. (2004d). *Report on the Observance of Standards and Codes (ROSC), Corporate Governance Country Assessment, Jordan, June.* World Bank. Retrieved from www.worldbank.org.

World Bank. (2004e). *Report on the Observance of Standards and Codes (ROSC), Corporate Governance Country Assessment, Panama, June.* World Bank. Retrieved from www.worldbank.org.

World Bank. (2004f). *Report on the Observance of Standards and Codes (ROSC), Corporate Governance Country Assessment, Republic of Peru, June.* World Bank. Retrieved from www.worldbank.org.

World Bank. (2005a). *Report on the Observance of Standards and Codes (ROSC), Corporate Governance Country Assessment, Brazil, May.* World Bank. Retrieved from www.worldbank.org.

World Bank. (2005b). *Report on the Observance of Standards and Codes (ROSC), Corporate Governance Country Assessment, Ghana, May.* World Bank. Retrieved from www.worldbank.org.

World Bank. (2005c). *Report on the Observance of Standards and Codes (ROSC), Corporate Governance Country Assessment, Malaysia, June.* World Bank. Retrieved from www.worldbank.org.

World Bank. (2005d). *Report on the Observance of Standards and Codes (ROSC), Corporate Governance Country Assessment, Nepal, April.* World Bank. Retrieved from www.worldbank.org.

World Bank. (2005e). *Report on the Observance of Standards and Codes (ROSC), Corporate Governance Country Assessment, Pakistan, June.* World Bank. Retrieved from www.worldbank.org.

World Bank. (2005f). *Report on the Observance of Standards and Codes (ROSC), Corporate Governance Country Assessment, Thailand, June.* World Bank. Retrieved from www.worldbank.org.

World Bank. (2005g). *Report on the Observance of Standards and Codes (ROSC), Corporate Governance Country Assessment, Uruguay. September.* World Bank. Retrieved from www.worldbank.org.

World Bank. (2006a). *Report on the Observance of Standards and Codes (ROSC), Corporate Governance Country Assessment, Bhutan, December.* World Bank. Retrieved from www. worldbank.org.

World Bank. (2006b). *Report on the Observance of Standards and Codes (ROSC), Corporate Governance Country Assessment, Philippines, May.* World Bank. Retrieved from www. worldbank.org.

World Bank. (2006c). *Report on the Observance of Standards and Codes (ROSC), Corporate Governance Country Assessment, Senegal, June.* World Bank. Retrieved from www.worldbank.org.

World Bank. (2006d). *Report on the Observance of Standards and Codes (ROSC), Corporate Governance Country Assessment, Vietnam, June.* World Bank. Retrieved from www. worldbank.org.

World Bank. (n.d.). *Report on the Observance of Standards and Codes (ROSC), Corporate Governance Country Assessment, Turkey.* World Bank. Retrieved from www.worldbank.org.

World Bank. (n.d.). *Report on the Observance of Standards and Codes (ROSC), Corporate Governance Country Assessment, Zimbabwe.* World Bank. Retrieved from www.worldbank.org.

Chapter 17
A Comparative Analysis of Corporate Governance Systems in Latin America: Argentina, Brazil, Chile, Colombia, and Venezuela

Ruth V. Aguilera

Introduction

This chapter analyzes corporate governance systems in five Latin American countries: Argentina, Brazil, Chile, Colombia, and Venezuela. We account for the broader institutional environment by explaining changes over time as well as existing corporate governance systems. We use a stakeholder definition of corporate governance that includes examining insiders such as owners and boards of directors as well as outsiders such as employees. This corporate governance perspective allows for a systematic cross-national comparison.

There exists an extensive literature on the Anglo-American corporate governance system, particularly from the finance field (e.g., Shleifer & Vishny, 1997; Keasey, Thompson, & Wright, 1999) as well as on comparative corporate governance among industrialized countries (e.g., Prowse, 1995; Rhodes & van Apeldoorn, 1998; Weimer & Pape, 1990; AMR special issue on corporate governance, 2003; Grandori, 2004; Gospel & Pendleton, 2005; Aguilera, Filatotchev, Gospel, & Jackson,2008).

There have also been some comparative corporate governance studies on eastern Europe (e.g., Federowicz & Aguilera, 2003) and east Asia (e.g., OECD, 2001; Zhuang & Edwards, 2001; Jacoby, 2004). This chapter seeks to fill a gap in comparative corporate governance research by systematically analyzing the main corporate governance characteristics in the five largest countries in Latin America[1]. Little comparative corporate governance research has been done on this region of the world despite its geographic importance and recent economic interest in creating a Free Trade Area of the Americas.

Studies of corporate governance examine how the rights and responsibilities within firms are distributed (Aguilera & Jackson, 2003). The institutions of corporate

R.V. Aguilera (✉)
University of Illinois at Champaign-Urbana, Champaign, IL, USA
e-mail: ruth-agu@uiuc.edu

[1] We exclude Mexico because it is part of a very different economic system given its close relationship and dependence with the U.S.

R.W. McGee (ed.), *Corporate Governance in Developing Economies*,
DOI 10.1007/978-0-387-84833-4_17, © Springer Science+Business Media, LLC 2009

governance are key factors in the long-term economic development of a country. These institutions have two main objectives: to stimulate the performance of corporations through a business environment that motivates productivity and to ensure corporate conformance between the interests of investors and society (Oman, 2003). Several scholars have discussed the positive relationship between effective national corporate governance systems and firm performance in emerging markets. For example, Klapper and Love (2002) demonstrate that efficient governance is highly correlated with better operating performance and market valuation, and Doidge, Karalyi, and Stulz (2004) show how country characteristics are key explanatory variables in governance ratings across firms in less-developed countries as opposed to firm characteristics in developed countries.

This chapter examines the largest and most productive five countries of South America (Argentina, Brazil, Chile, Colombia, and Venezuela). These are developing economies that have in common a tumultuous political and economic history of dictatorships and economic crises. Yet, these countries are in the process of modernizing their corporate governance systems, either as a condition in continuing to receive international aid or simply as a strategy to attract more foreign direct investment.

The comparative nature of this chapter allows us to tackle indirectly an important debate within corporate governance, that is, whether there is a convergence toward the Anglo-American model (Hansmann & Kraakman, 2001; Thomsen, 2004). This question has been addressed for transition economies such as Eastern Europe (Aguilera & Dabu, 2005), and more generally emerging markets. For example, an empirical analysis of 24 emerging countries by Khanna, Kogan, and Palepu (2002) indicates that corporate governance convergence is not imminent, although there is as yet no general consensus. Our chapter contributes to this debate by showing that, indeed, there is not full convergence as Latin American countries modernize their corporate governance system.

In this chapter, we first review the main political and economic trends of each of the five countries. This might seem unconventional for a study of corporate governance but since these five countries are in emerging markets, we believe it is particularly relevant to stress their broader political and economic conditions that undoubtedly shape their respective corporate governance patterns. Second, we systematically compare different aspects that define the systems of corporate governance in these countries.

Economic and Political Background

Outside observers tend to lump Latin American countries into a single category, when in reality these countries encompass a wide range of economic, political, and social histories. For example, Lenartowicz and Johnson (2003) show that common perceptions of Latin America as a culturally homogeneous region are stereotypical and incorrect. Table 17.1 highlights three key political events for each country: enactment of the latest constitution, date of the transition to democracy, and trading blocks.

Latin American governments have traditionally been defined as "paternalistic" because of their heavy-handed government intervention and protectionist policies toward workers.

Among investors, Latin American macroeconomic stability is the main concern since the region is characterized by high debt levels, high unemployment rates, high inflation levels, poor financial flows, and the constant need for foreign aid. Table 17.2 summarizes the main economic trends of the five countries.

Moreover, corruption has been a governance problem for most of these Latin American countries. In 2002, the Corruption Perception Index (CPI) by Transparency International listed the region of Latin America as one of the most, if not the most, corruption-plagued regions in the world, due to tax evasion, bribery, and dishonest practices that disadvantage foreign operators. In 2001–2002, the International Development Bank (IDB) offered loans in support of anticorruption and transparency initiatives to several of these countries. The IDB's Multilateral Investment Fund also approved a US $1.23 million grant in 2001 to Argentina, Brazil, Chile, and Venezuela to track and analyze transactions suspected of being money-laundering operations.

Table 17.1 Political context

	Constitution (1)	Democratic transition (1)	Trade blocks (1)	Population in 2006 (millions) (2)
Argentina	May 1853	1983	MERCOSUR and associate member of CAN	38.7
Brazil	October 1988	1985	MERCOSUR and associate member of CAN	190.5
Chile	September 1980 (but last amended in 1987)	1990	Associate member of CAN and MERCOSUR	16.4
Colombia	July 1991	1958	CAN and associate member of MERCOSUR	46.3
Venezuela, RB	December 1999	1958	MERCOSUR	27.1

Sources: (1) CIA Factbook; (2) GMID: Global Market Information Database.
MERCOSUR: Mercado Común del Sur (Argentina, Brazil, Paraguay, and Uruguay)
CAN: Comunidad Andina (Bolivia, Colombia, Ecuador, Peru, and Venezuela)

Table 17.2 Main economic factors

	Inflation rate (%) (1)	GDP real growth rate (%) (1)	GDP current (USD, in billions) (1)	Oil production (bbl/day) (million) (2)	External debt (% GDP) (3)	Internet sers (% of population) (3)	General Government Final Consumption Expenditure (% of GPD) (1)
	2006	2006	2006	2005	2006	2006	2006
Argentina	6.6	8.5	214	0.66	61	21.14	8
Brazil	4.2	3.7	1.068	1.63	18	22.42	20
Chile	3.4	4	146	0.004	42	25	N/A
Colombia	4.3	6.8	136	0.52	40	13	8
Venezuela, RB	13.7	10.3	182	3.12	24	16	11

Sources: (1) GMID; (2) OPEC; (3) CIA Factbook.

The debt crisis of the 1980s led many Latin American countries to adopt an export-oriented development strategy, implying major reforms in their economic and governance structures. Some of the most common policies developed are the privatization of the state-owned enterprises, trade liberalization, and cuts in the social spending. As argued by Cook (1998), even though these new policies improved the economies, they produced discomfort, particularly among labor unions.

Starting in the 1990s, massive inflows of foreign capital entered Latin American countries. A symbolic number is that after the big three state-owned oil companies (Pemex in Mexico, PDVSA in Venezuela, and Petrobras in Brazil), foreign owners dominate the list of the 50 largest firms in Latin America (Grosse, 2001, p. 669).

In the next section, I describe the main country characteristics, stressing the predicted future trends.

Argentina

Argentina, over the past decade, has suffered recurring economic problems of inflation, external debt, capital flight, and budget deficits. During the last 6 years the inflation rate has been unstable, changing from 1.1% in 2001 to 6.6% in 2006 with a peak of 25.9% in 2002 (GMID Country Profile, 2007a). This fact is a consequence of the economic collapse in 2001 and 2002, although it is slowly recovering and starting to show growing trends. Although the durability of Argentina's economic recovery is fragile because it depends primarily on volatile external factors rather than longer-lasting productivity gains. For example, Argentina has doubled its percentage of trade in the last decade, exporting agricultural products and importing intermediate goods (EIU, 2004).

Another important fact for the Argentinean economy is its debt. In 2005, it was huge and complex. It involved 152 varieties of paper denominated in 6 currencies and governed by 8 jurisdictions (GMID Country Profile, 2007a).

Argentina has generally encouraged inward FDI despite a government showing signs of interventionism in business activities. Furthermore, companies doing business in Argentina are charged one of the highest corporate tax rates in Latin America (35%) (GMID Business Environment, 2007b). The total tax rate as a percentage of profits reach 116% (the highest is Latin America and one of the most punitive in the world) – the OECD level is 46.8%. That means FDI rates decreased in 2005 ($4.7 billion) from 2000 ($10.4 billion) (WDI, 2007). Most of the investment has been made by local companies, explaining the 50.4% total annual growth during the 2002–2006 period (GMID Business Environment, 2007b). Lastly, Argentina still has government-imposed capital restrictions on the movement of capital in or out of the country.

From a positive angle, the CPI in 2006 (2.9) was better than in 2004 (Transparency International, 2006). Although, as we summarize in Table 17.3, in the 2002 survey, in Argentina, 90% or more of the people responded that corruption had increased "a lot" in the last 12 months.

Table 17.3 International trade and globalization

	FDI net inflows (% of GDP) (1)		Trade (% of GDP) (1)		Main destinations of exports (2)	Main origins of imports (2)
	1993	2005	1993	2006	2005	2005
Argentina	1	3	16	42	Brazil, 16.6%; US, 11.2%; Chile, 10.9%; China, 8.6%	Brazil, 33.8%; US, 15.7%; Germany, 5%; China, 5.1%
Brazil	0	2	29	26	US, 19.2%; Argentina, 8.4%; China, 5.8%; Germany, 4.2%	US, 17.5%; Argentina, 8.5%; China, 7.3%; the Netherlands, 0.8%
Chile	2	6	57	N/A	US, 18%; Asia, 32.7%; Europe, 31.7%; Latin America, 16.4%	Latin America, 38.5%; US, 18.5%; Europe, 18.3%; Asia, 17.5%
Colombia	2	8	35	41	US, 40.4%; Venezuela, 9.2%; Ecuador, 5.7%; Peru, 3.5%	US, 28.1%; Venezuela, 6.4%; Brazil, 5.5%; Mexico, 5.9%
Venezuela, RB	1	2	54	53	US, 57.8%; Canada, 2.9%; the Netherlands Antilles, 4.6%; Dominican Republic, 2.8%	US, 28.9%; Colombia, 8.4%; Brazil, 6%; China, 3.8%

Sources: (1) WDI; (2) EIU (2007).

It is predicted that Argentina will be the best performer in 2008 in GPD growth, among the countries of Latin America because real interest rates are on a decreasing trend, which is pushing household consumption and business investment up.

Brazil

The Brazilian currency (*real*) depreciated sharply in 2001 and 2002, leading to an inflation rate in 2003 of 15%. In 2006, the inflation rate was 4.2% (Table 17.2) demonstrating that the economy is recovering. Brazil's economy has been improving but the pace of growth is still somewhat disappointing. The public sector accounts for around 45% of GPD and is one of the main reasons why Brazil's performance does not match that of other large emerging markets (GMID Country Profile, 2007a).

FDI is recovering slowly from the crisis of 2002 and it is still one of the lowest percent of GPD of Latin America, repelling additional investments from foreign companies. Complexity of labor regulations is also threat for both domestic and foreign companies, and the tax burden for a medium-sized firm can reach 71.1% (GMID Business Environment, 2007b).

Another important fact is that the judicial system is dysfunctional and many of its judges are corrupt, with a 3.3% of corruption index (Transparency International, 2006).

A short-term future, tax cuts are planned for 2007 and 2008. And the private sector increased the investment between mid-2006 and 2007 (GMID Country Profile, 2007a).

Chile

Chile has performed very well over the last 15 years, after the effects of the 1999 recession. The inflation rate has declined in the last decade stabilising around 3.5% in 2006 (Table 17.2).

FDI in Chile as a percentage of GPD is one of the highest in Latin America, at a level of 6% in 2005 (Table 17.4). This is result of an open policy toward FDI and, that Chile's companies are benefiting from the most transparent and investor-friendly regulatory environment in Latin America. Chile was the leader in adopting open-market-oriented trade policies and fostering foreign direct investment in all economic sectors, including capital markets. Moreover, the Chilean government engages in a multitude of bilateral and multilateral free trade agreements with other countries – a policy that often irritates its Latin neighbors.

Although Chile is ranked as the world's most attractive destination for mining investment, the unemployment rate is still relatively high (7.8% in 2006) despite being the lowest rate in 8 years (Table 17.8). Moreover, a level of rigidity in the labor market could increase their cost.

Table 17.4 Corruption indicators

	Corruption perception index (2006) (1)	Critical areas of budget transparency (% of positive responses) (2)			Perception of change in the level of corruption (2)				Direct experience of corruption (%) (2)
		Citizen participation (% most critical)	Accountability (%)	Supervision of federal officials (%)	2000 – corruption increased (%)		2002 – corruption increased (%)		
					A lot	A little	A lot	A little	
Argentina	2.9	8	25	20	87	5	90	3	25
Brazil	3.3	11	24	33	85	5	78	6	61
Chile	7.3	21	39	37	60	15	58	13	13
Colombia	3.9	N/A	N/A	N/A	80	9	85	4	19
Venezuela, RB	2.3	N/A	N/A	N/A	54	11	73	7	27

Sources: (1) Transparency International (2006); (2) www.globalcorruptionreport.org

The public sector is generally honest and efficient. Chile is the least corrupt country in Latin America, with a perception index of corruption of 7.3% (Transparency International, 2006) – measured as transparency in the three main dimensions: citizen participation, accountability, and disclosure of purchase prices and supervision of federal officials.

Venezuela

Mr. Chávez, reelected in 2006, has made it very clear that he does not intend to privatize strategic economic activities, including oil production and the transmission and generation of hydroelectric power (EIU, Venezuela, 2004). As a consequence, the political climate of Venezuela is characterized by high levels of distrust, despite being among the world's top 10 crude oil producers (see Table 17.2).

The inflation rate has changed in the last 6 years, with a rate of 12.5% in 2001, a peak of 31.1% in 2003, and stabilising in 13.7% in 2006 (GMID Country Profile, 2007a).

Venezuela joined MERCOSUR in December 2005. On the other hand, Hugo Chavez announced in 2006 the separation from CAN, creating regional tension (EIU, Venezuela, 2007).

Venezuela's government intervenes openly in the economy, creating distortions in goods, services, and capital markets. As a consequence, inflows of FDI tend to stabilize because investors are concerned about the state control over the economy. Moreover, foreign participation in privatization is ruled by "special laws," requiring that between 10% and 20% of the shares of the privatized firm be reserved for the firms' current and retired workers. The government can also set aside a percentage of shares to be offered in local capital markets (PRS, Venezuela, 2003). As a consequence of this government "interventionism," 13 private Venezuelan companies have issued U.S. American Depository Receipts fearing government expropriation.

Companies doing business in Venezuela find a high level of corruption that can significantly increase their costs. The lowest index of perception of corruption among the five countries studied in this chapter is 2.3, with a score below 3 defined by Transparency International as "rampant corruption" (Transparency International, 2006). To conclude, it is important to highlight that Venezuelan GPD growth has been exceptionally high in the recent years, thanks to record high oil prices.

Colombia

President Uribe, elected in 2006, has focused on economic policies and democratic security strategies that have engendered a growing sense of confidence in the economy, particularly within the business sector. Colombia is showing incontestable signs of development – although it continues to struggle with the narco-terrorism problems. FDI has been increasing as a result of the government's sound policies, growing at a 20% annual rate during the period 2001–2006. Colombia's trade has increased, mostly due to oil exports (EIU, 2004). Unemployment is falling and the poverty rate has dropped to 49%.

On the negative side of things, the deficient tax structure and high tax rates affect business directly. The rate of corporate tax is the highest in Latin America at 39%. The total tax rate for a medium-sized company in Colombia is 82.8% of profits (GMID Business Environment, 2007b).

Mayors from Colombian regional capitals signed "transparency pacts," which were defined as public agreements between the elected officials and their constituents to implement efficiency and anticorruption programs (Wills and Ureña, 2006). The CPI has remained quite constant for the last few years at 3.9 (Transparency International, 2004).

To conclude, we examine how global these five countries are, given their increase in trade. From the last two columns in Table 17.3, we can see that in 2006 there was great dependence on the U.S., which ranked first (or second) as an import–export partner of all five countries. Recent policy analysis and the business press foresee a much closer trade relationships between Latin America and China as the latter needs for more natural and mineral resources.

Corporate Governance

The development and growth of Latin America is contingent on developing good corporate governance practices. These countries are at different stages in their transition to effective corporate governance, and this is directly related to their political governance. In order to succeed, a country needs both effective political and corporate governance. The characteristics of the country's legal institutions, the financial system (particularly the stock market), employment system, and structure of firm ownership define much of the country's corporate governance system. We discuss each of them in turn.

Legal System

The importance that the underlying legal systems have on various corporate-governance-related issues such as in the spread of codes of good governance (Aguilera and Cuervo-Cazurra, 2004) or creditor protection (Djankov, McLiesh, and Shleifer, 2004) is well established.

Law, in these five countries is based on French civil legal tradition that relies primarily on statutes and comprehensive codes (La Porta, Lopez-de-Silanes, & Shleifer, 1998). Table 17.5 shows that the time required to start a new business in terms of bureaucratic paperwork is fairly similar across these countries, with an average of 67 days. Chile has the lowest cost and Brazil and Venezuela the highest (Djankov, et al., 2000). According to the research by La Porta et al. (1998) summarized in Table 17.5, the judicial

Table 17.5 Business environment

	Time to start a new business (1)			Legal environment (2)				
	Number of procedures	Time (days)	Cost (GNP/ capita)	Efficiency of judicial system	Rule of law	Risk of expropriation	Rating on accounting standards	Anti-director rights
Argentina	12	71	0.232	6	5.35	5.91	45	4
Brazil	15	67	0.673	5.75	6.32	7.62	54	3
Chile	9	78	0.116	7.25	7.02	7.50	52	5
Colombia	17	55	0.124	7.25	2.08	6.95	50	3
Venezuela, RB	15	67	0.673	6.50	6.37	6.89	40	1

Sources: (1) Djankov, La Porta, Lopez-de-Silanes, and Shleifer (2000); (2) La Porta, Lopez-de-Silanes, Shleifer, and Vishny (1998).

system is also important, with the most efficiency and integrity in Chile and Colombia and the lowest in Brazil, although Colombia has a comparatively very low rule of law index, which captures the country's lack of law and order. Other key variables for corporate governance are the rating of accounting standards which reflects the transparency and disclosure of company annual reports and for which Brazil has the highest and Venezuela the lowest rating. "Anti-director rights," measuring the legal protection of minority shareholders, is the highest in Chile and the lowest in Venezuela.

Latin America is fully aware of the need to increase transparency and efficiency to their corporate governance systems in order to fully participate in the global economy. In 2001, Argentina enacted capital markets reform in a law that covers most firm-level corporate governance issues. Then, in 2002, FUNDECE and IDEA (two private-sector associations) established the *Instituto Argentino para el Gobierno de las Organizaciones* (IAGO), which aims to raise awareness of good governance and to provide director training.

The Brazilian Corporate Governance Institute (IBGC) launched its Code of Best Practices in 2001. Chile was the first country in Latin America to reform the legal and regulatory framework of corporate governance, including two main issues: banking regulation and the development of supervisory institutions. Colombia's private-sector efforts in corporate governance center on *Confecamaras* (Confederation of Chambers of Commerce) and its Corporate Governance Project is responsible for improving the awareness of good governance practices throughout the private sector. Finally, AVE (Venezuelan Executive Association) sponsors corporate governance awareness in Venezuela, and in 2003, with the participation of some private-sector and public-sector entities, AVE established an Executive Council for Corporate Best Practices. In a way, these positive efforts to improve corporate governance are minority shareholders engaging in "bonding" (Coffee, 1999) by committing themselves to play by international corporate governance rules.

Financial System

The banking system in Latin America is comparatively rather weak. For example, as shown in Table 17.6, private credit by commercial banks and other financial institutions as percentage of GDP is low (below 50%) in all five countries except Chile, which is higher. These ratios are low if we compare them with Spain (106%) or the United Kingdom (106%). In addition, the creditor index (Djankov et al., 2004), which measures four powers of secured lenders in bankruptcy, is 2 or below in four of the countries, 0 being poor creditor rights and 4 strong rights.

The comparative analysis of the banking system in the five Latin American countries shown in Table 17.6 also illustrates that there is concentration in the sector. There is a high incidence of foreign bank ownership, coupled with the recent decline of state-ownership that is the product of the liberalization of the sector. In

Table 17.6 Banking system

	Number of banks	Private foreign	Private domestic	Provincial public	National public	Private credit/GDP (2)	Creditors rights (2)
Argentina (1)	73	27 (37%)	32 (44%)	10 (13.5%)	4 (5.5%)	0.19	1

	Number of banks	Foreign-owned	State-owned	Private credit/GDP (2)	Creditors rights (2)
Brazil (1)	159	61 (38%)	98 (62%)	0.35	1

	Number of banks	Foreign-owned	Local banks	Private credit/GDP (2)	Creditors rights (2)
Chile (1)	25	12 (48%)	13 (52%)	0.61	2

	Sarmiento group (% of total assets)	Grupo Empresarial (% of total assets)	Banco Agrario (% of total assets)	Private banks: foreign and state-owned (% of total assets)	Private credit/GDP (2)	Creditors rights (2)
Colombia (1)	35	24	6	35	0.27	0

	Number of banks	Private banking institutions	Public banking institutions	Private credit/GDP (2)	Creditors rights (2)
Venezuela (1)	59	49 (83%)	10 (17%)	0.11	3

Sources: (1) EIU, 2007 (2) Djankov, Mc Liesh, and Shleifer (2004)

contrast to these trends, only three of Brazil's top 10 private banks were foreign-owned at the end of 2006: ABN Amro Real (Netherlands), Santander Banespa (Spain), and HSBC (UK) (EIU, 2007).

In Colombia the situation is similar: the two local financial groups (Sarmiento Group and Grupo Empresarial) own 59% of total assets, meanwhile the only remaining state-owned bank, Banco Agrario, accounts for merely 6%. On the contrary, Banco Santander, the first bank in Chile, accounts for 22% of total assets at the end of 2006, a clear example of the high incidence of foreign-ownership banks. Another example is Venezuela, where two of the four largest universal banks – universal banks account for around 75% of total financial-sector assets – are in majority Spanish-owned.

The capital markets of these countries are fairly underdeveloped, but not homogenous. The highly entrenched corporate ownership and the fact that private corporations are closed and family-owned are two characteristics influencing the Latin American structure of capital markets (Welch, 1993).

Argentina has the oldest stock market, founded in 1854, and Venezuela the newest (1947). Chile engages in the highest market capitalization of listed companies as percentage of GDP as shown in Table 17.7. The U.S. banks, and particularly, pension-fund managers are among the most dynamic players in Chilean capital markets. In 2001, the Brazilian stock market (BOVESPA) created three new market segments requiring different degrees of corporate governance.[2] The Brazilian Novo Mercado has received active support from a number of Brazilian governmental organizations, as well as from the International Finance Corporation, the World Bank, the Organisation for Economic Co-operation and Development (OECD), the Private Sector Advisory Group on Corporate Governance, and the Global Corporate Governance Forum (Santana, 2003). In Brazil there are about 6,000 companies with over 250 employees, only 120 of those companies are listed and regularly traded on the Sâo Paulo Stock Exchange (BOVESPA).

The market capitalization of listed companies and total value traded in Argentina and Venezuela is at minimum levels as shown in Table 17.7. This is explained by the lack of investor confidence in the economic and political stability of these two countries. The largest stock markets in Latin America, according to FIBV, are Brazil and Chile. Colombia's capital market is underdeveloped, but it has improved in the last 3 years and the exchange rate has been in appreciation since 2003, increasing market capitalization by US $42.7 billion.

---

[2] These include: (a) Special Corporate Governance Level 1, which requires companies to become more transparent by disclosing information such as financial statements, insider trading and self dealing (28 listed companies); (b) Special Corporate Governance Level 2, which requires companies to abide by all of the obligations set forth in the stricter regulations for the Novo Mercado with a few key exceptions; and (c) Novo Mercado, inaugurated in 2002, where many private companies and future IPOs will contemplate listing, although the process has slowed down due to the stagnation of Brazilian capital markets.

Table 17.7 Stock market

| | Stock exchange foundation | Total value stocks traded (% of GDP) (1) | | Stocks traded, turnover ratio (%) (1) | | Market capitalization of listed companies (% of GDP) (1) | | Firms with ADRs (2) | Publicly traded firms (3) | | | |
| | | | | | | | | | 1998 | | 2003 | |
		1993	2006	1993	2006	1993	2006		Domestic	Foreign	Domestic	Foreign
Argentina	1854	4	2	33	7	19	37	9	131	0	106	4
Brazil	1890	13	24	33	43	23	67	32	534	1	389	2
Chile	1893	6	20	7	19	100	120	17	287	0	240	1
Colombia	1929	1	8	10	22	17	41	1	118	0	108	0
Venezuela, RB	1947	4	0	24	9	13	5	13	162	1	57	2

Employment System

Latin American labor laws are based on a paternalistic model. Historically, Latin America has been characterized by high levels of state intervention and poor civil society action. This is the main reason why labor unions have developed strong ties with political parties and, even in some cases, the country's president comes from populist labor-based parties (Argentina, Brazil, and Venezuela). Similarly, union activism has been critical in resisting military regimes. Unions are active in Latin America in comparison with other developing countries and with the more industrialized world, and they tend to negotiate at the national or sectoral level. Argentina, and particularly Venezuela, have witnessed the most massive general strikes. For example, in December 2003 the CTV and FEDECAMARAS (business organization) in Venezuela called for a national strike, and most companies answered the call. For almost 2 months, Venezuela's oil company PDVSA (one of the world's largest, and ranked number 76 in the 2004 Fortune 500 World's largest corporations) shut down almost 100% of its production, distribution, and exportation of oil. The strike ended with strikers gaining a referendum for presidential elections.

Unemployment rates increased dramatically in the early 2000s reaching above the 10% mark in 2002 for all countries except Chile, as shown in Table 17.8. At present, the rates are making satisfactory downward progress, except Chile's unemployment rate which is keeping stable. Argentina has the highest unemployment rate of all five countries, and, of course, Brazil, the largest labor force.

The common denominator in these five countries is recent labor reforms, as shown in Table 17.8. Murillo (2004) argues, however, that economic pressures are not the sole cause of labor reform because Argentina, Venezuela, and Chile had different levels of trade liberalization, labor costs, and rates of unionization prior to their labor reforms. For example, Chile had the lowest labor cost of the three, and Venezuela the highest. Argentina and Venezuela have the highest rates of unionization followed by Brazil and Chile. In spite of these differences, these countries passed reforms of individual labor regulation in a politically uncertain climate.

All five countries have undertaken recent reforms in their labor laws, some of them also reflected in their constitutions. According to Cook (1998), three kinds of changes have occurred in Latin America's labor law. First, flexible laws deregulate labor markets and reduce employer costs. Second, liberal reforms strengthen the autonomy of the unions and employer organizations from the state as well as support pluralism; and, finally, reforms are based on the protection of the workers through national legislation rather than leaving it at the mercy of individual firms. Cook (1998) argues that Argentina has changed its labor law from protective to flexible, Brazil from liberal to flexible and then to protective, Chile from protective to liberal, and Colombia from protective to flexible. Venezuela, under Hugo Chavez, has adopted a retroactive reform. For example, in 2002, the *inamovilidad* decree (prohibiting firms from laying off employees) was enforced.

The strength and organization of the labor movement varies across countries. Argentina's labor movement is one of the strongest in Latin America. Colombia's

Table 17.8 Employment relations

	Labor force (millions) (1)			Unemployment rate (%)			Labor law reforms	Principal unions 2003 (3)	Members per union (millions) 2003 (3)	Unionized work force (%) (4)		
	1998	2002	2006	1998 (1)	2002 (1)	2006 (2)				1993	1998	2002
Argentina	14.3	16	18.7	12.8	15.6	11.4	2000	CGT (General Confederation of Labor), CTA (Argentine Workers Central)	CGT=3 CTA=0.6	28	28	28
Brazil	76.6	82.7	92.7	9	10.5	10	1988	CGT (General Confederation of Workers), CUT (Central Workers Union), The Union Force	These account for more than 60% of the unionized workforce	22	22	22
Chile	5.9	6.6	6.6	7.2	8.5	7.8	2001	CUT (Central Workers Union)	CUT=0.47	13	13	22
Colombia	17.5	19.8	22.5	15	14.2	11	2002	CUT (Central Workers Union), CDTC (General Confederation of Colombian Democratic Workers), CTC (Confederation of Colombian Workers)	8% of Colombian labor force is unionized	8	8	8
Venezuela, RB	9.3	8	10.7	11.2	18.4	8.8	1997 (with changes in 1999)	CTV (Confederation of Venezuelan Workers)	One fifth of workers are affiliate with some union	32	32	32

Sources: (1) WDI; (2) EIU (2006); (3) EIU (2004–2005); (4) PRS (2003)

union representation is small and fragmented due to political instability and notorious drug-trafficking problems, corruption and guerrilla movements. At the beginning of Chile's democratization process, its unions were weak due to low membership, labor fragmentation, and political divisions, but through the years these factors have been changing, and the union density rate has increased.

Union density has been fairly stable in the pat decade, as shown in Table 17.8. In 2002, the union density rates are: 28% in Argentina, 22% in Brazil, 8% in Colombia, and 32% in Venezuela. Chile is the only country that experienced important changes in union rates, following the reestablishment of democracy, rising from 13% in 1998 to 22% in 2002. Table 17.8 also enumerates the main unions in each countries and their membership.

Firm Ownership Structure and Control

A common denominator among Latin American publicly traded firms is the high degree of ownership concentration. Families are the main owners, even among the largest companies (OECD, 2003). Often control is in the organizational form of a conglomerate or business group, defined as a group of firms that are related to each other through ownership relations and controlled by a local family, a group of investors or by a foreign company.

Apreda (2001) argues that before 1991, the largest Argentinean firms were diversified in terms of ownership; and after 1991 these companies were subject to significant economic reforms under the Menem administration and opened to foreign investors. Yafeh and Khanna's (2003) study confirms Apreda's findings, as they show that among the 40 largest listed Argentinean companies, 25 are foreign-owned, 14 family-owned, and 1 is state-owned, and among these 40 there are 11 conglomerates. Yafeh and Khanna (2003) studied 100 nonfinancial firms in Brazil and found that two have dispersed ownership, 29 are controlled by a local family group, 37 by a foreign firm, and 32 by the federal government.

Again, business groups are a predominant organizational form, totaling 38 business groups in these 100 firms. This is also the case in Chile, where 68% of the Chilean nonfinancial listed firms are controlled by one conglomerate (Lefort & Walker, 2000). Another similar fact happens in Venezuela, where half of the ownership of Venezuelan SMEs is concentrated in the hands of members of the same family: "56% of the companies are integrated by an individual shareholder or a partner, only 14% have three or five partners and the remaining 30% only have to partners" (INSOTEV industrial sector poll).

Data on Latin American firm ownership is either nonexistent or difficult to acquire. The OECD's (2003) *White Paper on Corporate Governance* systematically compares ownership structure of some of the countries, and we have added additional data for the countries not included (see Table 17.9). In the case of Argentina, even though it is a very limited sample for 2002, 90% of ownership is in the hands of the five largest owners, and a majority of ownership is in the hands of the largest

Table 17.9 Corporate governance: ownership dispersion and identity

	Ownership concentration				Owner identity				Number of groups (1997)	Percent of affiliation to groups (2002)
	Sample	Percent of largest shareholder	Percent of 3 largest shareholders	Percent of 5 largest shareholders	Domestic–private (%)	Foreign (%)	State (%)	Disperse ownership (%)		
Argentina*	15	61	82	90	38.6	59,1	2.3	0	11	93
Brazil	459	51	65	67	43	33	21	3	38	89
Chile	260	55	74	80	69	30	0.8	0	50	68
Colombia	74	44	65	73	N/A	N/A	N/A	N/A	7	50
Venezuela, RB	33	50	N/A	N/A	60*	20*	N/A	20*	N/A	N/A

Source: OECD (2003).
*Data from 20-F ADR filings.

owner. The OECD data also confirms that in most cases the owner is foreign, followed by a private domestic owner. Table 17.10 shows that for the same sample, most of the firms belong to pyramidal business groups, which is a mechanism to separate ownership and control. This is also reflected in the composition of the board, which has a minority of independent directors.

Brazilian corporations are mostly family-owned, and this has effects in the type of management that prevails. According to Oman (2003), there are two main constraints in Brazil's corporate governance: (1) a high level of shareholder expropriation and, (2) the nature of its legal system. Table 17.9 shows that in most firms the largest shareholder has majority control and that the main type of owner is domestic (presumably family-owned). Table 17.10 illustrates the limited power that shareholders have, with 87% of the firms having non-voting shares as well as few independent directors on the board.

Chilean firms are controlled by a few large business groups, which are structured in pyramidal style, with one or more investment companies as the center of control. Operating companies, which are on the top of the pyramid, usually are listed on the stock exchange and, therefore, have outsider shareholders (Oman, 2003). Ownership is slightly more dispersed and in the hands of domestic owners, as shown in Table 17.9. The percentage of shareholders without voting rights is low, and the governance system of the board of directors seems more in line with international standards, with a majority of independent directors (as shown in Table 17.10).

Data on Colombia and Venezuela is fairly limited and unreliable, as shown in Tables 17.9 and 17.10. In Colombia, the majority of firms are owned by the largest five owners, the boards being reportedly small as well as the percentage of shareholders without voting rights over those with voting rights. Finally, in 50% of a sample of Venezuelan firms, a single owner has majority ownership, and the most active firms (those that issue ADRs) are mostly domestically owned.

Table 17.10 Corporate governance: control and board structure

	Separation of ownership and control				Board structure		
	Percent of firms with non-voting shares	Non-voting/ voting shares	Percent of firms in pyramids	Percent cash flow rights of controller	Number of board member	Percent of independent members	Board member/ board seats
Argentina	3.9	0.14	93	68	8.10	38.8	1.2
Brazil	86.9	1.29	89	60	8.5	28.6	1.1
Chile	7.2	0.07	68	57	7.6	55	1.6
Colombia	7.1	0.09	50	N/A	5	50	N/A
Venezuela, RB	N/A	N/A	N/A	N/A	8.3*	36.6*	N/A

Source: OECD (2003)
*Venezuela's board structure data is from a sample of 10 companies.

Conclusions

The economic recovery in Latin America started in the early 1990s with the relaxation of trade barriers, the inflow of foreign capital and massive privatizations of state enterprises (Grosse, 2001). These economies had positive growth, as shown in Table 17.2, but the trajectory has been bumpy. For example, while in the 1990s, Argentina was considered among the top 10 most attractive investment locations in the world, this all changed with the economic (tequila) crisis that began in 2001 (FDI inflows fell 69% from 2001 to 2002) and provoked a severe recession, financial turmoil, and political instability. Even though Argentina still remains open to foreign investment, its high corruption levels and the weakness of the judicial system makes foreign and domestic investors reluctant to invest there. Argentina had the largest external debt in 2003, which is a consequence of financial crises and currency devaluation (WDI, 2003).

Brazil, the Latin American behemoth, has an active private economy, but as in most of the region this is accompanied with serious social problems. Current President Lula Da Silva has requested the help of businesses in strengthening Brazil's social agenda and in reining in government expenditure. He expects financial contributions from state-owned companies, specially the state oil company, Petrobras – which represents two-thirds of the country's primary surplus (PRS, 2003) and is ranked 144 in the 2004 *Fortune's* list of world's largest corporations. Chile is currently the most economically and politically stable country in Latin American. It was the first country in the region to liberalize its foreign investment regulations, which is a key factor in the financial system (Treviño and Mixon, 2004) and also adopted effective banking practices which raised investor confidence. Colombia and Venezuela lag far behind in terms of modernization of their corporate governance systems and the overall economy.

Latin American countries stand out for their recurrent macroeconomic uncertainty and political instability. In terms of corporate governance, they share high ownership concentration patterns (state- or family-owned), small and illiquid stock markets, and limited options for corporate financing. Business leaders and politicians are increasingly aware that efficient corporate governance through transparency, greater accountability, and effective protection for shareholders is necessary for economic development. Latin American countries should increase their corporate transparency requirements, strengthen their legal systems, prevent shareholder expropriation by developing effective minority shareholder protection, provide adequate access to investment resources for small- and medium-sized firms as well as long-term financing to foster firm competitiveness and growth, and, finally, allow more activism from institutional investors who are likely to demand higher corporate governance standards, as they did in the U.K.

Acknowledgment I am very grateful for the research assistantship help of Isabel Ermoli and Marga Mayol as well as the CIBER at the University of Illinois at Urbana-Champaign.

References

Aguilera, R. V., & Jackson, G. (2003). The cross-national diversity of corporate governance: dimensions and determinants. *Academy of Management Review, 28*(3), 447–465.

Aguilera, R. V., & Cuervo-Cazurra, A. (2004). The spread of codes of good governance worldwide: what's the trigger? *Organization Studies, 25*(3), 415–443.

Aguilera, R. V., Dabu, A. (2005). The transformation of employment relations in central and Eastern Europe. *Journal of Industrial Relations, 47*(1), 16–42.

Aguilera, R. V., Filatotchev, I., Gospel, H., & Jackson, G. (2008) Contingencies, complementarities, and costs in corporate governance models. *Organization Science, 19*(3), 475–492.

Apreda, R. (2001) Corporate governance in Argentina: The outcome of economic freedom (1991–2000). *Corporate Governance, 9*(4), 298–310.

Coffee, J. C. (1999). The future as history: The prospects of global convergence in corporate governance and its Implications. *University Law Review,* (November).

Cook, M. (1998) Toward flexible industrial relations? Neo-liberalism, democracy, and labor reform in Latin America. *Industrial Relations, 37*(3), 313–332.

Daily, C., Dalton, D., & Cannella, A. (2003). Corporate Governance: Decades of Dialogue and Data. *Academy of Management Review.* 28, s. 371–382.

Djankov, S., La Porta, R., Lopez-de-Silanes, F., & Shleifer, A. (2000) *The regulation of entry.* Cambridge, MA: National Bureau of Economic Research, , Working Paper 7892.

Djankov, S., McLiesh, C., & Shleifer, A. (2004). Private Credit in 129 Countries. Working Paper. http://ssrn.com/abstract=637301.

Doidge, C., Karalyi, G. A., & Stulz, R. M. (2004). *Why do countries matter so much for corporate governance?* ECGI Finance Working Paper, 50/2004.

The Economist Intelligence Unit (2004–2005) *Country commerce for: Argentina, Brazil, Chile, Colombia and Venezuela.* London: Author

The Economist Intelligence Unit (2007) *Country profile for: Argentina, Brazil, Chile, Colombia and Venezuela.* London: Author.

Federowicz, M., & Aguilera, R. V. (2003) *Corporate governance in a changing economic and political environment. Trajectories of institutional change on the Europe Continent.* London: Palgrave MacMillan.

Gospel, H., & Pendleton, A. (2005) *Corporate governance and labor management. An international comparison.* Oxford: Oxford University Press.

Grandori, A. (2004) *Corporate governance and firm organization.* New York, NY: Oxford University Press.

Grosse, R. (2001) International business in Latin America. In A. Rugman & T. Brewer (Eds.), *The Oxford handbook of international business.* Oxford: Oxford University Press.

Hansmann, H., & Kraakman, R. (2001). The end of history for corporate law. *Georgetown Law Journal, 89*, 439–468.

Jacoby, S. M. (2004) *The embedded corporation: Corporate governance and employment relations in Japan and the United States.* Princeton, NJ: Princeton University Press.

Keasey, K., Thompson, S., & Wright, M. (Eds.) (1999). *Corporate governance.* Northampton: Edward Elgar Publishing, Inc.

Khanna, T., Kogan, J., & Palepu, K. (2002) *Globalization and similarities in corporate governance: A cross-country analysis.* Harvard NOM Working Paper No. 02–31.

Klapper, L., & Love, L. (2002). *Corporate governance, investor protection, and Performance in emerging markets.* Washington, D.C.: World Bank, Development Research Group.

La Porta, R., Lopez-de-Silanes, F., & Shleifer, A. (1998) Law and finance. *Journal of Political Economy, 106*(6), 1115–1148.

Lefort, F., & Walker, E. 2000. Corporate governance: Challenges for Latin America. *ABANTE, 2*(2).

Lenartowicz, T., & Johnson, J. P. (2003), A cross-national assessment of the values of Latin America managers: contrasting hues or shades of gray? *Journal of International Business Studies, 34*, 266–281.

Murillo, M. (2004) *Partisanship amidst convergence: The politics of labor reform in Latin America.* New York: Columbia University.

Transparency International (2002) *Annual Report Transparency International 2002.* Berlin.

Transparency International (2004) *Annual Report Transparency International 2004.* Berlin.

Global Market Information Database (2007a) Country profile for: Argentina, Brazil, Chile, Colombia and Venezuela. GMID

Global Market Information Database (2007b) Business environment for: Brazil, Chile, Colombia and Venezuela. GMID

OECD (2001) *Corporate Governance in Asia: A comparative perspective.* Paris, Author.

OECD (2003) *Corporate Governance in Latin America.* Paris, Author.

Oman, C. (2003) *Corporate governance in development.* Paris, OECD.

Political Risk Services (2003) *For: Argentina, Brazil, Chile, Colombia and Venezuela New York,* The PRS Group, Inc. See www.prsgroup.com

Prowse, S. (1995). Corporate governance in an international perspective: A survey of corporate control mechanisms among large firms in the U.S., U.K. and Germany. *Financial Markets, Institutions and Instruments, 4*(1), 1–61.

Rhodes, M., & Van Apeldoorn B., (1998). Capital unbound? The transformation of European Corporate Governance. *Journal of European Public Policy, 5*(3), 406–427.

Santana, M. (2003) *Innovative strategies to institute Corporate Governance in Brazil: The BOVESPA and The Novo Mercado.* Brazil.

Shleifer, A., & Vishny, R. W. (1997). A survey of corporate governance. *Journal of Finance, 52*(2), 737–783.

Thomsen, S. (2004). Convergence of corporate governance during the stock market bubble? Towards Anglo-American or European Standards. In A. Grandori (Ed.) *Corporate governance and firm organization* (pp. 1–30). New York, NY: Oxford University Press.

Treviño, L., & Mixon, F. (2004) Strategic factors affecting foreign direct investment decisions by multi-national enterprises in Latin America. *Journal of World Business,* 39, 234–236.

WDI (World Development Indicators) (2003). World Bank. Washington, D.C.

WDI (World Development Indicators) (2008). World Bank. Washington, D.C.

Weimer, J., & Pape, J. C. (1990) A taxonomy of systems of corporate governance. *Corporate Governance, 7*(2), 152–167.

Welch, J. H. (1993) The new face of Latin America: Financial flows, markets and institutions in the 1990s. *Journal of Latin American Studies, 25*(1). Cambridge University Press.

Wills, E., & Ureña, C. (2006) South America. Global Corruption Report. Berlin, Germany. Retrieved from www.globalcorruptionreport.org

Yafeh, Y., & Khanna, T. (2003) Business groups and risk sharing around the World. HBS Strategy Working Paper.

Zhuang, J., & Edwards, D. (2001). *Corporate Governance and Finance in East Asia: Country studies: A study of Indonesia, Republic of Korea, Malaysia, Philippines, and Thailand.* Manila: Asian Development Bank.

Other Sources:

www.sourceoecd.com (database-source-oecd)
http://www.caracasstock.com
http://www.cia.gov/cia/publications/factbook
http://www.fibv.com
http://www.nyse.com
http://www.worldbank.org

Chapter 18
Corporate Governance in Africa and the Middle East: A Comparative Study

Robert W. McGee

Introduction

The World Bank has done six *Report on the Observance of Standards and Codes* (ROSC) studies of corporate governance for African or Middle Eastern countries. The template it used was based on the categories used in an Organisation for Economic Co-operation and Development publication (OECD, 2004).

The following pages summarize the findings of those studies and do a comparative analysis.

Methodology

The World Bank studies used a template to evaluate various corporate governance categories. It classified various aspects of corporate governance into five categories. The present study assigned weights to those categories, which makes it possible to quantify the various rankings that the World Bank studies assigned to each country. The categories and points assigned to each category are as follows:

> O = Observed (5 points)
> LO = Largely Observed (4 points)
> PO = Partially Observed (3 points)
> MNO = Materially Not Observed (2 points)
> NO = Not Observed (1 point)

Findings

The findings are subdivided into five categories and are also combined into a single corporate governance score.

R.W. McGee (✉)
Florida International University, Miami, FL, USA
e-mail: bob414@hotmail.com

R.W. McGee (ed.), *Corporate Governance in Developing Economies*,
DOI 10.1007/978-0-387-84833-4_18, © Springer Science+Business Media, LLC 2009

Table 18.1 Rights of shareholders (30 points = maximum score)

Country	Points	Percentage of possible
Egypt	24	80.0
Ghana	17	56.7
Jordan	21	70.0
Mauritius	16	53.3
Senegal	17	56.7
South Africa	22	73.3

Rights of Shareholders

Table 18.1 shows the scores in the category of rights of shareholders. The only country that hit 80 percent was Egypt. Mauritius had the lowest percentage score, at 53.3 percent.

The bar chart below shows how the countries fared graphically. Egypt had the most points, followed by South Africa. Mauritius had the lowest percentage score (53.3 percent).

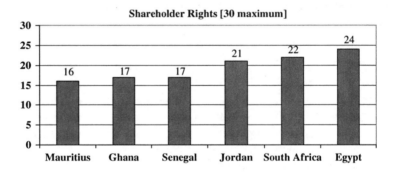

Equitable Treatment of Shareholders

None of the countries scored at least 80 percent. There was a three-way tie for the top percentage of 73.3. Senegal scored a miserable 40.0 percent. Table 18.2 shows the total points and percentage of possible points.

Table 18.2 Equitable treatment of shareholders (15 points = maximum score)

Country	Points	Percentage of possible
Egypt	11	73.3
Ghana	8	53.3
Jordan	11	73.3
Mauritius	9	60.0
Senegal	6	40.0
South Africa	11	73.3

The bar chart below shows the relative results for this category. Egypt, Jordan, and South Africa tied for first place. Senegal was in last place.

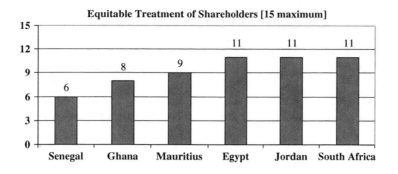

Equitable Treatment of Shareholders [15 maximum]

Role of Stakeholders in Corporate Governance

Table 18.3 shows the relative scores in the area of Role of Stakeholders in Corporate Governance. Some of the scores in this topical area were quite good. Jordan scored a perfect 100 percent, followed by Egypt and South Africa at 95 percent. Senegal had the lowest score at 55 percent.

The bar chart below shows how the countries stacked up against each other. This bar chart is almost like a bimodal distribution in that the high scores and low scores are clumped, with Jordan, South Africa, and Egypt at one extreme and Senegal and Mauritius at the other.

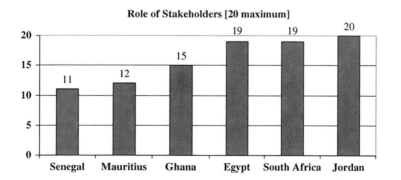

Role of Stakeholders [20 maximum]

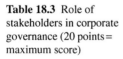

Table 18.3 Role of stakeholders in corporate governance (20 points = maximum score)

Country	Points	Percentage of possible
Egypt	19	95.0
Ghana	15	75.0
Jordan	20	100.0
Mauritius	12	60.0
Senegal	11	55.0
South Africa	19	95.0

Disclosure and Transparency

Table 18.4 shows the results of the category Disclosure and Transparency. Jordan was the only country that broke into the 80s. Egypt and Mauritius barely broke into the 70s. Senegal had the lowest score, at 45 percent.

The bar chart below shows the relative scores for each country. Jordan had the highest score; Senegal had the lowest.

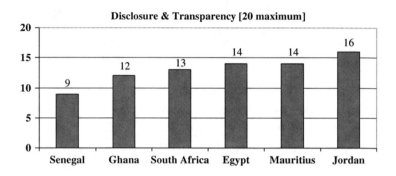

Responsibilities of the Board

Table 18.5 shows the scores in the category of Responsibilities of the Board. None of the countries broke the 80 percent barrier. Jordan and South Africa came the closest at 73.3 percent. Senegal came in last, with a score of 46.7 percent.

Table 18.4 Disclosure and transparency (20 points = maximum score)

Country	Points	Percentage of possible
Egypt	14	70.0
Ghana	12	60.0
Jordan	16	80.0
Mauritius	14	70.0
Senegal	9	45.0
South Africa	13	65.0

Table 18.5 Responsibilities of the board (30 points = maximum score)

Country	Points	Percentage of possible
Egypt	21	70.0
Ghana	18	60.0
Jordan	22	73.3
Mauritius	17	56.7
Senegal	14	46.7
South Africa	22	73.3

The bar chart below shows the relative scores graphically. South Africa and Jordan are tied, followed by Egypt.

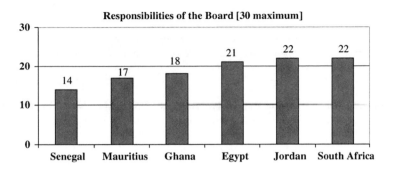

Overall Scores

Table 18.6 shows the overall scores for each country. None of them cracked the 80 percent barrier, although Jordan came close at 78.3 percent.

The bar chart below shows the relative scores graphically. Jordan had the highest number of points, followed closely by Egypt, then South Africa. Senegal had by far the fewest points.

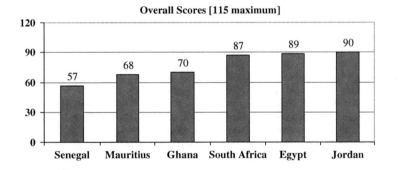

Table 18.6 Overall scores (115 points=maximum score)

Country	Points	Percentage of possible
Egypt	89	77.4
Ghana	70	60.9
Jordan	90	78.3
Mauritius	68	59.1
Senegal	57	49.6
South Africa	87	75.7

References

OECD (2004). *Principles of Corporate Governance*. Paris: Author.

World Bank. (2002). *Report on the Observance of Standards and Codes (ROSC), Corporate Governance Country Assessment, Mauritius, October.* World Bank. Retrieved from www.worldbank.org.

World Bank. (2003a). *Report on the Observance of Standards and Codes (ROSC), Corporate Governance Country Assessment, Chile, May.* World Bank. Retrieved from www.worldbank.org.

World Bank. (2003b). *Report on the Observance of Standards and Codes (ROSC), Corporate Governance Country Assessment, Colombia, August.* World Bank. Retrieved from www.worldbank.org.

World Bank. (2003c). *Report on the Observance of Standards and Codes (ROSC), Corporate Governance Country Assessment, Republic of Korea, September.* World Bank. Retrieved from www.worldbank.org.

World Bank. (2003d). *Report on the Observance of Standards and Codes (ROSC), Corporate Governance Country Assessment, Mexico, September.* World Bank. Retrieved from www.worldbank.org.

World Bank. (2003e). *Report on the Observance of Standards and Codes (ROSC), Corporate Governance Country Assessment, Republic of South Africa, July.* World Bank. Retrieved from www.worldbank.org.

World Bank. (2004a). *Report on the Observance of Standards and Codes (ROSC), Corporate Governance Country Assessment, Egypt, March.* World Bank. Retrieved from www.worldbank.org.

World Bank. (2004b). *Report on the Observance of Standards and Codes (ROSC), Corporate Governance Country Assessment, India, April.* World Bank. Retrieved from www.worldbank.org.

World Bank. (2004c). *Report on the Observance of Standards and Codes (ROSC), Corporate Governance Country Assessment, Republic of Indonesia, April.* World Bank. Retrieved from www.worldbank.org.

World Bank. (2004d). *Report on the Observance of Standards and Codes (ROSC), Corporate Governance Country Assessment, Jordan, June.* World Bank. Retrieved from www.worldbank.org.

World Bank. (2004e). *Report on the Observance of Standards and Codes (ROSC), Corporate Governance Country Assessment, Panama, June.* World Bank. Retrieved from www.worldbank.org.

World Bank. (2004f). *Report on the Observance of Standards and Codes (ROSC), Corporate Governance Country Assessment, Republic of Peru, June.* World Bank. Retrieved from www.worldbank.org.

World Bank. (2005a). *Report on the Observance of Standards and Codes (ROSC), Corporate Governance Country Assessment, Brazil, May.* World Bank. Retrieved from www.worldbank.org.

World Bank. (2005b). *Report on the Observance of Standards and Codes (ROSC), Corporate Governance Country Assessment, Ghana, May.* World Bank. Retrieved from www.worldbank.org.

World Bank. (2005c). *Report on the Observance of Standards and Codes (ROSC), Corporate Governance Country Assessment, Malaysia, June.* World Bank. Retrieved from www.worldbank.org.

World Bank. (2005d). *Report on the Observance of Standards and Codes (ROSC), Corporate Governance Country Assessment, Nepal, April.* World Bank. Retrieved from www.worldbank.org.

World Bank. (2005e). *Report on the Observance of Standards and Codes (ROSC), Corporate Governance Country Assessment, Pakistan, June.* World Bank. Retrieved from www.worldbank.org.

World Bank. (2005f). *Report on the Observance of Standards and Codes (ROSC), Corporate Governance Country Assessment, Thailand, June.* World Bank. Retrieved from www.worldbank.org.

World Bank. (2005g). *Report on the Observance of Standards and Codes (ROSC), Corporate Governance Country Assessment, Uruguay. September.* World Bank. Retrieved from www.worldbank.org.

World Bank. (2006a). *Report on the Observance of Standards and Codes (ROSC), Corporate Governance Country Assessment, Bhutan, December.* World Bank. Retrieved from www.worldbank.org.

World Bank. (2006b). *Report on the Observance of Standards and Codes (ROSC), Corporate Governance Country Assessment, Philippines, May.* World Bank. Retrieved from www. worldbank.org.

World Bank. (2006c). *Report on the Observance of Standards and Codes (ROSC), Corporate Governance Country Assessment, Senegal, June.* World Bank. Retrieved from www. worldbank.org.

World Bank. (2006d). *Report on the Observance of Standards and Codes (ROSC), Corporate Governance Country Assessment, Vietnam, June.* World Bank. Retrieved from www.worldbank.org.

World Bank. (n.d.). *Report on the Observance of Standards and Codes (ROSC), Corporate Governance Country Assessment, Turkey.* World Bank. www.worldbank.org.

World Bank. (n.d.). *Report on the Observance of Standards and Codes (ROSC), Corporate Governance Country Assessment, Zimbabwe.* World Bank. Retrieved from www.worldbank.org.

Chapter 19
International Influence on Accountancy in Vietnam

Robert H.S. Sarikas, Vu Dinh Hien, and Arsen M. Djatej

Introduction

This chapter concerns Vietnamese accountancy, an important element in Vietnamese corporate governance. Vietnamese accountancy is important to Vietnam because Vietnam has an increasingly market-driven economy that requires significant economic growth to meet the needs of its large and youthful population. In the twenty-first century the Vietnamese government opened two separate stock exchanges in Vietnam in order to contribute to the long-term economic success of Vietnam. Additionally, a third informal and largely unregulated market in unlisted stocks has appeared in Vietnam. Just as the long-run prosperity of Vietnam is likely linked to the success of the stock markets of Vietnam, similarly the long-term success of the stock markets of Vietnam is likely linked to the success of Vietnamese accountancy. Accountants provide financial and other information that many stock market participants believe are necessary to the success of such markets. This chapter about Vietnamese accountancy examines Vietnamese accountancy from the perspective of how different nations and their economic and accountancy cultures and systems have influenced Vietnamese accountancy. Vietnam has long valued its sovereignty, and it has successfully preserved its pride, language, and national culture throughout its challenging history. Nonetheless, Vietnam, like all nations, has been from time to time been profoundly impacted by other national cultures. We believe that at this point in history it very useful and appropriate to try to understand Vietnamese accountancy from the perspective of how Vietnamese

R.H.S. Sarikas (✉)
Ohio University, Athens, OH, USA
e-mail: sarikas@ohio.edu

V.D. Hien (✉)
National Economics University, Hanoi, Vietnam
e-mail: vdhien@fpt.vn

A.M. Djatej (✉)
Eastern Washington University, Cheney, WA, USA
e-mail: adjatej@ewu.edu

R.W. McGee (ed.), *Corporate Governance in Developing Economies*,
DOI 10.1007/978-0-387-84833-4_19, © Springer Science+Business Media, LLC 2009

accountancy has been influenced by the economic, political, and accounting systems of other nation states.

The Vietnamese Economy and the Vietnamese Stock Markets

The Socialist Republic of Vietnam is a developing country seeking to be an increasingly active and successful participant in the international economy. Traditionally the Vietnamese economy has been a command economy that relied heavily on state enterprises funded and managed by the state to achieve national economic goals. Today all successful national economies are mixed economies with a blend of market economy elements and state-owned enterprises. The national leadership of Vietnam has sought to improve the national economy and the lives of the Vietnamese people by evolving to a mixed economy that is an independent an autonomous economy with a significant market economy sector. Market economy elements of the Vietnamese national economy are increasingly important since the ruling party and the national leadership began economic restructuring (Do Moi) in 1986. At that time the Vietnamese economy was in terrible shape and the national government and the ruling party wisely sought change and modification of Vietnam's traditional socialist economic model.

The market economy sector of the Vietnamese national economy remains a work in process. The Communist Party of Vietnam is the ruling party in Vietnam and the Central Committee's Political Report at the IX Party Congress (2001, p. 11) included as a goal to develop rapidly capital markets, especially a safe and efficient stock market. The Ho Chi Minh City Securities Trading Center was opened by the national government in July of the prior year (2000) with only two listed equity securities (stocks). As is typical in Vietnamese economic change since 1986, the intent by the government is to proceed step by step so as to carefully accomplish meaningful change. It is intended by the Ministry of Finance that ultimately this exchange in Ho Chi Minh City serve the Vietnamese economy in a manner equivalent to how the New York Stock Exchange serves the United States economy. In July 2005, a start-up exchange designed to serve smaller companies was opened in Hanoi by the Ministry of Finance. The intent of the Ministry of Finance is that in the long run this Hanoi Securities Trading Center will serve Vietnam in a manner similar to the economic role played by the NASDAQ exchange in the United States. Additionally, there is an informal, largely unregulated market in stocks that occurs in unlisted stocks on the internet, and the sidewalks, streets, and cafes of Vietnam. It is the considered opinion of the authors that it is unlikely that this market will remain totally unregulated in the future.

In 2007, the stock exchange of the Ho Chi Minh City Securities Market (bonds are also traded) gained 23%. However, as of January 28, 2008, the index had fallen 16% for 2008 (McCool, 2008). By June 19, 2008, the Ho Chi Minh City index was down 60% from the start of the year, with inflation apparently a key concern according to Amy Kazmin (2008, p. 26). She believes that as the Vietnamese government moves to address the national inflation problem that the stock market may have reached a turning point and not suffer further losses. Earlier that month (June 6, 2008) a Than Nien News story posted on the website of the Vietnamese Embassy in Washington included a pledge by the Vietnamese government to improve the business environment in Vietnam. Specifically, Deputy Prime Minister Hoang Trung was quoted as offering, "an open and transparent environment" for investors. Presumably this transparency would include better financial information that would come from improvements in Vietnamese accountancy and financial reporting. Earlier, Chris Kamm (2004) has commented that in his opinion the financial and company information available to investors in the Vietnam stock market has only been "rudimentary." Kamm also desired that audits of the financial statements of listed companies be required to be, "by international standards."

It should be noted that auditing improvements in Vietnam are also proceeding step by step as no meaningful long-term improvements are possible instantly. All listed companies are required to be audited by professional auditors. Vietnamese auditors who audit listed companies in Vietnam have work procedures and work product that increasingly approach international standards. Nonetheless, the international accounting firms in Vietnam are waiting for the Ho Chi Minh City stock market to reach a new level of maturity with the largest and most successful Vietnamese enterprises listed on the exchange before actively competing for audits for listed companies. Currently the listed companies are generally not large enough to generate an audit fee substantial enough on a risk-adjusted basis to interest international accounting firms.

Johnson (2007) has commented on the back alley trading of unlisted securities in Vietnam. He reports there are 3,600 partially privatized companies issuing shares that are not listed on any official exchange. The Vietnamese government is encouraging this privatization process as a step toward the future listing of many of these enterprises on the stock exchanges in order to increase their access to capital. Individuals who hold such unlisted shares often trade them. Sometimes, the buyers of unlisted stocks rely only on a bill of sale, and fail to register the newly purchased stock. Until recently, the financial statements of such unlisted, but partially privatized companies did not have to be audited or presented to the Vietnamese State Securities Commission. Recently enacted reforms, Johnson notes, do require properly documented audits for the financial statements of unlisted but privatized companies. The financial statements of such companies must now be posted with the Vietnamese Securities Commission.

We do not mean to indicate that the current problems of the Vietnamese stock markets are primarily the result of poor Vietnamese accounting statements. In our opinion, the major causes of the 2008 downturn in the Vietnamese stock markets are the result of the growth of inflation in the Vietnamese economy, and the bursting of a speculative bubble that formed in the Vietnamese securities markets as a result of many individual investors adopting a speculative type investing pattern based on a momentum-based investment strategy.

Concerning these two major issues, the inflation in Vietnam is similar to spurts of inflation that have occurred in other economies that are growing rapidly. The government is now taking active measures to address the inflation problem. As to the speculative investment bubble caused by significant and excessive momentum-based investing, it should be noted that other countries have also had to suffer a sudden downward adjustment in the markets after the collapse of a bubble. There were some warning signs evident that a kind of speculative bubble was forming in the Vietnam stock markets. Johnson (2007) explained that many investors in unlisted stocks relied on a kind of low-information momentum investing strategy. Troung, Veeraraghavan, and Nguyen (2007, p. 6) have prepared an academic working paper that states, "There are significant momentum profits for investment horizons of 1–20 days" on the Ho Chi Minh City stock market. The United States stock exchanges have also recently experienced the bursting of a speculative bubble that had grown on large on speculative investing. Similar to the contemporary situation in Vietnam, this American speculative bubble had in large measure been fueled by the widespread adoption of momentum investing strategies by investors.

Even though we believe that less than perfect accounting was not a major problem in recent stock market losses in Vietnam, we do believe that the long-term improvement of the operating environment for listed stocks in Vietnam ought to include improvements in accounting and financial reporting. For this to proceed efficiently and effectively we also believe that increased international assistance in the development of Vietnamese accountancy may be useful and desirable. However, it is important, in our opinion, that a basic introduction to the appreciation of the history of past international influence on Vietnamese accountancy be available. Attempts to help are unlikely to be successful if outsiders do not appreciate the details of the contemporary Vietnamese environment. A recent example of international assistance to Vietnam was reported in a Vietnam News Briefs (2004) in which it was disclosed that the UK Association of Chartered Certified Accountants (ACCA) will assist the Vietnamese Ministry of Finance to draft changes to Vietnamese accounting and auditing standards. In addition, the Ministry of Finance and the ACCA will jointly provide examinations for auditors, with successful candidates receiving both Vietnamese and ACCA certificates. The international accounting firms in Vietnam have for some time encouraged young Vietnamese professional staff to acquire the ACCA credential. In Vietnam it is considered very positive that the ACCA examinations can be taken in an international accounting standards format.

The next section will review briefly the influence of France on Vietnamese accounting. It will be the first of several sections of this chapter that review specific examples of international influence on Vietnamese accountancy.

International Influence on Vietnamese Accountancy: France

Adams and Do (2003, p. 8) state that historically Vietnamese accountancy in 1954 began with a system inherited from France, the former colonial power in Vietnam. This inherited French accounting system was soon modified because Vietnam installed a socialist economy characterized by state ownership of the means of production and centralized economic planning.

In 1989, after Vietnam had begun efforts at economic reform, the French presented the Vietnamese with a Vietnamese translation of the current French accounting system. Visits to Vietnam were made by French accounting experts in an attempt to get the Vietnamese to adopt the French system. The French also provided training to Vietnamese government-employed auditors and Ministry of Finance employees concerning the French *Plan Comptable General (PCG)*. The impression that some observers had in the early to mid-1990s was that Vietnam was going to adopt the French accounting system for the non-state sector. Laurent Aleonard (1997) wrote a chapter (18) in the John Wiley book *Accounting in the Asia-Pacific Region* edited by Nabil Baydoun, Akira Nishamura, and Roger Willet. In his chapter on Vietnamese accounting, he indicated that Vietnam was going to be adopting an accounting system closely based on the French *PCG*. The book *Accounting in the Asia-Pacific Region* was reviewed by Susan Teo (1999, pp. 459–461) in the *International Journal of Accounting*. She spent one-third of her review discussing Vietnamese accounting and the fact that it was going to follow the French system. Amusingly, at this point in time the idea of adopting the French accounting system had already been abandoned by the Vietnamese Ministry of Finance.

However, Vietnamese accounting still retains elements of French accounting practice. The Vietnamese chart of accounts is largely a Soviet legacy, although the idea of a national chart of accounts can be viewed as a French legacy that was put in place by the French in the colonial period. Also the inclusion of separate income statement sections for operations, financial activities, and "other" activities seems to be the product of French influence. As one might expect, Vietnamese Ministry of Finance officials with recent French training have been more positive about French accounting concepts and approaches than some other officials. Officials at the Vietnamese Ministry of Finance who have had significant Soviet accounting training seem to have similarly favored the Soviet accounting approach at the Ministry of Finance. The next section of the chapter will discuss the very significant influence of Soviet accounting on Vietnamese accounting.

International Influence on Vietnamese Accountancy: The Soviet Union

The Soviet Union's influence on Vietnam in the period from 1954 to 1991 has been intense and comprehensive in scope. Vietnam adopted the political, economic, and military structures of the Soviet Union. Massive amounts of military and civilian equipment were "sold" to Vietnam. For many years this issue was a major item on the diplomatic agenda for Russia when it dealt with Vietnam. This delicate situation was aggravated when in 1996–1997 the Socialist Republic of Vietnam paid millions of dollars of war debt to the United States government that had been owed by the defunct Saigon regime. This cost was a requirement for full diplomatic relations that was established by the United States Congress. In 1998, the Vietnamese Foreign Minister Nguyen Manh Cam met with his counterpart, Yevgeny Primakov, in Moscow. Military issues were no longer important, and it was also decided at this meeting that the debt repayment issues would also no longer be treated as an important issue. The focus of the meeting of prime ministers was to try and increase trade, and to discuss the role of Vietnam as the coordinator for Russian relations with the Association of Southeast Asian Nations (ASEAN) (Nguyen Manh Cam, 1998, p. 5). Vietnam continues to have cordial relationships with Russia, in part because of long-term Vietnamese gratitude for past Soviet help and in part because many senior Vietnamese officials had Soviet training and they continue to maintain long-standing personal relationships.

To fully understand the influence of Soviet accounting on Vietnamese accountancy, it is necessary to understand the economic structures of the former Soviet Union. When "accounting" is translated into English in a Soviet translation, it is translated most often as "cost accounting." For example, Allakhverdyan (1996, p. 132) states that "When Lenin examined the cost accounting method of organizing the activities of state enterprises, he directly linked it with increasing labor productivity, the avoiding of losses, and the profitability of enterprises." Note that Lenin directly suggests that accounting is a tool for increasing profitability, a notion that might surprise uniformed westerners who sometimes assume that Soviet economic institutions were consistently antiprofit. Allakhverdyan (1966, p. 19), explained the role of finance in the Soviet Union, "Finance in the USSR fulfils two basic functions: distribution and control." In the Soviet Union, accounting and its cousin, statistical record keeping, were the basic tools of control in efforts to manage a planned economy.

This control function remains in Vietnamese accounting, as Vu Mong Giao (1997, p. 3) then Vice Minister of Finance has noted, is seen to be the strict stipulation of accounting regulations and methods. For example, there is the statutory requirement for a mandated chart of accounts. There are also detailed regulations for certain journal entries, and very specific requirements to be met by the chief accountant of an enterprise. Article 23 of the Vietnamese Accounting System (Ministry of Finance, 1996) states that "the accounting books must be kept in order in a locked room or cabinet to prevent a loss." Article 24 provides some incentive for a chief accountant to follow Article 23 as well as all other articles. "Any entity or individual who breaks the accounting book policy *must be punished* (emphasis added)."

In recent years as the influence of the Soviet Union in Vietnam has declined, the influence of the United States of America has increased. This is also reflected in the fact that it is the English language that has replaced Russian as the second language of choice in Vietnam. The next section of the chapter discusses the influence of the United States of America on Vietnamese accountancy.

International Influence on Vietnamese Accountancy: The United States of America

In Vietnam, Americans are often viewed as arrogant and difficult. However, they are also viewed as being practical people who are very good at business. Because China to the north is perceived by the Vietnamese as having made significant economic progress by successfully dealing with Americans and imitating some of American economic institutions, it is seen as very possibly wise to do likewise. In addition, America is the home of more overseas Vietnamese than anywhere else, and these individuals are viewed by Vietnam as an important resource for capital and business relationships.

Given, the above, it is no surprise that the United States of America has had some influence on Vietnamese accountancy. The primary American influence seems to have been the adoption some years ago of the cash flow statement. Other aspects of influence would be the format of all the financial statements. Recently, the primary influence of the United States of America on Vietnamese accountancy has probably been the encouragement by the United States government officials and American business interests to adopt the International Financial Reporting Standards (IFRS) of the International Accounting Standards Committee.

American influence probably also is responsible, in part, for the availability for many years of English language translations of Vietnamese accounting standards and regulations. The economic institution related to accountancy that likely has had the most significant American influence have been the stock markets themselves. America is seen as having greatly benefited from its stock markets, and the development of Vietnamese stock markets from their small and obviously experimental beginning is clearly due to American influence and the Vietnamese thinking that the most significant long-term economic progress in Vietnam will not happen without successful stock markets in Vietnam. In some years it will likely be clear that Vietnamese accounting has evolved in important ways in order to serve the financial reporting needs of investors in the stock markets.

Europeans often act overseas through the European Union. This is especially true in Vietnam. The Europeans seek to ensure America's influence in Vietnam does not crowd out or any way limit the influence of individual European countries or the European Union itself. Even though IFRS are similar to United States Generally Accepted Accounting Principles (GAAP), it has always been a European concern to minimize the possibility that GAAP would be dominant in any nation outside of North America. The next section provides an overview of European Union efforts in Vietnam that have focused on Vietnamese accountancy.

International Influence on Vietnamese Accountancy: The European Union and International Financial Reporting Standards

Europeans, especially the France and Germany have been eager that American influence, in particular, be limited in Vietnam. Europeans including Sweden and others have allocated significant financial and other resources to assisting the evolution of the economic institutions of Vietnam in ways the European Union thought appropriate. The European Union made a special attempt to influence the evolution of Vietnamese accountancy through the European Union Technical Assistance

Program – Vietnam (EUROTAP-VIET) of the late 1990s. According to Godden (2000, p. 4), the EUROTAP-VIET programs commenced in September 1995 and ended in June 1998. Some of the most significant and important EURPTAP-VIET programs were programs conducted at many European Universities that were some months long and combined contemporary western accounting, auditing, economics, and finance. They were like a shortened master of accountancy degree program and were offered to Ministry of Finance officials, Ministry of Finance experts, and auditors working in government-owned audit firms. Vietnamese employees of international accounting firms were not eligible. The European Union was attempting to achieve an increased professionalism in Vietnamese accountancy in addition to encouraging the early adoption of International Accounting Standards by Vietnam.

It was a matter of major frustration for the European Union, when in 1997, after years of permitting international companies operating in Vietnam to use international accounting standards, Vietnam imposed on all international companies the requirement to use Vietnamese accounting, clearly rejecting the early adoption of international accounting standards. Phillepe Longerstaey, the French codirector of EUROTAP-VIET responded publicly with considerable frustration. He stated that "we are trying to make them (The Ministry of Finance) understand that they are cutting down the tree they're sitting on," (Dao, 1997, p. 10). The European Union aggressively tried to get the Vietnamese government and the Ministry of Finance to reconsider this rejection of international accounting standards. The Vietnamese government refused to reconsider. This was despite Sir Bryan Carsberg (1997, pp. 13–15) of the International Accounting Standards Committee stating publicly in a very direct way in Hanoi in January 1997 that any country which fails to timely adopt the international accounting standards can expect to pay an economic price. From its perspective, the Ministry of Finance had not rejected International Accounting Standards; they were merely keeping such standards under a continuing and ongoing evaluation. By 1999, some international firms operating in Vietnam were still not using Vietnamese accounting because they either had formal or informal exemptions. By the end of 2000, however, all such exemptions had ceased according to Adams and Do (2003, p. 12).

At the very end of 2001, the first four new Vietnamese Accounting Standards (VAS) based on the IFRS were issued. This was clearly a victory for the European Union, albeit delayed and incomplete. The victory can be viewed as incomplete because the Vietnamese Ministry of Finance did not choose to adopt, as the European Union desired, all IFRS of the international accounting standards without modification. The Vietnamese Ministry of Finance instead endeavored to adopt downsized versions of the certain select existing international standards such that training for professional Vietnamese accountants on these standards would be minimized. The general process was if IFRS offered the financial statement preparer several options on presenting some financial material under the terms of a financial reporting standard, then the Vietnamese Ministry of Finance would likely select only one of the available choices as suitable for Vietnam. To the extent this procedure was followed, Vietnamese accounting would be IFRS compliant. However, certain financial statements that are IFRS-compliant financial statements prepared on the basis of undownsized IFRS would not be compliant with Vietnamese accounting rules. Thus, Vietnam, as well as many other nations, is choosing to create a kind of country-specific jurisdictional specific version of IFRS. This is a frustration for some professional accountants such as Wright (2003, p. 30) who has warned about the suboptimal nature of such "nationally divergent" IFRS. We authors believe that IFRS that is the same everywhere will only occur after a long process of harmonization. Wright and others simply must understand that many nations, such as Vietnam, will choose for their own reasons to exercise their sovereignty by creating IFRS tailored to meet perceived specific national needs and priorities.

The next section is on China and its influence on Vietnamese accountancy. China is a country that is much respected in Vietnam for its power, its ancient culture and its advanced civilization.

International Influence on Vietnamese Accountancy: China

Adams and Do (2003, p. 4) state that that the traditional model of socialist accounting came to Vietnam from both the Soviet Union and China. We view it as a better explanation that the traditional socialist accounting model came from the Soviet Union directly, and also indirectly through China. China is most critical to Vietnamese developments today, and China rightly has a separate section in this chapter because it is the most influential nation for Vietnam that today. China shares a border with Vietnam, and has a similar culture, government, and economic system. It is true to say that American, Accounting and IFRS would have not has so much impact on Vietnam, were it not for China. The simple fact that China has used American and International Financial Reporting systems as a guide in revising its own accounting standards has guaranteed that Vietnam would consider similar behavior.

The concluding section of this chapter consists of a brief conclusion and a thought about possible further research.

Conclusion and Suggestions for Further Research

The Socialist Republic of Vietnam is a developing country seeking to expand its economy for the long-term benefit of the Vietnamese people. Because Vietnam now has functioning stock markets, it is important that Vietnamese accountancy evolve in such a way that stock market investors are better served with improved financial reporting for companies listed on the stock markets. It is, however, useful for any international individual or institution involved in assisting Vietnam with improvements in Vietnamese accountancy to understand how past international influence has impacted Vietnamese accountancy as is outlined in this brief chapter.

Further research is needed in to how Vietnamese accountancy can improve the financial reporting available to investors in shares listed on the Vietnam stock markets. Research is also needed in to how other improvements might made corporate governance in Vietnam.

References

Adams, H. A., & Do, L. T. (2003) *Vietnamese accounting standards* (pp. 4, 8, and 12). Hanoi, Vietnam: ACW.

Aleonard, L. (1997). Systems of accounting in Vietnam. In N. Baydoun, A. Nishimura, & R. Willet (Eds.), *Accounting in the Asia-Pacific Region.*, Singapore: John Wiley & Sons (Asia).

Allakhverdyan, D. A., (1966). *Soviet financial system* (pp. 19 and 132). Moscow: Progress Publishers.

Carsberg, B. (1997). *The role and future plans of the international accounting standards committee.* International Accounting Conference, Hanoi, Vietnam, 13–15 January.

Central Committee at the IX Congress (2001). *Political Report of the Central Committee at the IX Congress.* Retrieved from http://www.vietnamembassy.us/story,php?d=20010420012402& print=yes 6/11/2008.

Dao, A., (1997). EU office to assist trade. *Vietnam Investment Review,* 17–23 March, 10.

Godden, T. (2000). *Financial management and governance issues in Vietnam – volume one* (p. 4). Manila: Asian Development Bank.

Johnson, K., (2007). Vietnam stock-market madness. *Time,* Thursday February 22. Retrieved from http://www.time.com/time/printout/0,8816,1592579,00.html 6/11/2008

Kamm, C., (2004). Stocks: Sleeping dragon. *InternationalReports.net / The Washington Times.* Retrieved from http://www.internationalreports.net/asiapacific/Vietnam/2004/stock.html

Kazmin, A., (2008) Inflation juggernaut bears down on Vietnam bourse. *Financial Times* Thursday June 19, 26.

Ministry of Finance. (1996). Vietnamese accounting system. Hanoi: Finance Publishing House, English translation by Coopers & Lybrand – AISC

McCool, G. (2008). Early optimism dims for Vietnam stock, market. *International Herald Tribune,* Monday January 28. Retrived from http://www.iht.com/bin/printfriendly.php?id=9522471.

Nguyen Manh Cam, (1998). New heights in Vietnam Russia relations.*"Vietnam Economic News,* 9 May, 5.

Teo, S. (1999). Book review: Accounting in the Asian Pacific Region. *The International Journal of Accountancy,* 34(3), 459–461

Troung, C., Veeraraghavan, M., & Nguyen, M. T. T. (2007). Delayed price discovery and momentum strategies: Evidence from Vietnam. 2007 Working paper from the Department of Accounting and Finance of the University of Auckland, New Zealand, p. 6.

Vietnam News Briefs. (2004). Banking and finance: UK's ACCA helps Vietnam draft accounting, auditing standards. June 1, 2004, Financial Times Information Lexis Nexis Document

Wright, I., (2003). Avoid Interpretations GAAP Trap. *World Watch,* (1), 2003 p. 30.

Part III
Country Studies

Chapter 20
An Overview of Corporate Governance Practices in Bhutan

Robert W. McGee

Introduction

The World Bank has published a series of reports on corporate governance as part of its project on the *Reports on the Observance of Standards and Codes* (ROSC). The corporate governance principles in its ROSC are benchmarked against the OECD's *Principles of Corporate Governance* (OECD, 2004). The main categories of principles are discussed below.

Methodology

The corporate governance topics discussed in the World Bank's ROSC were classified into categories based on the extent of compliance with the OECD's *Principles of Corporate Governance* (OECD, 2004). Points were then assigned to each category as follows:

O = Observed = 5 points
LO = Largely Observed = 4 points
PO = Partially Observed = 3 points
MNO = Materially Not Observed = 2 points
NO = Not Observed = 1 point

Summary of Findings

Table 20.1 summarizes the scores in the various categories. The table categorizes compliance with corporate governance principles into five categories.

R.W. McGee (✉)
Florida International University, Miami, FL, USA
e-mail: bob414@hotmail.com

R.W. McGee (ed.), *Corporate Governance in Developing Economies*,
DOI 10.1007/978-0-387-84833-4_20, © Springer Science+Business Media, LLC 2009

Table 20.1 Summary of scores by category

		O	LO	PO	MNO	NO
I	**Rights of shareholders**					
A	Protect shareholder rights			X		
B	Shareholders have the right to participate in, and to be sufficiently informed on, decisions concerning fundamental corporate changes			X		
C	Shareholders should have the opportunity to participate effectively and vote in general shareholder meetings				X	
D	Capital structures and arrangements that allow disproportionate control			X		
E	Markets for corporate control should be allowed to function in an efficient and transparent manner					X
F	Shareholders should consider the costs and benefits of exercising their voting rights			X		
II	**Equitable treatment of shareholders**					
A	The corporate governance framework should ensure the equitable treatment of all shareholders, including minority and foreign shareholders			X		
B	Insider trading and abusive self-dealing should be prohibited			X		
C	Board members and managers should be required to disclose material interests in transactions or matters affecting the corporation			X		
III	**Role of stakeholders in corporate governance**					
A	The corporate governance framework should recognize the rights of stakeholders			X		
B	Stakeholders should have the opportunity to obtain effective redress for violation of their rights			X		
C	The corporate governance framework should permit performance-enhancement mechanisms for stakeholder participation			X		
D	Stakeholders should have access to relevant information				X	
IV	**Disclosure and transparency**					
A	The corporate governance framework should ensure that timely and accurate disclosure is made on all material matters			X		
B	Information should be prepared, audited, and disclosed in accordance with high quality standards of accounting, financial and nonfinancial disclosure, and audit			X		
C	An independent audit should be conducted by an independent auditor			X		
D	Channels for disseminating information should provide for fair, timely, and cost-effective access to relevant information by users				X	
V	**The responsibility of the board**					
A	Board members should act on a fully informed basis, in good faith, with due diligence and care, and in the best interests of the company and the shareholders		X			

Table 20.1 (continued)

		O	LO	PO	MNO	NO
B	The board should treat all shareholders fairly			X		
C	The board should ensure compliance with applicable law and take into account the interests of stakeholders			X		
D	The board should fulfill certain board functions			X		
E	The board should be able to exercise objective judgment on corporate affairs independent from management				X	
F	Board members should have access to accurate, relevant, and timely information			X		

Table 20.2 Corporate governance scores

Category	Total points	Number of items	Average
Rights of shareholders	15	6	2.50
Equitable treatment of shareholders	9	3	3.00
Role of stakeholders in corporate governance	11	4	2.75
Disclosure and transparency	11	4	2.75
The responsibility of the board	18	6	3.00
Overall average			2.78

Table 20.2 shows the scores for each subcategory. The overall average was 2.78.

The chart below shows the relative scores graphically. As can be seen, none of the scores are particularly high, but the scores for treatment and board are relatively high.

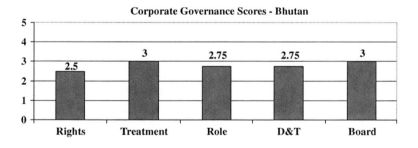

Corporate Governance Scores - Bhutan

Recommendations

The ROSC made several recommendations. The Companies Act needs to be revised to have a new law for capital markets. Enforcement needs to be strengthened. There should be more protection of shareholder rights and more transparency. The registrar needs more resources in order to inspect all companies annually.

Other institutions also need to be strengthened in order to have a strong and functioning capital market. Judges need better training in order to more fully understand capital market concepts.

A code of corporate governance should be created that supplements the Companies Act. It should also raise awareness of corporate governance issues and hopefully result in spreading good corporate governance practices.

The law should make it easier for foreign investors to invest in Bhutan. The fact that Bhutan has a small capital market makes matters more difficult, but foreign participation could be facilitated by reform of the process.

Shareholders need to be protected from abusive transactions. More disclosure is needed to determine who the large shareholders are. All documents filed with the registrar should be placed on the company's website as a means of increasing transparency. There should be more training programs for accountants and auditors. Domestic accounting and audit capacity needs to be expanded.

There should be more independent directors. Training programs are necessary to educate directors as to their duties and responsibilities.

References

OECD. (2004). *OECD Principles of Corporate Governance.* Paris: Author. Retrieved from www.oecd.org/dataoecd/32/18/31557724.pdf.

World Bank. (2006). *Report on the Observance of Standards and Codes (ROSC), Corporate Governance Country Assessment: Bhutan,. December.*

World Bank. (2008). *Reports on the Observance of Standards and Codes (ROSC) for Corporate Governance.* Retrieved from www.worldbank.org/ifa/rosc_cg.html

Chapter 21
An Overview of Corporate Governance Practices in India

Robert W. McGee

Introduction

The World Bank has published a series of reports on corporate governance as part of its project on the *Reports on the Observance of Standards and Codes* (ROSC). The corporate governance principles in its ROSC are benchmarked against the OECD's *Principles of Corporate Governance* (OECD, 2004). The main categories of principles are discussed below.

Methodology

The corporate governance topics discussed in the World Bank's ROSC were classified into categories based on the extent of compliance with the OECD's *Principles of Corporate Governance* (OECD, 2004). Points were then assigned to each category, as follows:

O = Observed = 5 points
LO = Largely Observed = 4 points
PO = Partially Observed = 3 points
MNO = Materially Not Observed = 2 points
NO = Not Observed = 1 point

Summary of Findings

Table 21.1 summarizes the scores in the various categories. The table categorizes compliance with corporate governance principles into five categories.

R.W. McGee (✉)
Florida International University, Miami, FL, USA
e-mail: bob414@hotmail.com

R.W. McGee (ed.), *Corporate Governance in Developing Economies*,
DOI 10.1007/978-0-387-84833-4_21, © Springer Science+Business Media, LLC 2009

Table 21.1 Summary of scores by category

		O	LO	PO	MNO	NO
I	**Rights of shareholders**					
A	Protect shareholder rights	X				
B	Shareholders have the right to participate in, and to be sufficiently informed on, decisions concerning fundamental corporate changes	X				
C	Shareholders should have the opportunity to participate effectively and vote in general shareholder meetings	X				
D	Capital structures and arrangements that allow disproportionate control		X			
E	Markets for corporate control should be allowed to function in an efficient and transparent manner	X				
F	Shareholders should consider the costs and benefits of exercising their voting rights				X	
II	**Equitable treatment of shareholders**					
A	The corporate governance framework should ensure the equitable treatment of all shareholders, including minority and foreign shareholders			X		
B	Insider trading and abusive self-dealing should be prohibited			X		
C	Board members and managers should be required to disclose material interests in transactions or matters affecting the corporation			X		
III	**Role of stakeholders in corporate governance**					
A	The corporate governance framework should recognize the rights of stakeholders	X				
B	Stakeholders should have the opportunity to obtain effective redress for violation of their rights			X		
C	The corporate governance framework should permit performance-enhancement mechanisms for stakeholder participation	X				
D	Stakeholders should have access to relevant information	X				
IV	**Disclosure and transparency**					
A	The corporate governance framework should ensure that timely and accurate disclosure is made on all material matters			X		
B	Information should be prepared, audited, and disclosed in accordance with high quality standards of accounting, financial and nonfinancial disclosure, and audit			X		
C	An independent audit should be conducted by an independent auditor				X	
D	Channels for disseminating information should provide for fair, timely, and cost-effective access to relevant information by users	X				
V	**The responsibility of the board**					
A	Board members should act on a fully informed basis, in good faith, with due diligence and care, and in the best interests of the company and the shareholders			X		
B	The board should treat all shareholders fairly			X		

Table 21.1 (continued)

		O	LO	PO	MNO	NO
C	The board should ensure compliance with applicable law and take into account the interests of stakeholders	X				
D	The board should fulfill certain board functions		X			
E	The board should be able to exercise objective judgment on corporate affairs independent from management			X		
F	Board members should have access to accurate, relevant, and timely information		X			

Table 21.2 Corporate governance scores

Category	Total points	Number of items	Average
Rights of shareholders	26	6	4.33
Equitable treatment of shareholders	9	3	3.00
Role of stakeholders in corporate governance	18	4	4.50
Disclosure and transparency	15	4	3.75
The responsibility of the board	25	6	4.17
Overall average			4.04

Table 21.2 shows the scores for each subcategory. The weighted average was a relatively high at 4.04.

The graph below shows the relative scores. Three of the scores are above 4.00. The best score is in the category of Role.

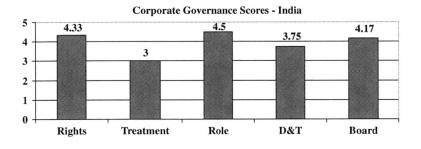

Recommendations

The ROSC made several recommendations. Some of the sanction and enforcement rules need to be adjusted, since they are inadequate at present. Monetary sanctions are especially in need of adjustment.

Sanctions imposed by the stock exchange include warnings, suspension of trading and delisting, but not fines. The ROSC recommends the ability to impose fines that are sufficiently high to deter noncompliance.

There is a three-tiered regulatory mechanism in place. The stock exchange and two other entities share jurisdiction over listed companies. This structure results in weak performance and creates the possibility of regulatory arbitrage. The ROSC recommends clarifying responsibilities as a means of strengthening the regulatory structure.

The present system includes a high degree of rubber stamping of management decisions by the board. The ROSC recommends moving away from this rubber-stamping approach, but in order to do so, board members must have a clear idea of what is expected of them. The structure could be improved if the law and relevant regulations made it clear what the responsibility of directors are, so they could know what is expected of them.

Institutional investors could play a positive role if they took a more active interest in the companies they invest in. At present, they tend to be apathetic when it comes to voting. They prefer exit over voice if they are dissatisfied with a corporation's policies or performance. Institutional investors that act in a fiduciary capacity should be encouraged to attend shareholder meetings and vote. Doing so might tend to increase shareholder activism, which is an important impetus for change.

References

OECD. (2004). *OECD Principles of Corporate Governance.* Paris: Author. Retrieved from www.oecd.org/dataoecd/32/18/31557724.pdf.

World Bank. (2004). *Report on the Observance of Standards and Codes (ROSC), Corporate Governance Country Assessment: India.*

World Bank. (2008). *Reports on the Observance of Standards and Codes (ROSC) for Corporate Governance.* Retrieved from www.worldbank.org/ifa/rosc_cg.html.

Chapter 22
An Overview of Corporate Governance Practices in Indonesia

Robert W. McGee

Introduction

The World Bank has published a series of reports on corporate governance as part of its project on the *Reports on the Observance of Standards and Codes* (ROSC). The corporate governance principles in its ROSC are benchmarked against the OECD's *Principles of Corporate Governance* (OECD, 2004). The main categories of principles are discussed below.

Methodology

The corporate governance topics discussed in the World Bank's ROSC were classified into categories based on the extent of compliance with the OECD's *Principles of Corporate Governance* (OECD, 2004). Points were then assigned to each category, as follows:

O = Observed = 5 points
LO = Largely Observed = 4 points
PO = Partially Observed = 3 points
MNO = Materially Not Observed = 2 points
NO = Not Observed = 1 point

Summary of Findings

Table 22.1 summarizes the scores in the various categories. The table categorizes compliance with corporate governance principles into five categories.

R.W. McGee (✉)
Florida International University, Miami, FL, USA
e-mail: bob414@hotmail.com

R.W. McGee (ed.), *Corporate Governance in Developing Economies*,
DOI 10.1007/978-0-387-84833-4_22, © Springer Science+Business Media, LLC 2009

Table 22.1 Summary of scores by category

		O	LO	PO	MNO	NO
I	**Rights of shareholders**					
A	Protect shareholder rights			X		
B	Shareholders have the right to participate in, and to be sufficiently informed on, decisions concerning fundamental corporate changes		X			
C	Shareholders should have the opportunity to participate effectively and vote in general shareholder meetings		X			
D	Capital structures and arrangements that allow disproportionate control				X	
E	Markets for corporate control should be allowed to function in an efficient and transparent manner				X	
F	Shareholders should consider the costs and benefits of exercising their voting rights				X	
II	**Equitable treatment of shareholders**					
A	The corporate governance framework should ensure the equitable treatment of all shareholders, including minority and foreign shareholders			X		
B	Insider trading and abusive self-dealing should be prohibited			X		
C	Board members and managers should be required to disclose material interests in transactions or matters affecting the corporation			X		
III	**Role of stakeholders in corporate governance**					
A	The corporate governance framework should recognize the rights of stakeholders			X		
B	Stakeholders should have the opportunity to obtain effective redress for violation of their rights			X		
C	The corporate governance framework should permit performance-enhancement mechanisms for stakeholder participation			X		
D	Stakeholders should have access to relevant information			X		
IV	**Disclosure and transparency**					
A	The corporate governance framework should ensure that timely and accurate disclosure is made on all material matters			X		
B	Information should be prepared, audited, and disclosed in accordance with high quality standards of accounting, financial and nonfinancial disclosure, and audit			X		
C	An independent audit should be conducted by an independent auditor.			X		
D	Channels for disseminating information should provide for fair, timely, and cost-effective access to relevant information by users			X		

Table 22.1 (continued)

		O	LO	PO	MNO	NO
V	**The responsibility of the board**					
A	Board members should act on a fully informed basis, in good faith, with due diligence and care, and in the best interests of the company and the shareholders			X		
B	The board should treat all shareholders fairly			X		
C	The board should ensure compliance with applicable law and take into account the interests of stakeholders			X		
D	The board should fulfill certain board functions			X		
E	The board should be able to exercise objective judgment on corporate affairs independent from management			X		
F	Board members should have access to accurate, relevant, and timely information			X		

Table 22.2 shows the scores for each subcategory. The weighted average score was 2.96.

The graph below shows the relative scores. None of the scores were particularly high. Four of the scores were identical (3.00) and the other score was only slightly lower (2.83).

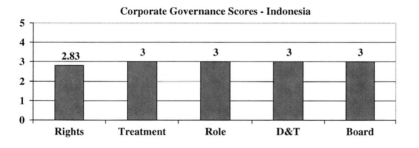

Corporate Governance Scores - Indonesia

Table 22.2 Corporate governance scores

Category	Total points	Number of items	Average
Rights of shareholders	17	6	2.83
Equitable treatment of shareholders	9	3	3.00
Role of stakeholders in corporate governance	12	4	3.00
Disclosure and transparency	12	4	3.00
The responsibility of the board	18	6	3.00
Overall average			2.96

Recommendations

The ROSC made several recommendations. In the area of basic shareholder rights, minority shareholders should have a greater voice in the selection of directors. Cumulative voting was recommended as a means of achieving this goal. Listed companies should establish nomination and remuneration committees.

Companies should strengthen shareholder access to information, especially for the items that are to be discussed at the general shareholders' meeting. Minority shareholders should be able to make proposals in connection with that meeting.

There should be adequate disclosure where disproportionate control exists. A study should be conducted to determine how the market for corporate control can work more efficiently. Institutional voters should disclose their voting policy.

In order to achieve the goal of treating all shareholders equally, steps should be taken to make it easier for shareholders and investors to file class action lawsuits. The threshold for filing lawsuits should also be lowered.

As a means of respecting stakeholder rights, there should be a requirement that pledged shares be reported and registered in the company share register. Information should be available and accessible to all stakeholders. Publication of annual reports and other relevant information should be posted on the company's website. Companies should fully adopt International Financial Reporting Standards and International Standards on Auditing. In order to make the disclosure of financial data more timely, companies should consider reducing the period for submission of their annual reports.

References

OECD. (2004). *OECD Principles of Corporate Governance.* Paris: Author. Retrieved from www. oecd.org/dataoecd/32/18/31557724.pdf.

World Bank. (2004). *Report on the Observance of Standards and Codes (ROSC), Corporate Governance Country Assessment: Republic of Indonesia..*

World Bank. (2008). *Reports on the Observance of Standards and Codes (ROSC) for Corporate Governance.* Retrieved from www.worldbank.org/ifa/rosc_cg.html.

Chapter 23
An Overview of Corporate Governance Practices in the Republic of Korea

Robert W. McGee

Introduction

The World Bank has published a series of reports on corporate governance as part of its project on the *Reports on the Observance of Standards and Codes* (ROSC). The corporate governance principles in its ROSC are benchmarked against the OECD's *Principles of Corporate Governance* (OECD, 2004). The main categories of principles are discussed below.

Methodology

The corporate governance topics discussed in the World Bank's ROSC were classified into categories based on the extent of compliance with the OECD's *Principles of Corporate Governance* (OECD, 2004). Points were then assigned to each category, as follows:

O = Observed = 5 points
LO = Largely Observed = 4 points
PO = Partially Observed = 3 points
MNO = Materially Not Observed = 2 points
NO = Not Observed = 1 point

Summary of Findings

Table 23.1 summarizes the scores in the various categories. The table categorizes compliance with corporate governance principles into five categories.

R.W. McGee (✉)
Florida International University, Miami, FL, USA
e-mail: bob414@hotmail.com

R.W. McGee (ed.), *Corporate Governance in Developing Economies*,
DOI 10.1007/978-0-387-84833-4_23, © Springer Science+Business Media, LLC 2009

Table 23.1 Summary of scores by category

		O	LO	PO	MNO	NO
I	**Rights of shareholders**					
A	Protect shareholder rights		X			
B	Shareholders have the right to participate in, and to be sufficiently informed on, decisions concerning fundamental corporate changes	X				
C	Shareholders should have the opportunity to participate effectively and vote in general shareholder meetings		X			
D	Capital structures and arrangements that allow disproportionate control		X			
E	Markets for corporate control should be allowed to function in an efficient and transparent manner		X			
F	Shareholders should consider the costs and benefits of exercising their voting rights			X		
II	**Equitable treatment of shareholders**					
A	The corporate governance framework should ensure the equitable treatment of all shareholders, including minority and foreign shareholders		X			
B	Insider trading and abusive self-dealing should be prohibited			X		
C	Board members and managers should be required to disclose material interests in transactions or matters affecting the corporation			X		
III	**Role of stakeholders in corporate governance**					
A	The corporate governance framework should recognize the rights of stakeholders			X		
B	Stakeholders should have the opportunity to obtain effective redress for violation of their rights	X				
C	The corporate governance framework should permit performance-enhancement mechanisms for stakeholder participation		X			
D	Stakeholders should have access to relevant information	X				
IV	**Disclosure and transparency**					
A	The corporate governance framework should ensure that timely and accurate disclosure is made on all material matters		X			
B	Information should be prepared, audited, and disclosed in accordance with high quality standards of accounting, financial and nonfinancial disclosure, and audit			X		
C	An independent audit should be conducted by an independent auditor		X			
D	Channels for disseminating information should provide for fair, timely, and cost-effective access to relevant information by users	X				

Table 23.1 (continued)

		O	LO	PO	MNO	NO
V	**The responsibility of the board**					
A	Board members should act on a fully informed basis, in good faith, with due diligence and care, and in the best interests of the company and the shareholders	X				
B	The board should treat all shareholders fairly			X		
C	The board should ensure compliance with applicable law and take into account the interests of stakeholders			X		
D	The board should fulfill certain board functions	X				
E	The board should be able to exercise objective judgment on corporate affairs independent from management			X		
F	Board members should have access to accurate, relevant, and timely information.			X		

Table 23.2 shows the scores for each subcategory. The weighted average score was 3.78.

The graph below shows the relative scores. Role had the highest score (4.25). All of the scores were above 3.00.

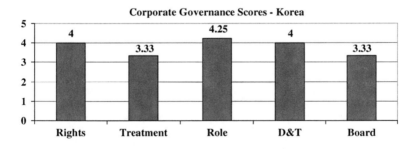

Corporate Governance Scores - Korea

Table 23.2 Corporate governance scores

Category	Total points	Number of items	Average
Rights of shareholders	24	6	4.00
Equitable treatment of shareholders	10	3	3.33
Role of stakeholders in corporate governance	17	4	4.25
Disclosure and transparency	16	4	4.00
The responsibility of the board	20	6	3.33
Overall average			3.78

Recommendations

The ROSC made several recommendations. Companies should give minority share-holders a greater voice in corporate governance. One area where more voice is needed is in the selection of directors. Cumulative voting is suggested as a way of achieving this goal. Ways should be found to facilitate foreign investor voting.

The process for nominating independent directors should be improved. There should be a requirement that at least two-thirds of outside nomination committees should be independent directors.

Shareholders and investors should be able to file class action lawsuits against directors, managers, and auditors for violations of the law and breaches of duty. Companies should consider the possibility of allowing shareholders to vote electronically. There should be full disclosure for related party transactions. Self-dealing and insider trading rules should be strengthened by excluding inside directors from making decisions that involve potential conflict of interest or related party transactions.

Companies should improve their accounting standards and auditing practices and should move in the direction of international standards and practices. They should improve the quality of disclosure in their quarterly and annual reports, especially in the areas of related party transactions, conflicts of interest, and nonfinancial information.

Companies should improve the effectiveness of their audit committees in ways that are consistent with international best practices. Statutory auditors should be replaced with audit committees in the case of smaller companies. The knowledge and skills of audit committees should be upgraded.

References

OECD. (2004). *OECD Principles of Corporate Governance*. Paris: Author. Retrieved from www.oecd.org/dataoecd/32/18/31557724.pdf.

World Bank. (2003). *Report on the Observance of Standards and Codes (ROSC), Corporate Governance Country Assessment: Republic of Korea.*.

World Bank. (2008). *Reports on the Observance of Standards and Codes (ROSC) for Corporate Governance*. Retrieved from www.worldbank.org/ifa/rosc_cg.html.

Chapter 24
An Overview of Corporate Governance Practices in Malaysia

Robert W. McGee

Introduction

The World Bank has published a series of reports on corporate governance as part of its project on the *Reports on the Observance of Standards and Codes* (ROSC). The corporate governance principles in its ROSC are benchmarked against the OECD's *Principles of Corporate Governance* (OECD, 2004). The main categories of principles are discussed below.

Methodology

The corporate governance topics discussed in the World Bank's ROSC were classified into categories based on the extent of compliance with the OECD's *Principles of Corporate Governance* (OECD, 2004). Points were then assigned to each category, as follows:

O = Observed = 5 points
LO = Largely Observed = 4 points
PO = Partially Observed = 3 points
MNO = Materially Not Observed = 2 points
NO = Not Observed = 1 point

Summary of Findings

Table 24.1 summarizes the scores in the various categories. The table categorizes compliance with corporate governance principles into five categories.

R.W. McGee (✉)
Florida International University, Miami, FL, USA
e-mail: bob414@hotmail.com

R.W. McGee (ed.), *Corporate Governance in Developing Economies*,
DOI 10.1007/978-0-387-84833-4_24, © Springer Science+Business Media, LLC 2009

Table 24.1 Summary of scores by category

		O	LO	PO	MNO	NO
I	**Rights of shareholders**					
A	Protect shareholder rights		X			
B	Shareholders have the right to participate in, and to be sufficiently informed on, decisions concerning fundamental corporate changes			X		
C	Shareholders should have the opportunity to participate effectively and vote in general shareholder meetings		X			
D	Capital structures andarrangements that allow disproportionate control		X			
E	Markets for corporate control should be allowed to function in an efficient and transparent manner		X			
F	Shareholders should consider the costs and benefits of exercising their voting rights			X		
II	**Equitable treatment of shareholders**					
A	The corporate governance framework should ensure the equitable treatment of all shareholders, including minority and foreign shareholders			X		
B	Insider trading and abusive self-dealing should be prohibited		X			
C	Board members and managers should be required to disclose material interests in transactions or matters affecting the corporation		X			
III	**Role of stakeholders in corporate governance**					
A	The corporate governance framework should recognize the rights of stakeholders		X			
B	Stakeholders should have the opportunity to obtain effective redress for violation of their rights		X			
C	The corporate governance framework should permit performance-enhancement mechanisms for stakeholder participation		X			

Table 24.1 (continued)

		O	LO	PO	MNO	NO
D	Stakeholders should have access to relevant information		X			
IV	**Disclosure and transparency**					
A	The corporate governance framework should ensure that timely and accurate disclosure is made on all material matters		X			
B	Information should be prepared, audited, and disclosed in accordance with high quality standards of accounting, financial and nonfinancial disclosure, and audit	X				
C	An independent audit should be conducted by an independent auditor		X			
D	Channels for disseminating information should provide for fair, timely, and cost-effective access to relevant information by users		X			
V	**The responsibility of the board**					
A	Board members should act on a fully informed basis, in good faith, with due diligence and care, and in the best interests of the company and the shareholders			X		
B	The board should treat all shareholders fairly		X			
C	The board should ensure compliance with applicable law and take into account the interests of stakeholders			X		
D	The board should fulfill certain board functions		X			
E	The board should be able to exercise objective judgment on corporate affairs independent from management		X			
F	Board members should have access to accurate, relevant, and timely information		X			

Table 24.2 Corporate governance scores

Category	Total points	Number of items	Average
Rights of shareholders	22	6	3.67
Equitable treatment of shareholders	11	3	3.67
Role of stakeholders in corporate governance	16	4	4.00
Disclosure and transparency	17	4	4.25
The responsibility of the board	22	6	3.67
Overall average			3.83

Table 24.2 shows the scores for each subcategory. The weighted average score was 3.83.

The graph below shows the relative scores. All the scores were above 3.50. The highest score was in the category of Disclosure and Transparency.

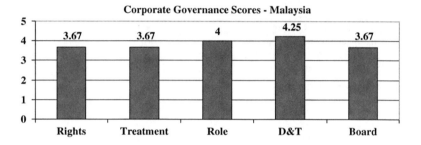

Corporate Governance Scores - Malaysia

Recommendations

The ROSC made several recommendations. Directors who are interested parties in related party transaction are at present not required to refrain from voting on the measure. The ROSC recommends that they be prevented from voting in such cases.

The present insider trading rules allow penalties of up to three times the inside trader's gain. The law includes civil penalties that allow those who suffer losses from insider trading to sue for full compensation. Such penalties should also be available for related party transactions, but they are not at present.

This particular recommendation requires further comment by the author. While related party transactions should be fully disclosed and the potential for abuses should be minimized, the penalties for engaging in insider trading are onerous, given the research on insider trading that seems to indicate that insider trading is often beneficial to both markets and shareholders. Research on this point has been cited elsewhere and will not be repeated here (McGee, 2008).

The ROSC also suggests making it easier for shareholders to vote by allowing voting by mail and proxy voting. It also suggests mandating longer notice periods and providing sufficient information for shareholders to make voting decisions.

The quality and effectiveness of the annual general meeting should also be improved. Doing so would help motivate institutional investors to attend and participate in those meetings. Attendance is not high at present and attendance is dominated by retail investors. The ROSC recommends adopting an approach similar to that of the Institute of Chartered Secretaries in the United Kingdom.

The ROSC recommends considering amending the law to provide for cumulative voting to choose company directors. Doing so would provide a stronger voice for minority shareholders. The law should require interested directors to abstain from voting on transactions in which they have an interest.

The external auditors should work more closely with the audit committee. At present there is a tendency to work more with management. There should be full disclosure of fees paid to auditors for nonaudit work.

Regulators should be more independent, both in appearance and fact, in order to maintain credibility with the public.

At present it is difficult for investors to institute actions against directors for breach of fiduciary duty. It is also difficult to bring derivative suits. The ROSC recommends making it easier to file such suits.

References

McGee, R. W. (2008). Insider trading regulation in transition economies. In R. W. McGee (Ed.), *Corporate governance in transition economies.* New York: Springer.

OECD. (2004). *OECD Principles of Corporate Governance.* Paris: Author. Retrieved from www. oecd.org/dataoecd/32/18/31557724.pdf.

World Bank. (2005). *Report on the Observance of Standards and Codes (ROSC), Corporate Governance Country Assessment: Malaysia..*

World Bank. (2008). *Reports on the Observance of Standards and Codes (ROSC) for Corporate Governance.* Retrieved from www.worldbank.org/ifa/rosc_cg.html.

Chapter 25
An Overview of Corporate Governance Practices in Nepal

Robert W. McGee

Introduction

The World Bank has published a series of reports on corporate governance as part of its project on the *Reports on the Observance of Standards and Codes* (ROSC). The corporate governance principles in its ROSC are benchmarked against the OECD's *Principles of Corporate Governance* (OECD, 2004). The main categories of principles are discussed below.

Methodology

The corporate governance topics discussed in the World Bank's ROSC were classified into categories based on the extent of compliance with the OECD's *Principles of Corporate Governance* (OECD, 2004). Points were then assigned to each category, as follows:

O = Observed = 5 points
LO = Largely Observed = 4 points
PO = Partially Observed = 3 points
MNO = Materially Not Observed = 2 points
NO = Not Observed = 1 point

Summary of Findings

Table 25.1 summarizes the scores in the various categories. The table categorizes compliance with corporate governance principles into five categories.

R.W. McGee (✉)
Florida International University, Miami, FL, USA
e-mail: bob414@hotmail.com

R.W. McGee (ed.), *Corporate Governance in Developing Economies*,
DOI 10.1007/978-0-387-84833-4_25, © Springer Science+Business Media, LLC 2009

Table 25.1 Summary of scores by category

		O	LO	PO	MNO	NO
I	**Rights of shareholders**					
A	Protect shareholder rights				X	
B	Shareholders have the right to participate in, and to be sufficiently informed on, decisions concerning fundamental corporate changes		X			
C	Shareholders should have the opportunity to participate effectively and vote in general shareholder meetings			X		
D	Capital structures and arrangements that allow disproportionate control				X	
E	Markets for corporate control should be allowed to function in an efficient and transparent manner				X	
F	Shareholders should consider the costs and benefits of exercising their voting rights				X	
II	**Equitable treatment of shareholders**					
A	The corporate governance framework should ensure the equitable treatment of all shareholders, including minority and foreign shareholders				X	
B	Insider trading and abusive self-dealing should be prohibited			X		
C	Board members and managers should be required to disclose material interests in transactions or matters affecting the corporation				X	
III	**Role of stakeholders in corporate governance**					
A	The corporate governance framework should recognize the rights of stakeholders		X			
B	Stakeholders should have the opportunity to obtain effective redress for violation of their rights		X			
C	The corporate governance framework should permit performance-enhancement mechanisms for stakeholder participation				X	
D	Stakeholders should have access to relevant information			X		
IV	**Disclosure and transparency**					
A	The corporate governance framework should ensure that timely and accurate disclosure is made on all material matters				X	
B	Information should be prepared, audited, and disclosed in accordance with high quality standards of accounting, financial and nonfinancial disclosure, and audit				X	
C	An independent audit should be conducted by an independent auditor				X	
D	Channels for disseminating information should provide for fair, timely, and cost-effective access to relevant information by users			X		

Table 25.1 (continued)

		O	LO	PO	MNO	NO
V	**The responsibility of the board**					
A	Board members should act on a fully informed basis, in good faith, with due diligence and care, and in the best interests of the company and the shareholders				X	
B	The board should treat all shareholders fairly		X			
C	The board should ensure compliance with applicable law and take into account the interests of stakeholders		X			
D	The board should fulfill certain board functions			X		
E	The board should be able to exercise objective judgment on corporate affairs independent from management		X			
F	Board members should have access to accurate, relevant, and timely information		X			

Table 25.2 Corporate governance scores

Category	Total points	Number of items	Average
Rights of shareholders	15	6	2.50
Equitable treatment of shareholders	7	3	2.33
Role of stakeholders in corporate governance	13	4	3.25
Disclosure and transparency	9	4	2.25
The responsibility of the board	21	6	3.50
Overall average			2.83

Table 25.2 shows the scores for each subcategory. The overall average is 2.83.

The graph below shows the corporate governance scores. Three categories are below 3.00. The best score is 3.5 in the Board category.

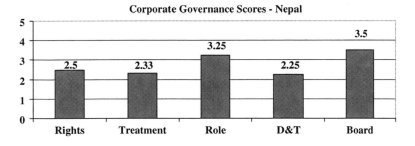

Corporate Governance Scores - Nepal

Recommendations

The ROSC made several recommendations. Nepal has started the reform process and the ROSC urges a continuation of the reforms. It recommends giving priority to strengthening the institutions that are charged with enforcing the new reform legislation. It recommends major reform of the Office of the Company Registrar (OCR), the institution that regulates corporate governance. It should be both willing and able to demand that companies hold annual general shareholder meeting and that they file the required documents. It should have both the resources and the political independence needed to fulfill its mission. The Securities and Exchange Board of Nepal needs similar independence and support.

The Nepal Stock Exchange should be privatized. Share registration is currently on a company basis. ROSC recommends replacing that with a centralized share registry, which would reduce conflicts of interest, reduce market abuses, and facilitate settlement.

The annual general shareholders' meeting also needs to be reformed. More emphasis should be placed on governance and less emphasis should be placed on using the meeting as an opportunity to receive gifts. The ROSC recommends banning all gifts at the meeting, including catered meals. Although some shareholders benefit by present practices, all shareholders have to pay the cost. The focus on gift giving distracts from the corporate governance function, which should be one of the main reasons for holding such meetings.

Shareholder rights may also be protected by creating transparent procedures for approving major and related party transactions. Shareholders should receive adequate notice and there should be direct shareholder approval for the most significant transactions.

The national standards for accounting and auditing should be mandatory for all listed companies to ensure transparency. Many more licensed accountants and auditors will be needed to implement those standards. They will need training. The national standard setting body should issue standards that are close to those of International Financial Reporting Standards.

References

OECD. (2004). *OECD Principles of Corporate Governance*. Paris: Author. Retrieved from www. oecd.org/dataoecd/32/18/31557724.pdf

World Bank. (2005). *Report on the Observance of Standards and Codes (ROSC), Corporate Governance Country Assessment: Nepal.*

World Bank. (2008). *Reports on the Observance of Standards and Codes (ROSC) for Corporate Governance*. Retrieved from www.worldbank.org/ifa/rosc_cg.html

Chapter 26
An Overview of Corporate Governance Practices in Pakistan

Robert W. McGee

Introduction

The World Bank has published a series of reports on corporate governance as part of its project on the *Reports on the Observance of Standards and Codes* (ROSC). The corporate governance principles in its ROSC are benchmarked against the OECD's *Principles of Corporate Governance* (OECD, 2004). The main categories of principles are discussed below.

Methodology

The corporate governance topics discussed in the World Bank's ROSC were classified into categories based on the extent of compliance with the OECD's *Principles of Corporate Governance* (OECD, 2004). Points were then assigned to each category, as follows:

    O=Observed=5 points
    LO=Largely Observed=4 points
    PO=Partially Observed=3 points
    MNO=Materially Not Observed=2 points
    NO=Not Observed=1 point

Summary of Findings

Table 26.1 summarizes the scores in the various categories. The table categorizes compliance with corporate governance principles into five categories.

R.W. McGee (✉)
Florida International University, Miami, FL, USA
e-mail: bob414@hotmail.com

R.W. McGee (ed.), *Corporate Governance in Developing Economies*,
DOI 10.1007/978-0-387-84833-4_26, © Springer Science+Business Media, LLC 2009

Table 26.1 Summary of scores by category

		O	LO	PO	MNO	NO
I	**Rights of shareholders**					
A	Protect shareholder rights		X			
B	Shareholders have the right to participate in, and to be sufficiently informed on, decisions concerning fundamental corporate changes		X			
C	Shareholders should have the opportunity to participate effectively and vote in general shareholder meetings		X			
D	Capital structures and arrangements that allow disproportionate control			X		
E	Markets for corporate control should be allowed to function in an efficient and transparent manner			X		
F	Shareholders should consider the costs and benefits of exercising their voting rights				X	
II	**Equitable treatment of shareholders**					
A	The corporate governance framework should ensure the equitable treatment of all shareholders, including minority and foreign shareholders		X			
B	Insider trading and abusive self-dealing should be prohibited			X		
C	Board members and managers should be required to disclose material interests in transactions or matters affecting the corporation		X			
III	**Role of stakeholders in corporate governance**					
A	The corporate governance framework should recognize the rights of stakeholders	X				
B	Stakeholders should have the opportunity to obtain effective redress for violation of their rights			X		
C	The corporate governance framework should permit performance-enhancement mechanisms for stakeholder participation	X				
D	Stakeholders should have access to relevant information		X			
IV	**Disclosure and transparency**					
A	The corporate governance framework should ensure that timely and accurate disclosure is made on all material matters		X			
B	Information should be prepared, audited, and disclosed in accordance with high quality standards of accounting, financial and nonfinancial disclosure, and audit		X			
C	An independent audit should be conducted by an independent auditor		X			
D	Channels for disseminating information should provide for fair, timely, and cost-effective access to relevant information by users		X			

Table 26.1 (continued)

		O	LO	PO	MNO	NO
V	**The responsibility of the board**					
A	Board members should act on a fully informed basis, in good faith, with due diligence and care, and in the best interests of the company and the shareholders			X		
B	The board should treat all shareholders fairly			X		
C	The board should ensure compliance with applicable law and take into account the interests of stakeholders		X			
D	The board should fulfill certain board functions			X		
E	The board should be able to exercise objective judgment on corporate affairs independent from management			X		
F	Board members should have access to accurate, relevant, and timely information	X				

Table 26.2 Corporate governance scores

Category	Total points	Number of items	Average
Rights of shareholders	20	6	3.33
Equitable treatment of shareholders	11	3	3.67
Role of stakeholders in corporate governance	17	4	4.25
Disclosure and transparency	16	4	4.00
The responsibility of the board	21	6	3.50
Overall average			3.70

Table 26.2 shows the scores for each subcategory. The overall average was 3.70. The graph below shows the relative scores. All of the scores are at least 3.33 or higher. The top score was in the category of Role (4.25).

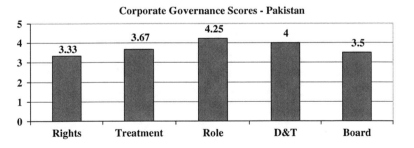

Corporate Governance Scores - Pakistan

Recommendations

The ROSC made several recommendations. It recognizes the major reforms that Pakistan has made in the last few years and urges the reforms to continue. The Securities and Exchange Commission of Pakistan (SECP) should take as its primary priority compliance in the following three areas: (1) the disclosure of beneficial ownership and control by shareholders and by companies; (2) reporting-related party transactions; and (3) compliance with regard to the annual general shareholders' meeting.

The ROSC recommends building the enforcement authority of the SECP in order to achieve these goals. Raising the technical level of its legal and accounting experts was also recommended.

The accounting and audit professions are currently self-regulated. The ROSC believes that self-regulation will not be adequate in the future. It recommends independent oversight.

The present situation in Pakistan involves a wide variety of listed companies with varying corporate governance rules. Board independence is a controversial issue. The ROSC recommends developing a new corporate governance listing tier. Companies that list on that tier would agree to comply with all code provisions, including board independence, mandatory director certification, and strengthened audit committees. It is hoped that the differentiation provided by this tier will, over time, encourage companies to upgrade to international standards.

Institutional investors should play a more active role in monitoring companies and should demand governance changes. Those that are acting in a fiduciary role should disclose their voting and corporate governance policies.

References

OECD. (2004). *OECD Principles of Corporate Governance*. Paris: Author. Retrieved from www. oecd.org/dataoecd/32/18/31557724.pdf

World Bank. (2005). *Report on the Observance of Standards and Codes (ROSC), Corporate Governance Country Assessment: Pakistan.*.

World Bank. (2008). *Reports on the Observance of Standards and Codes (ROSC) for Corporate Governance*. Retrieved from www.worldbank.org/ifa/rosc_cg.html

Chapter 27
An Overview of Corporate Governance Practices in the Philippines

Robert W. McGee

Introduction

The World Bank has published a series of reports on corporate governance as part of its project on the *Reports on the Observance of Standards and Codes* (ROSC). The corporate governance principles in its ROSC are benchmarked against the OECD's *Principles of Corporate Governance* (OECD, 2004). The main categories of principles are discussed below.

Methodology

The corporate governance topics discussed in the World Bank's ROSC were classified into categories based on the extent of compliance with the OECD's *Principles of Corporate Governance* (OECD, 2004). Points were then assigned to each category, as follows:

O = Observed = 5 points
LO = Largely Observed = 4 points
PO = Partially Observed = 3 points
MNO = Materially Not Observed = 2 points
NO = Not Observed = 1 point

Summary of Findings

Table 27.1 summarizes the scores in the various categories. The table categorizes compliance with corporate governance principles into five categories.

R.W. McGee (✉)
Florida International University, Miami, FL, USA
e-mail: bob414@hotmail.com

R.W. McGee (ed.), *Corporate Governance in Developing Economies*,
DOI 10.1007/978-0-387-84833-4_27, © Springer Science+Business Media, LLC 2009

Table 27.1 Summary of scores by category

		O	LO	PO	MNO	NO
I	**Rights of shareholders**					
A	Protect shareholder rights		X			
B	Shareholders have the right to participate in, and to be sufficiently informed on, decisions concerning fundamental corporate changes		X			
C	Shareholders should have the opportunity to participate effectively and vote in general shareholder meetings			X		
D	Capital structures and arrangements that allow disproportionate control			X		
E	Markets for corporate control should be allowed to function in an efficient and transparent manner			X		
F	Shareholders should consider the costs and benefits of exercising their voting rights			X		
II	**Equitable treatment of shareholders**					
A	The corporate governance framework should ensure the equitable treatment of all shareholders, including minority and foreign shareholders			X		
B	Insider trading and abusive self-dealing should be prohibited			X		
C	Board members and managers should be required to disclose material interests in transactions or matters affecting the corporation			X		
III	**Role of stakeholders in corporate governance**					
A	The corporate governance framework should recognize the rights of stakeholders		X			
B	Stakeholders should have the opportunity to obtain effective redress for violation of their rights			X		
C	The corporate governance framework should permit performance-enhancement mechanisms for stakeholder participation			X	X	
D	Stakeholders should have access to relevant information			X		
IV	**Disclosure and transparency**					
A	The corporate governance framework should ensure that timely and accurate disclosure is made on all material matters			X		
B	Information should be prepared, audited, and disclosed in accordance with high quality standards of accounting, financial and nonfinancial disclosure, and audit		X			
C	An independent audit should be conducted by an independent auditor			X		
D	Channels for disseminating information should provide for fair, timely, and cost-effective access to relevant information by users			X		

Table 27.1 (continued)

		O	LO	PO	MNO	NO
V	**The responsibility of the board**					
A	Board members should act on a fully informed basis, in good faith, with due diligence and care, and in the best interests of the company and the shareholders			X		
B	The board should treat all shareholders fairly			X		
C	The board should ensure compliance with applicable law and take into account the interests of stakeholders			X		
D	The board should fulfill certain board functions			X		
E	The board should be able to exercise objective judgment on corporate affairs independent from management			X		
F	Board members should have access to accurate, relevant, and timely information		X			

Table 27.2 Corporate governance scores

Category	Total points	Number of items	Average
Rights of shareholders	20	6	3.33
Equitable treatment of shareholders	9	3	3.00
Role of stakeholders in corporate governance	13	4	3.25
Disclosure and transparency	13	4	3.25
The responsibility of the board	19	6	3.17
Overall average			3.22

Table 27.2 shows the scores for each subcategory. The overall average was 3.22. The corporate governance scores are shown graphically below. All scores were 3.00 or above. The highest score was in the category of Rights.

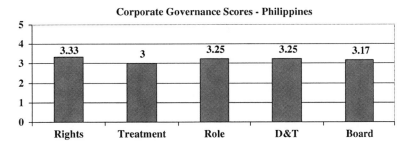

Corporate Governance Scores - Philippines

Recommendations

The ROSC made several recommendations. It gave high priority to strengthening enforcement of the existing legal requirements for independent directors, including the rules concerning conflict of interest. Although there is a requirement for companies to have independent directors, the rule is not effectively followed. Although conflict-of-interest rules for board members have been introduced, there continues to be a need to effectively implement the rules. The ROSC recommends considering a rule to require related party transactions to be approved by the independent directors. It also recommends considering increasing the ratio of independent directors from the present rule of "2 or 20 percent, whichever is less."

Another recommendation is to increase free float by raising the minimum 10 percent requirement of total registered shares to offer to the public. Companies should consider making it easier for shareholders to vote by allowing them to vote by mail or electronically.

Another high-priority item is to strengthen enforcement by the SEC and Philippine Stock Exchange of laws related to insider trading and tender offer rules. Information on enforcement actions should be posted on the SEC website. Additional resources should be provided to enhance the Philippine Stock Exchange's surveillance system.

Financial statements that are submitted by regulated companies are to be reviewed by regulators to ensure that they comply with all International Financial Reporting Standards and required disclosures. Noncompliance should result in sanctions.

At present the annual report does not require the disclosure of internal control systems. That should be changed. There should also be disclosures providing background information on the independent directors and a disclosure of the mission and vision of the company.

References

OECD. (2004). *OECD Principles of Corporate Governance*. Paris: Author. Retrieved from www.oecd.org/dataoecd/32/18/31557724.pdf

World Bank. (2006). *Report on the Observance of Standards and Codes (ROSC), Corporate Governance Country Assessment: Philippines*.

World Bank. (2008). *Reports on the Observance of Standards and Codes (ROSC) for Corporate Governance*. Retrieved from www.worldbank.org/ifa/rosc_cg.html

Chapter 28
An Overview of Corporate Governance Practices in Thailand

Robert W. McGee

Introduction

The World Bank has published a series of reports on corporate governance as part of its project on the *Reports on the Observance of Standards and Codes* (ROSC). The corporate governance principles in its ROSC are benchmarked against the OECD's *Principles of Corporate Governance* (OECD, 2004). The main categories of principles are discussed below.

Methodology

The corporate governance topics discussed in the World Bank's ROSC were classified into categories based on the extent of compliance with the OECD's *Principles of Corporate Governance* (OECD, 2004). Points were then assigned to each category, as follows:

O = Observed = 5 points
LO = Largely Observed = 4 points
PO = Partially Observed = 3 points
MNO = Materially Not Observed = 2 points
NO = Not Observed = 1 point

Summary of Findings

Table 28.1 summarizes the scores in the various categories. The table categorizes compliance with corporate governance principles into five categories.

R.W. McGee (✉)
Florida International University, Miami, FL, USA
e-mail: bob414@hotmail.com

R.W. McGee (ed.), *Corporate Governance in Developing Economies*,
DOI 10.1007/978-0-387-84833-4_28, © Springer Science+Business Media, LLC 2009

Table 28.1 Summary of scores by category

		O	LO	PO	MNO	NO
I	**Rights of shareholders**					
A	Protect shareholder rights		X			
B	Shareholders have the right to participate in, and to be sufficiently informed on, decisions concerning fundamental corporate changes			X		
C	Shareholders should have the opportunity to participate effectively and vote in general shareholder meetings		X			
D	Capital structures and arrangements that allow disproportionate control		X			
E	Markets for corporate control should be allowed to function in an efficient and transparent manner			X		
F	Shareholders should consider the costs and benefits of exercising their voting rights		X			
II	**Equitable treatment of shareholders**					
A	The corporate governance framework should ensure the equitable treatment of all shareholders, including minority and foreign shareholders			X		
B	Insider trading and abusive self-dealing should be prohibited		X			
C	Board members and managers should be required to disclose material interests in transactions or matters affecting the corporation		X			
III	**Role of stakeholders in corporate governance**					
A	The corporate governance framework should recognize the rights of stakeholders		X			
B	Stakeholders should have the opportunity to obtain effective redress for violation of their rights		X			
C	The corporate governance framework should permit performance-enhancement mechanisms for stakeholder participation		X			
D	Stakeholders should have access to relevant information		X			
IV	**Disclosure and transparency**					
A	The corporate governance framework should ensure that timely and accurate disclosure is made on all material matters		X			
B	Information should be prepared, audited, and disclosed in accordance with high quality standards of accounting, financial and nonfinancial disclosure, and audit			X		
C	An independent audit should be conducted by an independent auditor		X			
D	Channels for disseminating information should provide for fair, timely, and cost-effective access to relevant information by users		X			

Table 28.1 (continued)

		O	LO	PO	MNO	NO
V	**The responsibility of the board**					
A	Board members should act on a fully informed basis, in good faith, with due diligence and care, and in the best interests of the company and the shareholders			X		
B	The board should treat all shareholders fairly		X			
C	The board should ensure compliance with applicable law and take into account the interests of stakeholders			X		
D	The board should fulfill certain board functions			X		
E	The board should be able to exercise objective judgment on corporate affairs independent from management			X		
F	Board members should have access to accurate, relevant, and timely information		X			

Table 28.2 Corporate governance scores

Category	Total points	Number of items	Average
Rights of shareholders	22	6	3.67
Equitable treatment of shareholders	11	3	3.67
Role of stakeholders in corporate governance	16	4	4.00
Disclosure and transparency	15	4	3.75
The responsibility of the board	20	6	3.33
Overall average			3.65

Table 28.2 shows the scores for each subcategory. The overall score was 3.65. The scores for each category are shown below graphically. All scores were over 3.00. The highest score was in the category Role (4.00).

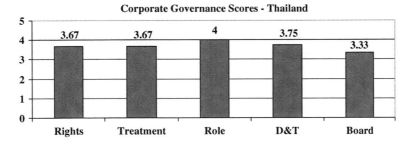

Recommendations

The ROSC made several recommendations. It mentioned that, although Thailand has made significant improvements in corporate governance in recent years, it should continue the reform process. The focus should be on implementation and on completing its regulatory and legislative agenda, enhancing financial reporting and disclosure in a manner consistent with international standards, improvement of legal enforcement and promoting business ethics, and good corporate practices.

There is a concern for the protection of minority shareholders and the strengthening of shareholder rights. Shareholders should be given more voice at the annual general shareholders' meeting. The legislative process has been slow and uncertain, which is a cause for concern.

Shareholders seeking redress of grievances should have cost-effective legal channels open to them. The class action lawsuit is one potential remedy. Directors should act for the benefit of all the shareholders. Director registration should be for a limited term, perhaps 3–5 years, and they should not be reregistered unless they complete refresher training.

The process of removal of a board member should be simplified. Cumulative voting should be considered as a means of giving a voice to minority shareholders. International good practice provides for the electronic appointment of proxies. Thailand should follow this practice.

In cases where legislative action is slow or uncertain, the reform process could be enhanced if the regulatory authorities and private-sector institutions take an active role in the reform process. For example, the stock exchange could require certain things in its listing requirements.

There are also recommendations for increasing the accountability of directors and management and further clarity regarding the fiduciary duties of directors. There is also a need to improve the quality and reliability of financial information and disclosures provided by public companies.

References

OECD. (2004). *OECD Principles of Corporate Governance*. Paris: Author. Retrieved from www. oecd.org/dataoecd/32/18/31557724.pdf

World Bank. (2005). *Report on the Observance of Standards and Codes (ROSC), Corporate Governance Country Assessment: Thailand.*

World Bank. (2008). *Reports on the Observance of Standards and Codes (ROSC) for Corporate Governance*. Retrieved form www.worldbank.org/ifa/rosc_cg.html

Chapter 29
An Overview of Corporate Governance Practices in Turkey

Robert W. McGee

Introduction

The World Bank has published a series of reports on corporate governance as part of its project on the *Reports on the Observance of Standards and Codes* (ROSC). The corporate governance principles in its ROSC are benchmarked against the OECD's *Principles of Corporate Governance* (OECD 2004). The main categories of principles are discussed below.

Methodology

The corporate governance topics discussed in the World Bank's ROSC were classified into categories on the basis of the extent of compliance with the OECD's *Principles of Corporate Governance* (OECD, 2004). The categories were:

Yes
No
N/A
Incomplete

Summary of Findings

Table 29.1 summarizes the scores in the various categories. The table categorizes compliance with corporate governance principles into five categories.

Since the World Bank template for Turkey was different from the template for the other countries, no meaningful comparisons can be made.

R.W. McGee (✉)
Florida International University, Miami, FL, USA
e-mail: bob414@hotmail.com

R.W. McGee (ed.), *Corporate Governance in Developing Economies*,
DOI 10.1007/978-0-387-84833-4_29, © Springer Science+Business Media, LLC 2009

Table 29.1 Summary of scores by category

		Yes	No	N/A	Incomplete
I	**Rights of shareholders**				
A	Protect shareholder rights	X			
B	Shareholders have the right to participate in, and to be sufficiently informed on, decisions concerning fundamental corporate changes	X			
C	Shareholders should have the opportunity to participate effectively and vote in general shareholder meetings	X			
D	Capital structures and arrangements that allow disproportionate control	X			
E	Markets for corporate control should be allowed to function in an efficient and transparent manner				X
F	Shareholders should consider the costs and benefits of exercising their voting rights			X	
II	**Equitable treatment of shareholders**				
A	The corporate governance framework should ensure the equitable treatment of all share-holders, including minority and foreign shareholders	X			
B	Insider trading and abusive self-dealing should be prohibited	X			
C	Board members and managers should be required to disclose material interests in transactions or matters affecting the corporation				X
III	**Role of stakeholders in corporate governance**				
A	The corporate governance framework should recognize the rights of stakeholders			X	
B	The corporate governance framework should permit performance-enhancement mecha-nisms for stakeholder participation			X	
C	The corporate governance framework should permit performance-enhancement mecha-nisms for stakeholder participation			X	
D	Stakeholders should have access to relevant information			X	
IV	**Disclosure and transparency**				
A	The corporate governance framework should ensure that timely and accurate disclosure is made on all material matters				X
B	Information should be prepared, audited, and disclosed in accordance with high quality standards of accounting, financial and nonfinancial disclosure, and audit				X
C	An independent audit should be conducted by an independent auditor	X			
D	Channels for disseminating information should provide for fair, timely, and cost-effective access to relevant information by users	X			

Table 29.1 (continued)

		Yes	No	N/A	Incomplete
V	**The responsibility of the board**				
A	Board members should act on a fully informed basis, in good faith, with due diligence and care, and in the best interests of the company and the shareholders	X			
B	The board should treat all shareholders fairly	X			
C	The board should ensure compliance with applicable law and take into account the interests of stakeholders	X			
D	The board should fulfill certain board functions	X			
E	The board should be able to exercise objective judgment on corporate affairs independent from management				X
F	Board members should have access to accurate, relevant, and timely information	X			

Recommendations

The ROSC for Turkey did not make recommendations. It is in a different style and format than most of the other ROSC country reports. The Turkey report is more descriptive. It discloses basic information about the present state of corporate governance in Turkey. It is short on advice and recommendations.

References

OECD. (2004). *OECD Principles of Corporate Governance*. Paris: Author. Retrieved from www.oecd.org/dataoecd/32/18/31557724.pdf

World Bank (n.d.). *Report on the Observance of Standards and Codes (ROSC), Corporate Governance Country Assessment: Turkey*.

World Bank. (2008). *Reports on the Observance of Standards and Codes (ROSC) for Corporate Governance*. Retrieved from www.worldbank.org/ifa/rosc_cg.html

Chapter 30
An Overview of Corporate Governance Practices in Vietnam

Robert W. McGee

Introduction

The World Bank has published a series of reports on corporate governance as part of its project on the *Reports on the Observance of Standards and Codes* (ROSC). The corporate governance principles in its ROSC are benchmarked against the OECD's *Principles of Corporate Governance* (OECD, 2004). The main categories of principles are discussed below.

Methodology

The corporate governance topics discussed in the World Bank's ROSC were classified into categories based on the extent of compliance with the OECD's *Principles of Corporate Governance* (OECD, 2004). Points were then assigned to each category, as follows:

O = Observed = 5 points
LO = Largely Observed = 4 points
PO = Partially Observed = 3 points
MNO = Materially Not Observed = 2 points
NO = Not Observed = 1 point

Summary of Findings

Table 30.1 summarizes the scores in the various categories. The table categorizes compliance with corporate governance principles into five categories.

R.W. McGee (✉)
Florida International University, Miami, FL, USA
e-mail: bob414@hotmail.com

R.W. McGee (ed.), *Corporate Governance in Developing Economies*,
DOI 10.1007/978-0-387-84833-4_30, © Springer Science+Business Media, LLC 2009

Table 30.1 Summary of scores by category

		O	LO	PO	MNO	NO
I	**Rights of shareholders**					
A	Protect shareholder rights			X		
B	Shareholders have the right to participate in, and to be sufficiently informed on, decisions concerning fundamental corporate changes			X		
C	Shareholders should have the opportunity to participate effectively and vote in general shareholder meetings			X		
D	Capital structures and arrangements that allow disproportionate control			X		
E	Markets for corporate control should be allowed to function in an efficient and transparent manner				X	
F	Shareholders should consider the costs and benefits of exercising their voting rights				X	
II	**Equitable treatment of shareholders**					
A	The corporate governance framework should ensure the equitable treatment of all shareholders, including minority and foreign shareholders				X	
B	Insider trading and abusive self-dealing should be prohibited				X	
C	Board members and managers should be required to disclose material interests in transactions or matters affecting the corporation				X	
III	**Role of stakeholders in corporate governance**					
A	The corporate governance framework should recognize the rights of stakeholders			X		
B	Stakeholders should have the opportunity to obtain effective redress for violation of their rights			X		
C	The corporate governance framework should permit performance-enhancement mechanisms for stakeholder participation			X		
D	Stakeholders should have access to relevant information				X	
IV	**Disclosure and transparency**					
A	The corporate governance framework should ensure that timely and accurate disclosure is made on all material matters				X	
B	Information should be prepared, audited, and disclosed in accordance with high quality standards of accounting, financial and nonfinancial disclosure, and audit			X		
C	An independent audit should be conducted by an independent auditor			X		
D	Channels for disseminating information should provide for fair, timely, and cost-effective access to relevant information by users			X		

Table 30.1 (continued)

		O	LO	PO	MNO	NO
V	**The responsibility of the board**					
A	Board members should act on a fully informed basis, in good faith, with due diligence and care, and in the best interests of the company and the shareholders			X		
B	The board should treat all shareholders fairly				X	
C	The board should ensure compliance with applicable law and take into account the interests of stakeholders				X	
D	The board should fulfill certain board functions				X	
E	The board should be able to exercise objective judgment on corporate affairs independent from management				X	
F	Board members should have access to accurate, relevant, and timely information			X		

Table 30.2 Corporate governance scores

Category	Total points	Number of items	Average
Rights of shareholders	16	6	2.67
Equitable treatment of shareholders	6	3	2.00
Role of stakeholders in corporate governance	11	4	2.75
Disclosure and transparency	11	4	2.75
The responsibility of the board	14	6	2.33
Overall average			2.52

Table 30.2 shows the scores for each subcategory. The overall average was 2.52. The scores for each category are shown below graphically. None of the scores were above 3.00.

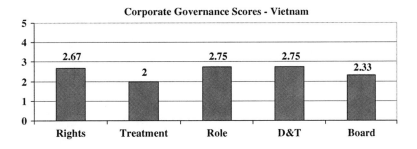

Corporate Governance Scores - Vietnam

Recommendations

The ROSC made several recommendations. The role of the State Securities Commission needs to be strengthened and its operations need to be reorganized. It should be able to act independently as a regulator. Staff needs to be trained to increase their skill level.

There are conflicts and inconsistencies in the law and regulations that impede their effectiveness. The Securities Trading Centers need to be upgraded to stock exchanges. The forms and roles of these organizations need to be clarified and they need to be upgraded to the status of self-regulatory organizations.

Investors need to be protected in both official and unofficial markets. The investment environment needs to be more transparent. Disclosure and transparency need to be promoted in both listed and nonlisted companies.

There is currently no regulation of the informal market. The ROSC advocates the establishment of a suitable regulatory framework, which would encourage companies in the informal market to enter the regulatory net. The definition of public companies needs to be expanded to include companies that are now excluded from the definition, which the ROSC deems to be too narrow.

Financial information should be released to the public and it should be audited by an independent, qualified auditor. Vietnamese Accounting Standards need comprehensive guidelines in order to avoid differing interpretations and differences in practice. Standards need to be applied consistently to improve the quality of financial information. Vietnamese Accounting Standards should be compatible with International Financial Reporting Standards. Although Vietnam has issued accounting and auditing standards that comply with international standards, those standards have not yet been fully implemented.

Although the country has adopted rules on corporate governance, there are no sanctions for failure to follow the rules. Proxy voting should be encouraged. Shareholders should be allowed to vote electronically.

References

OECD. (2004). *OECD Principles of Corporate Governance.* Paris: Author. Retrieved from www.oecd.org/dataoecd/32/18/31557724.pdf

World Bank. (2006). *Report on the Observance of Standards and Codes (ROSC), Corporate Governance Country Assessment: Vietnam.*

World Bank. (2008). *Reports on the Observance of Standards and Codes (ROSC) for Corporate Governance.* Retrieved from www.worldbank.org/ifa/rosc_cg.html

Chapter 31
An Overview of Corporate Governance Practices in Brazil

Robert W. McGee

Introduction

The World Bank has published a series of reports on corporate governance as part of its project on the *Reports on the Observance of Standards and Codes* (ROSC). The corporate governance principles in its ROSC are benchmarked against the OECD's *Principles of Corporate Governance* (OECD, 2004). The main categories of principles are discussed below.

Methodology

The corporate governance topics discussed in the World Bank's ROSC were classified into categories based on the extent of compliance with the OECD's *Principles of Corporate Governance* (OECD, 2004). Points were then assigned to each category, as follows:

O = Observed = 5 points
LO = Largely Observed = 4 points
PO = Partially Observed = 3 points
MNO = Materially Not Observed = 2 points
NO = Not Observed = 1 point

Summary of Findings

Table 31.1 summarizes the scores in the various categories. The table categorizes compliance with corporate governance principles into five categories.

R.W. McGee (✉)
Florida International University, Miami, FL, USA
e-mail: bob414@hotmail.com

R.W. McGee (ed.), *Corporate Governance in Developing Economies*,
DOI 10.1007/978-0-387-84833-4_31, © Springer Science+Business Media, LLC 2009

Table 31.1 Summary of scores by category

		O	LO	PO	MNO	NO
I	**Rights of shareholders**					
A	Protect shareholder rights		X			
B	Shareholders have the right to participate in, and to be sufficiently informed on, decisions concerning fundamental corporate changes		X			
C	Shareholders should have the opportunity to participate effectively and vote in general shareholder meetings			X		
D	Capital structures and arrangements that allow disproportionate control			X		
E	Markets for corporate control should be allowed to function in an efficient and transparent manner		X			
F	Shareholders should consider the costs and benefits of exercising their voting rights		X			
II	**Equitable treatment of shareholders**					
A	The corporate governance framework should ensure the equitable treatment of all shareholders, including minority and foreign shareholders			X		
B	Insider trading and abusive self-dealing should be prohibited		X			
C	Board members and managers should be required to disclose material interests in transactions or matters affecting the corporation			X		
III	**Role of stakeholders in corporate governance**					
A	The corporate governance framework should recognize the rights of stakeholders	X				
B	Stakeholders should have the opportunity to obtain effective redress for violation of their rights	X				
C	The corporate governance framework should permit performance-enhancement mechanisms for stakeholder participation		X			
D	Stakeholders should have access to relevant information		X			
IV	**Disclosure and transparency**					
A	The corporate governance framework should ensure that timely and accurate disclosure is made on all material matters			X		
B	Information should be prepared, audited, and disclosed in accordance with high quality standards of accounting, financial and nonfinancial disclosure, and audit			X		
C	An independent audit should be conducted by an independent auditor			X		
D	Channels for disseminating information should provide for fair, timely, and cost-effective access to relevant information by users	X				

Table 31.1 (continued)

		O	LO	PO	MNO	NO
V	**The responsibility of the board**					
A	Board members should act on a fully informed basis, in good faith, with due diligence and care, and in the best interests of the company and the shareholders			X		
B	The board should treat all shareholders fairly			X		
C	The board should ensure compliance with applicable law and take into account the interests of stakeholders		X			
D	The board should fulfill certain board functions			X		
E	The board should be able to exercise objective judgment on corporate affairs independent from management				X	
F	Board members should have access to accurate, relevant, and timely information		X			

Table 31.2 Corporate governance scores

Category	Total points	Number of items	Average
Rights of shareholders	22	6	3.67
Equitable treatment of shareholders	10	3	3.33
Role of stakeholders in corporate governance	18	4	4.5
Disclosure and transparency	14	4	3.5
The responsibility of the board	19	6	3.17
Overall average			3.61

Table 31.2 shows the scores for each subcategory. The overall average score is 3.61.

The graph below shows the relative scores for each category. The highest score is for Role. The lowest is for Board.

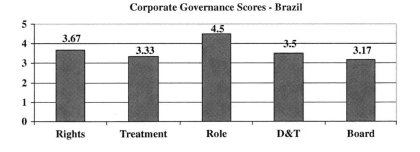

Corporate Governance Scores - Brazil

Recommendations

The ROSC made several recommendations. Good corporate governance already exists within the elite top tier of Brazilian companies. The trick is to make corporate governance reforms more widespread.

Directors who are appointed by pension funds generally have a close relationship with the pension fund. Thus, there is the perception that they lack independence. Often they do not have the training necessary to be an effective director. The ROSC recommends the introduction of independence requirements to help alleviate that problem.

Judges are not adequately educated to rule on financial and capital market issues. It was suggested that CVM, Brazil's securities regulator, act in an amicus curiae (friend of the court) capacity in such cases. Over the longer term, it was suggested that courses be added to the judges' curriculum on financial and capital markets issues.

Under the present structure, the same small group of investors may own listed companies and private firms and the ownership connections may not be known to outside investors because of a lack of transparency. Minority shareholders may not even know who the majority shareholders are. Current law allows the misuse of corporate assets.

It is difficult to recover debt in bankruptcy proceedings and covenant enforcement is difficult. The ROSC recommends that an effective, efficient insolvency framework be established and that an effective mechanism for the enforcement of creditors' rights be put in place.

References

OECD. (2004). *OECD Principles of Corporate Governance*. Paris: Author. Retrieved from www.oecd.org/dataoecd/32/18/31557724.pdf

World Bank. (2005). *Report on the Observance of Standards and Codes (ROSC), Corporate Governance Country Assessment: Brazil*.

World Bank. (2008). *Reports on the Observance of Standards and Codes (ROSC) for Corporate Governance*. Retrieved from www.worldbank.org/ifa/rosc_cg.html

Chapter 32
An Overview of Corporate Governance Practices in Chile

Robert W. McGee

Introduction

The World Bank has published a series of reports on corporate governance as part of its project on the *Reports on the Observance of Standards and Codes* (ROSC). The corporate governance principles in its ROSC are benchmarked against the OECD's *Principles of Corporate Governance* (OECD, 2004). The main categories of principles are discussed below.

Methodology

The corporate governance topics discussed in the World Bank's ROSC were classified into categories based on the extent of compliance with the OECD's *Principles of Corporate Governance* (OECD, 2004). Points were then assigned to each category, as follows:

O = Observed = 5 points
LO = Largely Observed = 4 points
PO = Partially Observed = 3 points
MNO = Materially Not Observed = 2 points
NO = Not Observed = 1 point

Summary of Findings

Table 32.1 summarizes the scores in the various categories. The table categorizes compliance with corporate governance principles into five categories.

R.W. McGee (✉)
Florida International University, Miami, FL, USA
e-mail: bob414@hotmail.com

R.W. McGee (ed.), *Corporate Governance in Developing Economies*,
DOI 10.1007/978-0-387-84833-4_32, © Springer Science+Business Media, LLC 2009

Table 32.1 Summary of scores by category

		O	LO	PO	MNO	NO
I	**Rights of shareholders**					
A	Protect shareholder rights		X			
B	Shareholders have the right to participate in, and to be sufficiently informed on, decisions concerning fundamental corporate changes	X				
C	Shareholders should have the opportunity to participate effectively and vote in general shareholder meetings		X			
D	Capital structures and arrangements that allow disproportionate control			X		
E	Markets for corporate control should be allowed to function in an efficient and transparent manner		X			
F	Shareholders should consider the costs and benefits of exercising their voting rights		X			
II	**Equitable treatment of shareholders**					
A	The corporate governance framework should ensure the equitable treatment of all shareholders, including minority and foreign shareholders		X			
B	Insider trading and abusive self-dealing should be prohibited			X		
C	Board members and managers should be required to disclose material interests in transactions or matters affecting the corporation		X			
III	**Role of stakeholders in corporate governance**					
A	The corporate governance framework should recognize the rights of stakeholders		X			
B	Stakeholders should have the opportunity to obtain effective redress for violation of their rights			X		
C	The corporate governance framework should permit performance-enhancement mechanisms for stakeholder participation		X			
D	Stakeholders should have access to relevant information	X				
IV	**Disclosure and transparency**					
A	The corporate governance framework should ensure that timely and accurate disclosure is made on all material matters			X		
B	Information should be prepared, audited, and disclosed in accordance with high quality standards of accounting, financial and nonfinancial disclosure, and audit			X		
C	An independent audit should be conducted by an independent auditor			X		
D	Channels for disseminating information should provide for fair, timely, and cost-effective access to relevant information by users		X			

Table 32.1 (continued)

		O	LO	PO	MNO	NO
V	**The responsibility of the board**					
A	Board members should act on a fully informed basis, in good faith, with due diligence and care, and in the best interests of the company and the shareholders			X		
B	The board should treat all shareholders fairly			X		
C	The board should ensure compliance with applicable law and take into account the interests of stakeholders		X			
D	The board should fulfill certain board functions			X		
E	The board should be able to exercise objective judgment on corporate affairs independent from management			X		
F	Board members should have access to accurate, relevant, and timely information		X			

Table 32.2 Corporate governance scores

Category	Total points	Number of items	Average
Rights of shareholders	24	6	4.00
Equitable treatment of shareholders	11	3	3.67
Role of stakeholders in corporate governance	16	4	4.00
Disclosure and transparency	13	4	3.25
The responsibility of the board	20	6	3.33
Overall average			3.65

Table 32.2 shows the scores for each subcategory. The overall average score was 3.65.

The chart below shows the relative scores. The categories of Rights and Role scored the highest. Disclosure and Transparency scored the lowest.

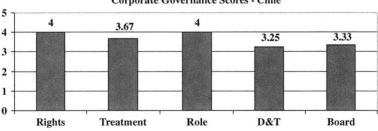

Recommendations

The ROSC made several recommendations. There is a need for legislative reform. The notice of the annual general shareholders' meeting needs to be extended to 30 days so that foreign shareholders can have adequate time to vote. Disclosure should be required for changes in equity, material foreseeable risks, management discussion and analysis, and governance policies. Penalties should be imposed for breaches of duty, care, and loyalty. Issuers should be allowed to disseminate information over the Internet and by e-mail.

Late filings should not be tolerated. The agency that regulates securities should be more accountable to the public and its enforcement powers should be increased. Its activities should be more transparent. It should prepare an annual report for submission to the parliament.

References

OECD. (2004). *OECD Principles of Corporate Governance.* Paris: Author. Retrieved from www.oecd.org/dataoecd/32/18/31557724.pdf

World Bank. (2003). *Report on the Observance of Standards and Codes (ROSC), Corporate Governance Country Assessment: Chile.*

World Bank. (2008). *Reports on the Observance of Standards and Codes (ROSC) for Corporate Governance.* Retrieved from www.worldbank.org/ifa/rosc_cg.html

Chapter 33
An Overview of Corporate Governance Practices in Colombia

Robert W. McGee

Introduction

The World Bank has published a series of reports on corporate governance as part of its project on the *Reports on the Observance of Standards and Codes* (ROSC). The corporate governance principles in its ROSC are benchmarked against the OECD's *Principles of Corporate Governance* (OECD, 2004). The main categories of principles are discussed below.

Methodology

The corporate governance topics discussed in the World Bank's ROSC were classified into categories based on the extent of compliance with the OECD's *Principles of Corporate Governance* (OECD, 2004). Points were then assigned to each category, as follows:

O = Observed = 5 points
LO = Largely Observed = 4 points
PO = Partially Observed = 3 points
MNO = Materially Not Observed = 2 points
NO = Not Observed = 1 point

Summary of Findings

Table 33.1 summarizes the scores in the various categories. The table categorizes compliance with corporate governance principles into five categories.

R.W. McGee (✉)
Florida International University, Miami, FL, USA
e-mail: bob414@hotmail.com

R.W. McGee (ed.), *Corporate Governance in Developing Economies*,
DOI 10.1007/978-0-387-84833-4_33, © Springer Science+Business Media, LLC 2009

Table 33.1 Summary of scores by category

		O	LO	PO	MNO	NO
I	**Rights of shareholders**					
A	Protect shareholder rights		X			
B	Shareholders have the right to participate in, and to be sufficiently informed on, decisions concerning fundamental corporate changes			X		
C	Shareholders should have the opportunity to participate effectively and vote in general shareholder meetings			X		
D	Capital structures and arrangements that allow disproportionate control				X	
E	Markets for corporate control should be allowed to function in an efficient and transparent manner				X	
F	Shareholders should consider the costs and benefits of exercising their voting rights					X
II	**Equitable treatment of shareholders**					
A	The corporate governance framework should ensure the equitable treatment of all shareholders, including minority and foreign shareholders			X		
B	Insider trading and abusive self-dealing should be prohibited				X	
C	Board members and managers should be required to disclose material interests in transactions or matters affecting the corporation					X
III	**Role of stakeholders in corporate governance**					
A	The corporate governance framework should recognize the rights of stakeholders	X				
B	Stakeholders should have the opportunity to obtain effective redress for violation of their rights			X		
C	The corporate governance framework should permit performance-enhancement mechanisms for stakeholder participation		X			
D	Stakeholders should have access to relevant information	X				
IV	**Disclosure and transparency**					
A	The corporate governance framework should ensure that timely and accurate disclosure is made on all material matters			X		
B	Information should be prepared, audited, and disclosed in accordance with high quality standards of accounting, financial and nonfinancial disclosure, and audit				X	
C	An independent audit should be conducted by an independent auditor				X	
D	Channels for disseminating information should provide for fair, timely, and cost-effective access to relevant information by users	X				

Table 33.1 (continued)

		O	LO	PO	MNO	NO
V	**The responsibility of the board**					
A	Board members should act on a fully informed basis, in good faith, with due diligence and care, and in the best interests of the company and the shareholders			X		
B	The board should treat all shareholders fairly				X	
C	The board should ensure compliance with applicable law and take into account the interests of stakeholders		X			
D	The board should fulfill certain board functions			X		
E	The board should be able to exercise objective judgment on corporate affairs independent from management				X	
F	Board members should have access to accurate, relevant, and timely information	X				

Table 33.2 Corporate governance scores

Category	Total points	Number of items	Average
Rights of shareholders	15	6	2.50
Equitable treatment of shareholders	6	3	2.00
Role of stakeholders in corporate governance	17	4	4.25
Disclosure and transparency	12	4	3.00
The responsibility of the board	19	6	3.17
Overall average			3.00

Table 33.2 shows the scores for each subcategory. The overall average score is 3.00 but there is a great deal of fluctuation in scores.

The graph below illustrates the relative scores graphically. The best score was in the category of Role (4.25). The lowest score was for Treatment (2.00) and was considerably lower than the highest score.

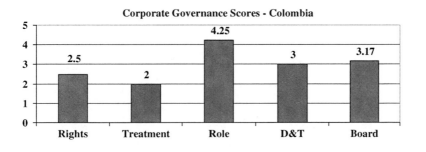

Recommendations

The ROSC made several recommendations. Colombian accounting standards are considered to be substandard. The authority to issue accounting standards should be taken away from the body that presently has that authority. A technical board should be created to issue accounting standards along the lines of those issued by the International Accounting Standards Board. The country should adopt IFRS and an independent audit oversight board dominated by nonpractitioners should be created.

Institutions are in need of strengthening. The laws, rules, and regulations issued by several different regulators are often confusing. Supervision is fragmented, which can lead to forum shopping. There is a lack of oversight for conglomerates. The regulatory framework needs to be streamlined and clear lines of responsibility need to be assigned to the various regulatory agencies.

Directors need to be trained. The training effort has begun. Thought should be given to accrediting directors.

References

OECD. (2004) *OECD Principles of Corporate Governance.* Paris: Author. Retrieved from www.oecd.org/dataoecd/32/18/31557724.pdf

World Bank. (2003). *Report on the Observance of Standards and Codes (ROSC), Corporate Governance Country Assessment: Colombia.*

World Bank. (2008). *Reports on the Observance of Standards and Codes (ROSC) for Corporate Governance.* Retrieved from www.worldbank.org/ifa/rosc_cg.html

Chapter 34
An Overview of Corporate Governance Practices in Mexico

Robert W. McGee

Introduction

The World Bank has published a series of reports on corporate governance as part of its project on the *Reports on the Observance of Standards and Codes* (ROSC). The corporate governance principles in its ROSC are benchmarked against the OECD's *Principles of Corporate Governance* (OECD, 2004). The main categories of principles are discussed below.

Methodology

The corporate governance topics discussed in the World Bank's ROSC were classified into categories based on the extent of compliance with the OECD's *Principles of Corporate Governance* (OECD, 2004). Points were then assigned to each category, as follows:

O = Observed = 5 points
LO = Largely Observed = 4 points
PO = Partially Observed = 3 points
MNO = Materially Not Observed = 2 points
NO = Not Observed = 1 point

Summary of Findings

Table 34.1 summarizes the scores in the various categories. The table categorizes compliance with corporate governance principles into five categories.

R.W. McGee (✉)
Florida International University, Miami, FL, USA
e-mail: bob414@hotmail.com

R.W. McGee (ed.), *Corporate Governance in Developing Economies*,
DOI 10.1007/978-0-387-84833-4_34, © Springer Science+Business Media, LLC 2009

Table 34.1 Summary of scores by category

		O	LO	PO	MNO	NO
I	**Rights of shareholders**					
A	Protect shareholder rights		X			
B	Shareholders have the right to participate in, and to be sufficiently informed on, decisions concerning fundamental corporate changes			X		
C	Shareholders should have the opportunity to participate effectively and vote in general shareholder meetings			X		
D	Capital structures and arrangements that allow disproportionate control			X		
E	Markets for corporate control should be allowed to function in an efficient and transparent manner		X			
F	Shareholders should consider the costs and benefits of exercising their voting rights					X
II	**Equitable treatment of shareholders**					
A	The corporate governance framework should ensure the equitable treatment of all shareholders, including minority and foreign shareholders			X		
B	Insider trading and abusive self-dealing should be prohibited		X			
C	Board members and managers should be required to disclose material interests in transactions or matters affecting the corporation			X		
III	**Role of stakeholders in corporate governance**					
A	The corporate governance framework should recognize the rights of stakeholders		X			
B	Stakeholders should have the opportunity to obtain effective redress for violation of their rights		X			
C	The corporate governance framework should permit performance-enhancement mechanisms for stakeholder participation		X			
D	Stakeholders should have access to relevant information	X				
IV	**Disclosure and transparency**					
A	The corporate governance framework should ensure that timely and accurate disclosure is made on all material matters		X			
B	Information should be prepared, audited, and disclosed in accordance with high quality standards of accounting, financial and nonfinancial disclosure, and audit			X		
C	An independent audit should be conducted by an independent auditor			X		
D	Channels for disseminating information should provide for fair, timely, and cost-effective access to relevant information by users	X				

Table 34.1 (continued)

		O	LO	PO	MNO	NO
V	**The responsibility of the board**					
A	Board members should act on a fully informed basis, in good faith, with due diligence and care, and in the best interests of the company and the shareholders			X		
B	The board should treat all shareholders fairly			X		
C	The board should ensure compliance with applicable law and take into account the interests of stakeholders		X			
D	The board should fulfill certain board functions			X		
E	The board should be able to exercise objective judgment on corporate affairs independent from management			X		
F	Board members should have access to accurate, relevant, and timely information	X				

Table 34.2 Corporate governance scores

Category	Total points	Number of items	Average
Rights of shareholders	18	6	3.00
Equitable treatment of shareholders	10	3	3.33
Role of stakeholders in corporate governance	17	4	4.25
Disclosure and transparency	15	4	3.75
The responsibility of the board	21	6	3.50
Overall average			3.52

Table 34.2 shows the scores for each subcategory. The overall average was 3.52.
The graph below shows the relative scores. The highest score is in the category of Role. All scores are 3.00 or above.

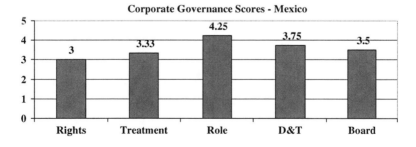

Recommendations

The ROSC made several recommendations. A training institution for the training of directors should be created. The organization should also serve a corporate governance advocacy role. Such an organization was being formed at the time the ROSC was issued.

Having corporate governance rules are one thing. Enforcing them is another. Enforcement is needed for the disclosure provisions and for the securities laws. The staff of the enforcement authority needs to be trained.

There should be more emphasis on the disclosure of ownership and related party transactions. The pension fund law should be revised to include a discussion of corporate governance roles and duties. Pension funds that hold shares should be required to disclose their voting policies.

There is a need to reform legislation to increase compliance with OECD guidelines. Certain provisions need to be clarified. An accounting oversight board needs to be created and its powers delineated. Accounting reform remains a high-priority item.

References

OECD. (2004). *OECD Principles of Corporate Governance*. Paris: Author. Retrieved from www. oecd.org/dataoecd/32/18/31557724.pdf

World Bank. (2003). *Report on the Observance of Standards and Codes (ROSC), Corporate Governance Country Assessment: Mexico*.

World Bank. (2008). *Reports on the Observance of Standards and Codes (ROSC) for Corporate Governance*. Retrieved from www.worldbank.org/ifa/rosc_cg.html

Chapter 35
An Overview of Corporate Governance Practices in Panama

Robert W. McGee

Introduction

The World Bank has published a series of reports on corporate governance as part of its project on the *Reports on the Observance of Standards and Codes* (ROSC). The corporate governance principles in its ROSC are benchmarked against the OECD's *Principles of Corporate Governance* (OECD, 2004). The main categories of principles are discussed below.

Methodology

The corporate governance topics discussed in the World Bank's ROSC were classified into categories based on the extent of compliance with the OECD's *Principles of Corporate Governance* (OECD, 2004). Points were then assigned to each category, as follows:

O=Observed=5 points
LO=Largely Observed=4 points
PO=Partially Observed=3 points
MNO=Materially Not Observed=2 points
NO=Not Observed=1 point

Summary of Findings

Table 35.1 summarizes the scores in the various categories. The table categorizes compliance with corporate governance principles into five categories.

R.W. McGee (✉)
Florida International University, Miami, FL, USA
e-mail: bob414@hotmail.com

R.W. McGee (ed.), *Corporate Governance in Developing Economies*,
DOI 10.1007/978-0-387-84833-4_35, © Springer Science+Business Media, LLC 2009

Table 35.1 Summary of scores by category

		O	LO	PO	MNO	NO
I	**Rights of shareholders**					
A	Protect shareholder rights		X			
B	Shareholders have the right to participate in, and to be sufficiently informed on, decisions concerning fundamental corporate changes			X		
C	Shareholders should have the opportunity to participate effectively and vote in general shareholder meetings			X		
D	Capital structures and arrangements that allow disproportionate control				X	
E	Markets for corporate control should be allowed to function in an efficient and transparent manner		X			
F	Shareholders should consider the costs and benefits of exercising their voting rights				X	
II	**Equitable treatment of shareholders**					
A	The corporate governance framework should ensure the equitable treatment of all shareholders, including minority and foreign shareholders				X	
B	Insider trading and abusive self-dealing should be prohibited		X			
C	Board members and managers should be required to disclose material interests in transactions or matters affecting the corporation		X			
III	**Role of stakeholders in corporate governance**					
A	The corporate governance framework should recognize the rights of stakeholders	X				
B	Stakeholders should have the opportunity to obtain effective redress for violation of their rights	X				
C	The corporate governance framework should permit performance-enhancement mechanisms for stakeholder participation		X			
D	Stakeholders should have access to relevant information	X				
IV	**Disclosure and transparency**					
A	The corporate governance framework should ensure that timely and accurate disclosure is made on all material matters			X		
B	Information should be prepared, audited, and disclosed in accordance with high quality standards of accounting, financial and nonfinancial disclosure, and audit			X		
C	An independent audit should be conducted by an independent auditor			X		
D	Channels for disseminating information should provide for fair, timely, and cost-effective access to relevant information by users	X				

Table 35.1 (continued)

		O	LO	PO	MNO	NO
V	**The responsibility of the board**					
A	Board members should act on a fully informed basis, in good faith, with due diligence and care, and in the best interests of the company and the shareholders	X				
B	The board should treat all shareholders fairly			X		
C	The board should ensure compliance with applicable law and take into account the interests of stakeholders	X				
D	The board should fulfill certain board functions			X		
E	The board should be able to exercise objective judgment on corporate affairs independent from management				X	
F	Board members should have access to accurate, relevant, and timely information		X			

Table 35.2 Corporate governance scores

Category	Total points	Number of items	Average
Rights of shareholders	18	6	3.00
Equitable treatment of shareholders	10	3	3.33
Role of stakeholders in corporate governance	19	4	4.75
Disclosure and transparency	14	4	3.50
The responsibility of the board	20	6	3.33
Overall average			3.52

Table 35.2 shows the scores for each subcategory. The overall average was 3.52.
The graph below shows the relative scores. All the scores are 3.00 or above. The highest score (4.75) was in the category of Role.

Corporate Governance Scores - Panama

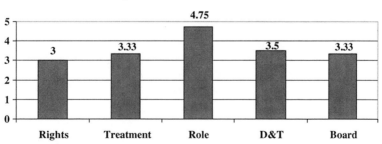

Recommendations

The ROSC made several recommendations. Legislators are reluctant to make changes to the law that would result in less flexibility. That being the case, the

ROSC recommends the introduction of corporate governance reforms for listed firms through amendments to the securities laws. The law should grant specific authority to regulate listed companies. Jurisdiction of the regulatory agency needs to be clarified and upheld.

Better disclosure of ultimate ownership interests needs to be strengthened so that significant owners can be identified. Enforcement of the securities laws is a priority, especially in the areas of disclosure and related party transactions. Directors need to be more accountable for their actions. The enforcement process should be streamlined by centralizing regulation in a single regulatory authority that would oversee banks, insurance companies, and pension funds.

Companies should have an audit committee and a director training organization should be created to educate directors on their duties and responsibilities.

References

OECD. (2004). *OECD Principles of Corporate Governance*. Paris: Author. Retrieved from www. oecd.org/dataoecd/32/18/31557724.pdf

World Bank (2004). *Report on the Observance of Standards and Codes (ROSC), Corporate Governance Country Assessment: Panama*.

World Bank. (2008). *Reports on the Observance of Standards and Codes (ROSC) for Corporate Governance*. Retrieved from www.worldbank.org/ifa/rosc_cg.html

Chapter 36
An Overview of Corporate Governance Practices in Peru

Robert W. McGee

Introduction

The World Bank has published a series of reports on corporate governance as part of its project on the *Reports on the Observance of Standards and Codes* (ROSC). The corporate governance principles in its ROSC are benchmarked against the OECD's *Principles of Corporate Governance* (OECD, 2004). The main categories of principles are discussed below.

Methodology

The corporate governance topics discussed in the World Bank's ROSC were classified into categories based on the extent of compliance with the OECD's *Principles of Corporate Governance* (OECD, 2004). Points were then assigned to each category, as follows:

O = Observed = 5 points
LO = Largely Observed = 4 points
PO = Partially Observed = 3 points
MNO = Materially Not Observed = 2 points
NO = Not Observed = 1 point

Summary of Findings

Table 36.1 summarizes the scores in the various categories. The table categorizes compliance with corporate governance principles into five categories.

R.W. McGee (✉)
Florida International University, Miami, FL, USA
e-mail: bob414@hotmail.com

R.W. McGee (ed.), *Corporate Governance in Developing Economies*,
DOI 10.1007/978-0-387-84833-4_36, © Springer Science+Business Media, LLC 2009

Table 36.1 Summary of scores by category

		O	LO	PO	MNO	NO
I	**Rights of shareholders**					
A	Protect shareholder rights		X			
B	Shareholders have the right to participate in, and to be sufficiently informed on, decisions concerning fundamental corporate changes		X			
C	Shareholders should have the opportunity to participate effectively and vote in general shareholder meetings			X		
D	Capital structures and arrangements that allow disproportionate control			X		
E	Markets for corporate control should be allowed to function in an efficient and transparent manner			X		
F	Shareholders should consider the costs and benefits of exercising their voting rights			X		
II	**Equitable treatment of shareholders**					
A	The corporate governance framework should ensure the equitable treatment of all shareholders, including minority and foreign shareholders			X		
B	Insider trading and abusive self-dealing should be prohibited				X	
C	Board members and managers should be required to disclose material interests in transactions or matters affecting the corporation				X	
III	**Role of stakeholders in corporate governance**					
A	The corporate governance framework should recognize the rights of stakeholders		X			
B	Stakeholders should have the opportunity to obtain effective redress for violation of their rights		X			
C	The corporate governance framework should permit performance-enhancement mechanisms for stakeholder participation			X		
D	Stakeholders should have access to relevant information		X			
IV	**Disclosure and transparency**					
A	The corporate governance framework should ensure that timely and accurate disclosure is made on all material matters			X		
B	Information should be prepared, audited, and disclosed in accordance with high quality standards of accounting, financial and nonfinancial disclosure, and audit			X		
C	An independent audit should be conducted by an independent auditor				X	
D	Channels for disseminating information should provide for fair, timely, and cost-effective access to relevant information by users			X		

Table 36.1 (continued)

		O	LO	PO	MNO	NO
V	**The responsibility of the board**					
A	Board members should act on a fully informed basis, in good faith, with due diligence and care, and in the best interests of the company and the shareholders			X		
B	The board should treat all shareholders fairly				X	
C	The board should ensure compliance with applicable law and take into account the interests of stakeholders		X			
D	The board should fulfill certain board functions			X		
E	The board should be able to exercise objective judgment on corporate affairs independent from management				X	
F	Board members should have access to accurate, relevant, and timely information.			X		

Table 36.2 Corporate Governance Scores-Peru

Category	Total points	Number of items	Average
Rights of shareholders	20	6	3.33
Equitable treatment of shareholders	7	3	2.33
Role of stakeholders in corporate governance	15	4	3.75
Disclosure and transparency	11	4	2.75
The responsibility of the board	17	6	2.83
Overall average			3.04

Table 36.2 shows the scores for each subcategory. The overall score was 3.04.

The graph below shows the relative scores. The highest score was in the category of Role (3.75).

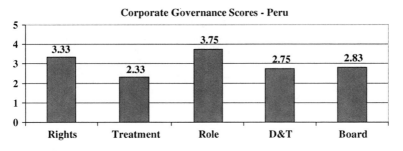

Recommendations

The ROSC made several recommendations. They fell into the four broad categories of legislative reform, institutional strengthening, enforcement, and voluntary/private initiatives.

On the legislative front, the law needs to be changed in several places to increase the degree of compliance with OECD principles. Calling annual general shareholders meetings should be required of all listed companies. Shareholder participation and involvement should be encouraged. The time period for meeting notices should be extended so that shareholders have more time to decide how to vote. Shareholders should be able to submit resolutions for the meetings. Companies should facilitate proxy voting. The approval process for large transactions should be more transparent. Redress mechanisms should be in place.

The securities regulator (CONASEV) needs to be more independent. Board nominations are currently subject to capture and conflicts of interest. One suggested solution is to appoint the CONASEV chair to a longer term than that of the executive office. Another suggestion is to institutionalize the bard by appointing board members from various government agencies and the central bank.

The internal governance structure needs to be strengthened. There should be guidelines that clearly define the duties of pension fund administrators. Firewalls should be put in place to prevent conflicts of interest.

Enforcement of the corporate governance rules remains a challenge. Enforcement is especially needed in the areas of disclosure and related party transactions.

Although the existing Peruvian code of good governance is quite similar to that of the OECD, it is too broad, provides insufficient detail and needs to be revised to more fully deal with Peruvian corporate governance issues. Special attention should be focused on board practices, director independence, special-purpose committees, and board duties. An institute needs to be established to train directors.

References

OECD. (2004). *OECD Principles of Corporate Governance*. Paris: Author. Retrieved form www. oecd.org/dataoecd/32/18/31557724.pdf

World Bank. (2004). *Report on the Observance of Standards and Codes (ROSC), Corporate Governance Country Assessment: Republic of Peru.*

World Bank. (2008). *Reports on the Observance of Standards and Codes (ROSC) for Corporate Governance*. Retrieved from www.worldbank.org/ifa/rosc_cg.html

Chapter 37
An Overview of Corporate Governance Practices in Uruguay

Robert W. McGee

Introduction

The World Bank has published a series of reports on corporate governance as part of its project on the *Reports on the Observance of Standards and Codes* (ROSC). The corporate governance principles in its ROSC are benchmarked against the OECD's *Principles of Corporate Governance* (OECD, 2004). The main categories of principles are discussed below.

Methodology

The corporate governance topics discussed in the World Bank's ROSC were classified into categories based on the extent of compliance with the OECD's *Principles of Corporate Governance* (OECD, 2004). Points were then assigned to each category, as follows:

O = Observed = 5 points
LO = Largely Observed = 4 points
PO = Partially Observed = 3 points
MNO = Materially Not Observed = 2 points
NO = Not Observed = 1 point

Summary of Findings

Table 37.1 summarizes the scores in the various categories. The table categorizes compliance with corporate governance principles into five categories.

R.W. McGee (✉)
Florida International University, Miami, FL, USA
e-mail: bob414@hotmail.com

R.W. McGee (ed.), *Corporate Governance in Developing Economies*,
DOI 10.1007/978-0-387-84833-4_37, © Springer Science+Business Media, LLC 2009

Table 37.1 Summary of scores by category

		O	LO	PO	MNO	NO
I	**Rights of shareholders**					
A	Protect shareholder rights			X		
B	Shareholders have the right to participate in, and to be sufficiently informed on, decisions concerning fundamental corporate changes			X		
C	Shareholders should have the opportunity to participate effectively and vote in general shareholder meetings			X		
D	Capital structures and arrangements that allow disproportionate control				X	
E	Markets for corporate control should be allowed to function in an efficient and transparent manner				X	
F	Shareholders should consider the costs and benefits of exercising their voting rights				X	
II	**Equitable treatment of shareholders**					
A	The corporate governance framework should ensure the equitable treatment of all shareholders, including minority and foreign shareholders			X		
B	Insider trading and abusive self-dealing should be prohibited				X	
C	Board members and managers should be required to disclose material interests in transactions or matters affecting the corporation			X		
III	**Role of stakeholders in corporate governance**					
A	The corporate governance framework should recognize the rights of stakeholders			X		
B	Stakeholders should have the opportunity to obtain effective redress for violation of their rights		X			
C	The corporate governance framework should permit performance-enhancement mechanisms for stakeholder participation			X		
D	Stakeholders should have access to relevant information				X	
IV	**Disclosure and transparency**					
A	The corporate governance framework should ensure that timely and accurate disclosure is made on all material matters				X	
B	Information should be prepared, audited, and disclosed in accordance with high quality standards of accounting, financial and nonfinancial disclosure, and audit			X		
C	An independent audit should be conducted by an independent auditor			X		
D	Channels for disseminating information should provide for fair, timely, and cost-effective access to relevant information by users		X			

Table 37.1 (continued)

		O	LO	PO	MNO	NO
V	**The responsibility of the board**					
A	Board members should act on a fully informed basis, in good faith, with due diligence and care, and in the best interests of the company and the shareholders		X			
B	The board should treat all shareholders fairly				X	
C	The board should ensure compliance with applicable law and take into account the interests of stakeholders				X	
D	The board should fulfill certain board functions				X	
E	The board should be able to exercise objective judgment on corporate affairs independent from management				X	
F	Board members should have access to accurate, relevant, and timely information			X		

Table 37.2 Corporate governance scores

Category	Total points	Number of items	Average
Rights of shareholders	15	6	2.50
Equitable treatment of shareholders	8	3	2.67
Role of stakeholders in corporate governance	12	4	3.00
Disclosure and transparency	12	4	3.00
The responsibility of the board	14	6	2.33
Overall average			2.65

Table 37.2 shows the scores for each subcategory. The overall average was 2.65. The scores are shown below graphically. None of the scores were above 3.00.

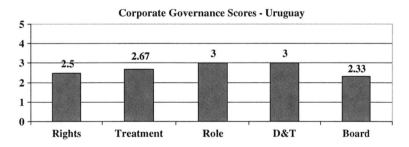

Recommendations

The ROSC made several recommendations. The key areas identified for reform are

- creation of a strong securities regulator,
- continued improvement of disclosure requirements,

- amending the corporate law to enhance companies' access to finance and protect shareholders,
- improvement of the functioning of the corporate board,
- strengthening company registration and reporting systems, and
- revamping the securities framework to spur capital markets development.

The capital market regulator in Uruguay does not have as much power as those of other countries and this is thought to be a bad thing. There is a need to protect shareholder rights and instill confidence in investors and issuers.

The securities regulator needs to improve training for its staff in order to be an effective regulator. There needs to be more disclosure. The external auditor should be present at the annual general shareholders' meeting and should be available to answer shareholder questions. The annual report should include a discussion of company objectives and a management discussion. Consideration should be given to requiring a full audit of the financial statements of economically significant companies. Companies should be permitted to publish their annual reports online as an alternative to publishing them in the national press.

The related party rules should be strengthened. There should be more transparency for large asset sales. Shareholder rights should be strengthened, especially the rights of minority shareholders. Proportional representation rules should be introduced for the election of directors. The notice for the annual general shareholders' meeting is currently 10 days. The ROSC recommends expanding it to 30 days, which is the international best practice.

References

OECD. (2004). *OECD Principles of Corporate Governance*. Paris: Author. Retrieved from www. oecd.org/dataoecd/32/18/31557724.pdf

World Bank. (2005). *Report on the Observance of Standards and Codes (ROSC), Corporate Governance Country Assessment: Uruguay.*

World Bank. (2008). *Reports on the Observance of Standards and Codes (ROSC) for Corporate Governance*. Retrieved from www.worldbank.org/ifa/rosc_cg.html

Chapter 38
An Overview of Corporate Governance Practices in Egypt

Robert W. McGee

Introduction

The World Bank has published a series of reports on corporate governance as part of its project on the *Reports on the Observance of Standards and Codes* (ROSC). The corporate governance principles in its ROSC are benchmarked against the OECD's *Principles of Corporate Governance* (OECD, 2004). The main categories of principles are discussed below.

Methodology

The corporate governance topics discussed in the World Bank's ROSC were classified into categories based on the extent of compliance with the OECD's *Principles of Corporate Governance* (OECD, 2004). Points were then assigned to each category, as follows:

O=Observed=5 points
LO=Largely Observed=4 points
PO=Partially Observed=3 points
MNO=Materially Not Observed=2 points
NO=Not Observed=1 point

Summary of Findings

Table 38.1 summarizes the scores in the various categories. The table categorizes compliance with corporate governance principles into five categories.

R.W. McGee (✉)
Florida International University, Miami, FL, USA
e-mail: bob414@hotmail.com

R.W. McGee (ed.), *Corporate Governance in Developing Economies*,
DOI 10.1007/978-0-387-84833-4_38, © Springer Science+Business Media, LLC 2009

Table 38.1 Summary of scores by category

		O	LO	PO	MNO	NO
I	**Rights of shareholders**					
A	Protect shareholder rights	X				
B	Shareholders have the right to participate in, and to be sufficiently informed on, decisions concerning fundamental corporate changes		X			
C	Shareholders should have the opportunity to participate effectively and vote in general shareholder meetings		X			
D	Capital structures and arrangements that allow disproportionate control		X			
E	Markets for corporate control should be allowed to function in an efficient and transparent manner		X			
F	Shareholders should consider the costs and benefits of exercising their voting rights			X		
II	**Equitable treatment of shareholders**					
A	The corporate governance framework should ensure the equitable treatment of all shareholders, including minority and foreign shareholders		X			
B	Insider trading and abusive self-dealing should be prohibited			X		
C	Board members and managers should be required to disclose material interests in transactions or matters affecting the corporation		X			
III	**Role of stakeholders in corporate governance**					
A	The corporate governance framework should recognize the rights of stakeholders	X				
B	Stakeholders should have the opportunity to obtain effective redress for violation of their rights	X				
C	The corporate governance framework should permit performance-enhancement mechanisms for stakeholder participation	X				
D	Stakeholders should have access to relevant information		X			
IV	**Disclosure and transparency**					
A	The corporate governance framework should ensure that timely and accurate disclosure is made on all material matters			X		
B	Information should be prepared, audited, and disclosed in accordance with high quality standards of accounting, financial and nonfinancial disclosure, and audit		X			
C	An independent audit should be conducted by an independent auditor			X		
D	Channels for disseminating information should provide for fair, timely, and cost-effective access to relevant information by users		X			
V	**The responsibility of the board**					
A	Board members should act on a fully informed basis, in good faith, with due diligence and care, and in the best interests of the company and the shareholders		X			

Table 38.1 (continued)

		O	LO	PO	MNO	NO
B	The board should treat all shareholders fairly			X		
C	The board should ensure compliance with applicable law and take into account the interests of stakeholders		X			
D	The board should fulfill certain board functions			X		
E	The board should be able to exercise objective judgment on corporate affairs independent from management				X	
F	Board members should have access to accurate, relevant, and timely information	X				

Table 38.2 Corporate governance scores

Category	Total points	Number of items	Average
Rights of shareholders	24	6	4.00
Equitable treatment of shareholders	11	3	3.67
Role of stakeholders in corporate governance	19	4	4.75
Disclosure and transparency	14	4	3.50
The responsibility of the board	21	6	3.50
Overall average			3.87

Table 38.2 shows the scores for each subcategory. The overall score was 3.87.

The graph below shows the relative scores graphically. The highest score was in the category of Role. The lowest scores were for Disclosure and Transparency (D&T) and Board.

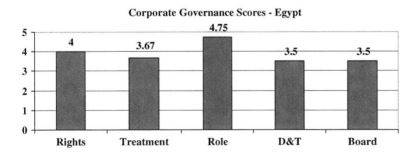

Corporate Governance Scores - Egypt

Recommendations

The ROSC made several recommendations. They focused on three particular areas: legislative reform, institutional strengthening, and voluntary/private initiatives.

Several areas were identified where a change in the law would enhance compliance with the OECD guidelines. Many of the issues may be resolved by updating the accounting and auditing laws. Changing the laws will result in some technical problems that can be resolved through workshops.

Enforcement of the corporate governance rules continues to be a challenge. Enforcement of the disclosure provisions is especially important. The capacity to monitor disclosure needs to be strengthened. Staff needs to be trained to become aware of the issues and the possible abuses. More focus should be placed on the mid-caps.

The private sector should develop training capabilities so that directors may be educated regarding their duties and responsibilities.

References

OECD. (2004). *OECD Principles of Corporate Governance*. Paris: Author. Retrieved from www.oecd.org/dataoecd/32/18/31557724.pdf

World Bank. (2004). *Report on the Observance of Standards and Codes (ROSC), Corporate Governance Country Assessment: Egypt.*

World Bank. (2008). *Reports on the Observance of Standards and Codes (ROSC) for Corporate Governance*. Retrieved from www.worldbank.org/ifa/rosc_cg.html

Chapter 39
An Overview of Corporate Governance Practices in Ghana

Robert W. McGee

Introduction

The World Bank has published a series of reports on corporate governance as part of its project on the *Reports on the Observance of Standards and Codes* (ROSC). The corporate governance principles in its ROSC are benchmarked against the OECD's *Principles of Corporate Governance* (OECD, 2004). The main categories of principles are discussed below.

Methodology

The corporate governance topics discussed in the World Bank's ROSC were classified into categories based on the extent of compliance with the OECD's *Principles of Corporate Governance* (OECD, 2004). Points were then assigned to each category, as follows:

O = Observed = 5 points
LO = Largely Observed = 4 points
PO = Partially Observed = 3 points
MNO = Materially Not Observed = 2 points
NO = Not Observed = 1 point

Summary of Findings

Table 39.1 summarizes the scores in the various categories. The table categorizes compliance with corporate governance principles into five categories.

R.W. McGee (✉)
Florida International University, Miami, FL, USA
e-mail: bob414@hotmail.com

R.W. McGee (ed.), *Corporate Governance in Developing Economies*,
DOI 10.1007/978-0-387-84833-4_39, © Springer Science+Business Media, LLC 2009

Table 39.1 Summary of scores by category

		O	LO	PO	MNO	NO
I	**Rights of shareholders**					
A	Protect shareholder rights				X	
B	Shareholders have the right to participate in, and to be sufficiently informed on, decisions concerning fundamental corporate changes		X			
C	Shareholders should have the opportunity to participate effectively and vote in general shareholder meetings		X			
D	Capital structures and arrangements that allow disproportionate control			X		
E	Markets for corporate control should be allowed to function in an efficient and transparent manner				X	
F	Shareholders should consider the costs and benefits of exercising their voting rights				X	
II	**Equitable treatment of shareholders**					
A	The corporate governance framework should ensure the equitable treatment of all shareholders, including minority and foreign shareholders			X		
B	Insider trading and abusive self-dealing should be prohibited			X		
C	Board members and managers should be required to disclose material interests in transactions or matters affecting the corporation				X	
III	**Role of stakeholders in corporate governance**					
A	The corporate governance framework should recognize the rights of stakeholders		X			
B	Stakeholders should have the opportunity to obtain effective redress for violation of their rights			X		
C	The corporate governance framework should permit performance-enhancement mechanisms for stakeholder participation	X				
D	Stakeholders should have access to relevant information			X		
IV	**Disclosure and transparency**					
A	The corporate governance framework should ensure that timely and accurate disclosure is made on all material matters			X		
B	Information should be prepared, audited, and disclosed in accordance with high quality standards of accounting, financial and nonfinancial disclosure, and audit			X		
C	An independent audit should be conducted by an independent auditor				X	
D	Channels for disseminating information should provide for fair, timely, and cost-effective access to relevant information by users		X			

Table 39.1 (continued)

		O	LO	PO	MNO	NO
V	**The responsibility of the board**					
A	Board members should act on a fully informed basis, in good faith, with due diligence and care, and in the best interests of the company and the shareholders			X		
B	The board should treat all shareholders fairly					X
C	The board should ensure compliance with applicable law and take into account the interests of stakeholders		X			
D	The board should fulfill certain board functions		X			
E	The board should be able to exercise objective judgment on corporate affairs independent from management				X	
F	Board members should have access to accurate, relevant, and timely information.		X			

Table 39.2 Corporate governance scores

Category	Total points	Number of items	Average
Rights of shareholders	17	6	2.83
Equitable treatment of shareholders	8	3	2.67
Role of stakeholders in corporate governance	15	4	3.75
Disclosure and transparency	12	4	3.00
The responsibility of the board	18	6	3.00
Overall average			3.04

Table 39.2 shows the scores for each subcategory. The weighted average score was 3.04.

The graph below shows the relative scores. The best score was in the category of Role. The scores for the other categories were about the same, ranging from 2.67 to 3.00.

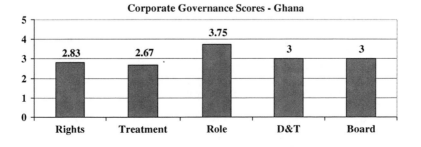

Recommendations

The ROSC made several recommendations. They centered on the following broad areas:

- overhaul the institutional framework,
- continue the legislative review and modernization, and
- increase awareness of corporate governance issues.

The Securities and Exchange Commission (SEC) needs to be strengthened in order to become compliant with International Organization of Securities Commissions (IOSCO) requirements. It should have a separate enforcement department to focus on the SEC-monitoring efforts. SEC personnel need more training. There needs to be more transparency.

Speedier dispute resolution is needed in the High Court and that process has started. However, its expertise and specialization need to be addressed. There is a new Commercial Court but it needs to demonstrate improvement in functioning. More training and resources are needed and there should be monitoring for quality. Private arbitration should be considered as an alternative to the official dispute resolution mechanism.

A central registry system needs to be developed for equities. The SEC should assert jurisdiction over the registry system. A clearance system for brokers would accelerate the processing of share trades.

The governance of state-owned enterprises (SOE) needs to be improved. The capital markets laws are being reformed and the ROSC urged the continuation of the reforms. The companies code needs to be updated in order to be harmonized with SEC regulations. There are two codes on mergers and they need to be harmonized.

The board representation and nomination process needs to be improved. Related party transactions need to be regulated or prohibited based on international best practices. Disclosure rules for beneficial ownership need to be adopted. There is a regulatory vacuum in some areas.

Ghana should promote director and executive training. There should be increased awareness and more institutional investor activism.

References

OECD. (2004). *OECD Principles of Corporate Governance*. Paris: Author. Retrieved from www.oecd.org/dataoecd/32/18/31557724.pdf

World Bank. (2005). *Report on the Observance of Standards and Codes (ROSC), Corporate Governance Country Assessment: Ghana.*

World Bank. (2008). *Reports on the Observance of Standards and Codes (ROSC) for Corporate Governance*. Retrieved from www.worldbank.org/ifa/rosc_cg.html

Chapter 40
An Overview of Corporate Governance Practices in Jordan

Robert W. McGee

Introduction

The World Bank has published a series of reports on corporate governance as part of its project on the *Reports on the Observance of Standards and Codes* (ROSC). The corporate governance principles in its ROSC are benchmarked against the OECD's *Principles of Corporate Governance* (OECD, 2004). The main categories of principles are discussed below.

Methodology

The corporate governance topics discussed in the World Bank's ROSC were classified into categories based on the extent of compliance with the OECD's *Principles of Corporate Governance* (OECD 2004). Points were then assigned to each category, as follows:

O=Observed=5 points
LO=Largely Observed=4 points
PO=Partially Observed=3 points
MNO=Materially Not Observed=2 points
NO=Not Observed=1 point

Summary of Findings

Table 40.1 summarizes the scores in the various categories. The table categorizes compliance with corporate governance principles into five categories.

R.W. McGee (✉)
Florida International University, Miami, FL, USA
e-mail: bob414@hotmail.com

R.W. McGee (ed.), *Corporate Governance in Developing Economies*,
DOI 10.1007/978-0-387-84833-4_40, © Springer Science+Business Media, LLC 2009

Table 40.1 Summary of scores by category

		O	LO	PO	MNO	NO
I	**Rights of shareholders**					
A	Protect shareholder rights		X			
B	Shareholders have the right to participate in, and to be sufficiently informed on, decisions concerning fundamental corporate changes		X			
C	Shareholders should have the opportunity to participate effectively and vote in general shareholder meetings		X			
D	Capital structures and arrangements that allow disproportionate control			X		
E	Markets for corporate control should be allowed to function in an efficient and transparent manner			X		
F	Shareholders should consider the costs and benefits of exercising their voting rights			X		
II	**Equitable treatment of shareholders**					
A	The corporate governance framework should ensure the equitable treatment of all shareholders, including minority and foreign shareholders			X		
B	Insider trading and abusive self-dealing should be prohibited		X			
C	Board members and managers should be required to disclose material interests in transactions or matters affecting the corporation		X			
III	**Role of stakeholders in corporate governance**					
A	The corporate governance framework should recognize the rights of stakeholders	X				
B	Stakeholders should have the opportunity to obtain effective redress for violation of their rights	X				
C	The corporate governance framework should permit performance-enhancement mechanisms for stakeholder participation	X				
D	Stakeholders should have access to relevant information	X				
IV	**Disclosure and transparency**					
A	The corporate governance framework should ensure that timely and accurate disclosure is made on all material matters			X		
B	Information should be prepared, audited, and disclosed in accordance with high quality standards of accounting, financial and nonfinancial disclosure, and audit	X				
C	An independent audit should be conducted by an independent auditor			X		
D	Channels for disseminating information should provide for fair, timely, and cost-effective access to relevant information by users		X			

Table 40.1 (continued)

		O	LO	PO	MNO	NO
V	**The responsibility of the board**					
A	Board members should act on a fully informed basis, in good faith, with due diligence and care, and in the best interests of the company and the shareholders	X				
B	The board should treat all shareholders fairly		X			
C	The board should ensure compliance with applicable law and take into account the interests of stakeholders	X				
D	The board should fulfill certain board functions	X				
E	The board should be able to exercise objective judgment on corporate affairs independent from management				X	
F	Board members should have access to accurate, relevant, and timely information	X				

Table 40.2 Corporate governance scores

Category	Total points	Number of items	Average
Rights of shareholders	21	6	3.50
Equitable treatment of shareholders	11	3	3.67
Role of stakeholders in corporate governance	20	4	5.00
Disclosure and transparency	16	4	4.00
The responsibility of the board	22	6	3.67
Overall average			3.91

Table 40.2 shows the scores for each subcategory. The weighted average score is 3.91.

The graph below shows the relative scores. Jordan earned a perfect 5.00 score in the Role category. The lowest score was in the Rights category (3.50).

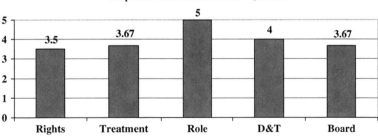

Corporate Governance Scores - Jordan

Recommendations

The ROSC made several recommendations. A code of corporate governance should be developed in a joint effort of the private sector and various government entities.

Such a code could help build a national consensus on the role, duties, and functions of the board. Emphasis should also be placed on the protection of minority shareholder rights. Issuers might be given the option of complying with the various code provisions or explaining why they do not comply.

Institutions need to be strengthened. Enforcement of the corporate governance rules continues to be a challenge. The ROSC recommends continued enforcement of the disclosure provisions in particular. More emphasis should be placed on disclosure of ownership and related party transactions.

There are overlaps in regulatory jurisdiction. The ROSC recommends a high-level strategic review of the different functions of the JSC and controller so that functional responsibilities can be better aligned. Doing so would reduce regulatory duplication and would reduce the regulatory burden on businesses.

References

OECD. (2004). *OECD Principles of Corporate Governance*. Paris: Author. Retrieved from www.oecd.org/dataoecd/32/18/31557724.pdf.

World Bank. (2004). *Report on the Observance of Standards and Codes (ROSC), Corporate Governance Country Assessment: Jordan*.

World Bank. (2008). *Reports on the Observance of Standards and Codes (ROSC) for Corporate Governance*. Retrieved from www.worldbank.org/ifa/rosc_cg.html

Chapter 41
An Overview of Corporate Governance Practices in Mauritius

Robert W. McGee

Introduction

The World Bank has published a series of reports on corporate governance as part of its project on the *Reports on the Observance of Standards and Codes* (ROSC). The corporate governance principles in ROSC are benchmarked against the OECD's *Principles of Corporate Governance* (OECD, 2004). The main categories of principles are discussed below.

Methodology

The corporate governance topics discussed in the World Bank's ROSC were classified into categories based on the extent of compliance with the OECD's *Principles of Corporate Governance* (OECD, 2004). Points were then assigned to each category, as follows:

O = Observed = 5 points
LO = Largely Observed = 4 points
PO = Partially Observed = 3 points
MNO = Materially Not Observed = 2 points
NO = Not Observed = 1 point

Summary of Findings

Table 41.1 summarizes the scores in the various categories. The table categorizes compliance with corporate governance principles into five categories.

R.W. McGee (✉)
Florida International University, Miami, FL, USA
e-mail: bob414@hotmail.com

R.W. McGee (ed.), *Corporate Governance in Developing Economies*,
DOI 10.1007/978-0-387-84833-4_41, © Springer Science+Business Media, LLC 2009

Table 41.1 Summary of scores by category

		O	LO	PO	MNO	NO
I	**Rights of shareholders**					
A	Protect shareholder rights			X		
B	Shareholders have the right to participate in, and to be sufficiently informed on, decisions concerning fundamental corporate changes			X		
C	Shareholders should have the opportunity to participate effectively and vote in general shareholder meetings			X		
D	Capital structures and arrangements that allow disproportionate control			X		
E	Markets for corporate control should be allowed to function in an efficient and transparent manner			X		
F	Shareholders should consider the costs and benefits of exercising their voting rights					X
II	**Equitable treatment of shareholders**					
A	The corporate governance framework should ensure the equitable treatment of all shareholders, including minority and foreign shareholders			X		
B	Insider trading and abusive self-dealing should be prohibited			X		
C	Board members and managers should be required to disclose material interests in transactions or matters affecting the corporation			X		
III	**Role of stakeholders in corporate governance**					
A	The corporate governance framework should recognize the rights of stakeholders			X		
B	Stakeholders should have the opportunity to obtain effective redress for violation of their rights			X		
C	The corporate governance framework should permit performance-enhancement mechanisms for stakeholder participation				X	
D	Stakeholders should have access to relevant information		X			
IV	**Disclosure and transparency**					
A	The corporate governance framework should ensure that timely and accurate disclosure is made on all material matters			X		
B	Information should be prepared, audited, and disclosed in accordance with high quality standards of accounting, financial and nonfinancial disclosure, and audit		X			
C	An independent audit should be conducted by an independent auditor			X		
D	Channels for disseminating information should provide for fair, timely, and cost-effective access to relevant information by users		X			

Table 41.1 (continued)

		O	LO	PO	MNO	NO
V	**The responsibility of the board**					
A	Board members should act on a fully informed basis, in good faith, with due diligence and care, and in the best interests of the company and the shareholders			X		
B	The board should treat all shareholders fairly			X		
C	The board should ensure compliance with applicable law and take into account the interests of stakeholders			X		
D	The board should fulfill certain board functions			X		
E	The board should be able to exercise objective judgment on corporate affairs independent from management				X	
F	Board members should have access to accurate, relevant, and timely information			X		

Table 41.2 Corporate governance scores

Category	Total points	Number of items	Average
Rights of shareholders	16	6	2.67
Equitable treatment of shareholders	9	3	3.00
Role of stakeholders in corporate governance	12	4	3.00
Disclosure and transparency	14	4	3.50
The responsibility of the board	17	6	2.83
Overall average			2.96

Table 41.2 shows the scores for each subcategory. The overall average was 2.96.

The graph below shows the relative scores by category. The highest score was in the category of Disclosure and Transparency (D&T).

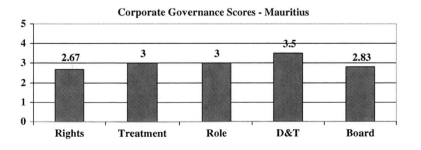

Recommendations

The ROSC made several recommendations. Shareholder protections were enhanced with the passage of the Companies Act of 2001. This piece of legislation enhanced other areas of corporate governance as well. But the ROSC believes that a number of other legal improvements are also needed.

Shareholders still are not always adequately protected in cases where one dominant family has a controlling interest in a company. There are also inefficient pyramid structures and holding companies.

Institutions need to be strengthened. Although several corporate governance statutes have been passed, enforcing them is sometimes another story. There are problems with lower-level management in the regulatory agency. More training is needed and the possibility of retaining the services of foreign experts should be considered. Compensation for regulatory agency personnel needs to be sufficiently high to be competitive with the private sector.

Board members are not always adequately qualified and they often lack independence. Most are executive directors or controlling shareholder representatives. Training needs to be improved. In some cases, training should be industry specific.

The ROSC calls for a voluntary code of corporate governance. However, listed companies should be required to disclose how closely they comply with the code.

References

OECD. (2004). *OECD Principles of Corporate Governance.* Paris: Author. Retrieved from www.oecd.org/dataoecd/32/18/31557724.pdf

World Bank. (2002). *Report on the Observance of Standards and Codes (ROSC), Corporate Governance Country Assessment: Mauritius.*

World Bank. (2008). *Reports on the Observance of Standards and Codes (ROSC) for Corporate Governance.* Retrieved from www.worldbank.org/ifa/rosc_cg.html

Chapter 42
An Overview of Corporate Governance Practices in Senegal

Robert W. McGee

Introduction

The World Bank has published a series of reports on corporate governance as part of its project on the *Reports on the Observance of Standards and Codes* (ROSC). The corporate governance principles in ROSC are benchmarked against the OECD's *Principles of Corporate Governance* (OECD, 2004). The main categories of principles are discussed below.

Methodology

The corporate governance topics discussed in the World Bank's ROSC were classified into categories based on the extent of compliance with the OECD's *Principles of Corporate Governance* (OECD, 2004). Points were then assigned to each category, as follows:

O=Observed=5 points
LO=Largely Observed=4 points
PO=Partially Observed=3 points
MNO=Materially Not Observed=2 points
NO=Not Observed=1 point

Summary of Findings

Table 42.1 summarizes the scores in the various categories. The table categorizes compliance with corporate governance principles into five categories.

R.W. McGee (✉)
Florida International University, Miami, FL, USA
e-mail: bob414@hotmail.com

R.W. McGee (ed.), *Corporate Governance in Developing Economies*,
DOI 10.1007/978-0-387-84833-4_42, © Springer Science+Business Media, LLC 2009

Table 42.1 Summary of scores by category

		O	LO	PO	MNO	NO
I	**Rights of shareholders**					
A	Protect shareholder rights		X			
B	Shareholders have the right to participate in, and to be sufficiently informed on, decisions concerning fundamental corporate changes		X			
C	Shareholders should have the opportunity to participate effectively and vote in general shareholder meetings		X			
D	Capital structures and arrangements that allow disproportionate control			X		
E	Markets for corporate control should be allowed to function in an efficient and transparent manner					X
F	Shareholders should consider the costs and benefits of exercising their voting rights					X
II	**Equitable treatment of shareholders**					
A	The corporate governance framework should ensure the equitable treatment of all shareholders, including minority and foreign shareholders				X	
B	Insider trading and abusive self-dealing should be prohibited					X
C	Board members and managers should be required to disclose material interests in transactions or matters affecting the corporation			X		
III	**Role of stakeholders in corporate governance**					
A	The corporate governance framework should recognize the rights of stakeholders			X		
B	Stakeholders should have the opportunity to obtain effective redress for violation of their rights			X		
C	The corporate governance framework should permit performance-enhancement mechanisms for stakeholder participation			X		
D	Stakeholders should have access to relevant information				X	
IV	**Disclosure and transparency**					
A	The corporate governance framework should ensure that timely and accurate disclosure is made on all material matters				X	
B	Information should be prepared, audited, and disclosed in accordance with high quality standards of accounting, financial and nonfinancial disclosure, and audit			X		
C	An independent audit should be conducted by an independent auditor			X		
D	Channels for disseminating information should provide for fair, timely, and cost-effective access to relevant information by users					X

Table 42.1 (continued)

		O	LO	PO	MNO	NO
V	**The responsibility of the board**					
A	Board members should act on a fully informed basis, in good faith, with due diligence and care, and in the best interests of the company and the shareholders				X	
B	The board should treat all shareholders fairly				X	
C	The board should ensure compliance with applicable law and take into account the interests of stakeholders			X		
D	The board should fulfill certain board functions				X	
E	The board should be able to exercise objective judgment on corporate affairs independent from management				X	
F	Board members should have access to accurate, relevant, and timely information.			X		

Table 42.2 Corporate governance scores

Category	Total points	Number of items	Average
Rights of shareholders	17	6	2.83
Equitable treatment of shareholders	6	3	2.00
Role of stakeholders in corporate governance	11	4	2.75
Disclosure and transparency	9	4	2.25
The responsibility of the board	14	6	2.33
Overall average			2.48

Table 42.2 shows the scores for each subcategory. The overall average was 2.48. The corporate governance scores are shown graphically below. None of the scores were over 3.00.

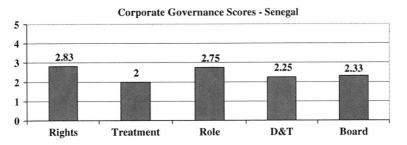

Recommendations

The ROSC made several recommendations. It breaks down the recommendations into two categories: steps that can be taken by the government and the private sector and those that require action at the community or regional level.

Senegal should draft a voluntary corporate governance code that establishes a set of basic principles. The scope should include all public interest entities, such as listed companies, financial institutions, and significant state enterprises.

Since most corporate governance regulation is established at the community level it is difficult to adopt a code that has any mandatory provisions, or even a code that has a "comply or explain" provision.

The code should focus on the board of directors. Specifically, it should state that the directors owe loyalty to the company and to all stakeholders. Minority shareholders should be able to nominate board representatives and it should encourage a transparent nomination process. It should list board responsibilities that are in line with OECD principles. Responsibilities of the board should be distinguished from those of management.

Having a code can increase the demand for high-quality financial reporting. Auditors should be independent and audits should be carried out in compliance with International Standards on Auditing. The internal audit function should be reinvigorated and the internal auditor should report to the board of directors, not management. There should be a separate audit committee for listed companies, banks, and large state-owned enterprises. Full financial statements should be posted on the company's website.

References

OECD. (2004). *OECD Principles of Corporate Governance.* Paris: Author. Retrieved from www. oecd.org/dataoecd/32/18/31557724.pdf

World Bank. (2006). *Report on the Observance of Standards and Codes (ROSC), Corporate Governance Country Assessment: Senegal.*

World Bank. (2008). *Reports on the Observance of Standards and Codes (ROSC) for Corporate Governance.* Retrieved from www.worldbank.org/ifa/rosc_cg.html

Chapter 43
An Overview of Corporate Governance Practices in South Africa

Robert W. McGee

Introduction

The World Bank has published a series of reports on corporate governance as part of its project on the *Reports on the Observance of Standards and Codes* (ROSC). The corporate governance principles in ROSC are benchmarked against the OECD's *Principles of Corporate Governance* (OECD, 2004). The main categories of principles are discussed below.

Methodology

The corporate governance topics discussed in the World Bank's ROSC were classified into categories based on the extent of compliance with the OECD's *Principles of Corporate Governance* (OECD, 2004). Points were then assigned to each category, as follows:

O = Observed = 5 points
LO = Largely Observed = 4 points
PO = Partially Observed = 3 points
MNO = Materially Not Observed = 2 points
NO = Not Observed = 1 point

Summary of Findings

Table 43.1 summarizes the scores in the various categories. The table categorizes compliance with corporate governance principles into five categories.

R.W. McGee (✉)
Florida International University, Miami, FL, USA
e-mail: bob414@hotmail.com

R.W. McGee (ed.), *Corporate Governance in Developing Economies*,
DOI 10.1007/978-0-387-84833-4_43, © Springer Science+Business Media, LLC 2009

Table 43.1 Summary of scores by category

		O	LO	PO	MNO	NO
I	**Rights of shareholders**					
A	Protect shareholder rights	X				
B	Shareholders have the right to participate in, and to be sufficiently informed on, decisions concerning fundamental corporate changes		X			
C	Shareholders should have the opportunity to participate effectively and vote in general shareholder meetings			X		
D	Capital structures and arrangements that allow disproportionate control	X				
E	Markets for corporate control should be allowed to function in an efficient and transparent manner		X			
F	Shareholders should consider the costs and benefits of exercising their voting rights					X
II	**Equitable treatment of shareholders**					
A	The corporate governance framework should ensure the equitable treatment of all shareholders, including minority and foreign shareholders			X		
B	Insider trading and abusive self-dealing should be prohibited	X				
C	Board members and managers should be required to disclose material interests in transactions or matters affecting the corporation			X		
III	**Role of stakeholders in corporate governance**					
A	The corporate governance framework should recognize the rights of stakeholders	X				
B	Stakeholders should have the opportunity to obtain effective redress for violation of their rights	X				
C	The corporate governance framework should permit performance-enhancement mechanisms for stakeholder participation		X			
D	Stakeholders should have access to relevant information	X				
IV	**Disclosure and transparency**					
A	The corporate governance framework should ensure that timely and accurate disclosure is made on all material matters			X		
B	Information should be prepared, audited, and disclosed in accordance with high quality standards of accounting, financial and nonfinancial disclosure, and audit			X		
C	An independent audit should be conducted by an independent auditor			X		
D	Channels for disseminating information should provide for fair, timely, and cost-effective access to relevant information by users		X			

Table 43.1 (continued)

		O	LO	PO	MNO	NO
V	**The responsibility of the board**					
A	Board members should act on a fully informed basis, in good faith, with due diligence and care, and in the best interests of the company and the shareholders			X		
B	The board should treat all shareholders fairly		X			
C	The board should ensure compliance with applicable law and take into account the interests of stakeholders	X				
D	The board should fulfill certain board functions			X		
E	The board should be able to exercise objective judgment on corporate affairs independent from management			X		
F	Board members should have access to accurate, relevant, and timely information		X			

Table 43.2 Corporate governance scores

Category	Total points	Number of items	Average
Rights of shareholders	22	6	3.67
Equitable treatment of shareholders	11	3	3.67
Role of stakeholders in corporate governance	19	4	4.75
Disclosure and transparency	13	4	3.25
The responsibility of the board	22	6	3.67
Overall average			3.78

Table 43.2 shows the scores for each subcategory. The overall average was 3.78. The scores are shown below graphically. All the scores were above 3.00. The highest score was in the category of Role (4.75).

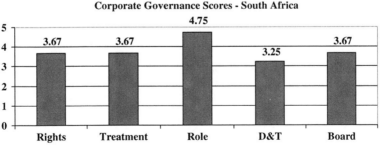

Corporate Governance Scores - South Africa

Recommendations

The ROSC made several recommendations. In the area of shareholder rights, the ROSC calls for amendment of the Companies Act to require a higher quorum of share capital and voting rights for all fundamental corporate changes. Shareholders should be able to make resolutions. Voting should be by ballot unless it is agreed that voting is by a show of hands. Shareholders should have the authority to approve or reject antitakeover devices.

Pension funds should be required to disclose their voting policies. South Africa should consider expanding the powers of the securities regulator in order to have more oversight over issuers. Accounting should be transparent. Failure to disclose beneficial ownership should result in withholding dividends or disenfranchising voting rights.

The definition of independence should be clarified and the external auditor's independence should be insured.

References

OECD. (2004). *OECD Principles of Corporate Governance*. Paris: Author. Retrieved from www.oecd.org/dataoecd/32/18/31557724.pdf

World Bank. (2003). *Report on the Observance of Standards and Codes (ROSC), Corporate Governance Country Assessment: Republic of South Africa*.

World Bank. (2008). *Reports on the Observance of Standards and Codes (ROSC) for Corporate Governance*. Retrieved from www.worldbank.org/ifa/rosc_cg.html

Chapter 44
An Overview of Corporate Governance Practices in Zimbabwe

Robert W. McGee

Introduction

The World Bank has published a series of reports on corporate governance as part of its project on the *Reports on the Observance of Standards and Codes* (ROSC). The corporate governance principles in ROSC are benchmarked against the OECD's *Principles of Corporate Governance* (OECD, 2004). The main categories of principles are discussed below.

Methodology

The corporate governance topics discussed in the World Bank's ROSC were classified into categories on the basis of the extent of compliance with the OECD's *Principles of Corporate Governance* (OECD, 2004). The categories were:

Yes
No
N/A
Incomplete

Summary of Findings

Table 44.1 summarizes the scores in the various categories. The table categorizes compliance with corporate governance principles into four categories. The template for Zimbabwe is different than the template for the other countries in the ROSC reports, making it impossible to make comparisons.

R.W. McGee (✉)
Florida International University, Miami, FL, USA
e-mail: bob414@hotmail.com

R.W. McGee (ed.), *Corporate Governance in Developing Economies*,
DOI 10.1007/978-0-387-84833-4_44, © Springer Science+Business Media, LLC 2009

Table 44.1 Summary of scores by category

		Yes	No	N/A	Incomplete
I	**Rights of shareholders**				
A	Protect shareholder rights	X			
B	Shareholders have the right to participate in, and to be sufficiently informed on, decisions concerning fundamental corporate changes	X			
C	Shareholders should have the opportunity to participate effectively and vote in general shareholder meetings	X			
D	Capital structures and arrangements that allow disproportionate control		X		
E	Markets for corporate control should be allowed to function in an efficient and transparent manner		X		
F	Shareholders should consider the costs and benefits of exercising their voting rights			X	
II	**Equitable treatment of shareholders**				
A	The corporate governance framework should ensure the equitable treatment of all shareholders, including minority and foreign shareholders	X			
B	Insider trading and abusive self-dealing should be prohibited		X		
C	Board members and managers should be required to disclose material interests in transactions or matters affecting the corporation				X
III	**Role of stakeholders in corporate governance**				
A	The corporate governance framework should recognize the rights of stakeholders			X	
B	Stakeholders should have the opportunity to obtain effective redress for violation of their rights			X	
C	The corporate governance framework should permit performance-enhancement mechanisms for stakeholder participation			X	
D	Stakeholders should have access to relevant information			X	
IV	**Disclosure and transparency**				
A	The corporate governance framework should ensure that timely and accurate disclosure is made on all material matters			X	
B	Information should be prepared, audited, and disclosed in accordance with high quality standards of accounting, financial and nonfinancial disclosure, and audit	X			
C	An independent audit should be conducted by an independent auditor.	X			
D	Channels for disseminating information should provide for fair, timely, and cost-effective access to relevant information by users			X	

Table 44.1 (continued)

		Yes	No	N/A	Incomplete
V	**The responsibility of the board**				
A	Board members should act on a fully informed basis, in good faith, with due diligence and care, and in the best interests of the company and the shareholders	X			
B	The board should treat all shareholders fairly	X			
C	The board should ensure compliance with applicable law and take into account the interests of stakeholders			X	
D	The board should fulfill certain board functions		X		X
E	The board should be able to exercise objective judgment on corporate affairs independent from management			X	
F	Board members should have access to accurate, relevant, and timely information			X	

Recommendations

The ROSC did not make many recommendations. The report was more descriptive in nature. One recommendation was that the registrar of companies and the high court need to have their monitoring and enforcement capacities enhanced in order to better implement principles of corporate governance.

References

OECD. (2004). *OECD Principles of Corporate Governance*. Paris: Author. Retrieved from www.oecd.org/dataoecd/32/18/31557724.pdf

World Bank. (n.d.). *Report on the Observance of Standards and Codes (ROSC), Corporate Governance Country Assessment: Zimbabwe*.

World Bank. (2008). *Reports on the Observance of Standards and Codes (ROSC) for Corporate Governance*. Retrieved website www.worldbank.org/ifa/rosc_cg.html

Index